D1006771

HE MOVED
WEST *with*
AMERICA

HE MOVED WEST *with* AMERICA

The Life and Times of Wm. Carr Lane:
1789–1863

St. Louis Mayor and New Mexico Governor
Militiaman and Surgeon's Mate
Doctor and Businessman

WILLIAM C. CARSON

ARCHWAY
PUBLISHING

Archway Publishing books may be ordered through booksellers or by contacting:

Archway Publishing
1663 Liberty Drive
Bloomington, IN 47403
www.archwaypublishing.com
1 (888) 242-5904

Because of the dynamic nature of the Internet, any web addresses or
links contained in this book may have changed since publication and
may no longer be valid. The views expressed in this work are solely those
of the author and do not necessarily reflect the views of the publisher,
and the publisher hereby disclaims any responsibility for them.

Portrait of William Carr Lane. Oil painting by A.J. Conant after Chester
Harding, 1881. Missouri History Museum Art Collections. 1950-087-0001.

ISBN: 978-1-4808-3703-4 (sc)
ISBN: 978-1-4808-3702-7 (hc)
ISBN: 978-1-4808-3704-1 (e)

Library of Congress Control Number: 2016915584

Print information available on the last page.

Archway Publishing rev. date: 11/10/2016

FOR GEORGIA

MY WIFE OF SIXTY YEARS

Contents

Prologue

On February 28, 1853, Governor Wm. Carr Lane set out for the southern part of the Territory of New Mexico in a carriage pulled by four mules. His official translator, a thirty-six-year-old Virginian, sat beside him, while three other men—two Black servants from St. Louis and a Tesuque Pueblo Indian—rode horses alongside. The party traveled fifteen miles to Delgado's Ranch, where they spent the night. Fifty-eight days later the governor returned to Santa Fe to be greeted by a "cavalcade of citizens."[1]

The tumult in New Mexico was far greater than Lane had anticipated when he arrived in Santa Fe from St. Louis on September 9 of the previous year. The commander of the US Army in New Mexico, Colonel Edwin Vose Sumner, thought little of the place. He had written to the War Department the previous May that the territory was worthless and the United States should return New Mexico, which then included present-day Arizona, to the Mexicans and Indians. Sumner departed for Albuquerque on September 10 with all the available government funds and the American flag, which had flown over the Palace of the Governors since General Stephen Watts Kearny's conquest of the territory in 1846. Sumner did not believe there should be a civil government. Nevertheless, Lane was inaugurated as governor on the plaza, with prayers and cannon salutes, on September 13, 1852. His address was brief, but in December after traveling through most of the territory, he outlined his hopes and plans for the territory, though it "was run over with red and white thieves and robbers."[2] The governor had made some progress in organizing the government and securing peace with the Navajo, but "turmoil" was still an accurate description of conditions in the territory that February.

Lane intended, during the southern trip, to establish American ownership of the more than twenty-nine million acres of land claimed by Mexico because of major errors in the map used to establish the boundary between the two countries by the Treaty of Guadalupe Hidalgo, which ended the Mexican War. He had no help from Colonel Sumner, who was still in Albuquerque, and no authority from Washington for the territorial claim. He also aimed to make peace with the Apache in the Mimbres Mountains, who were supporting themselves by crossing the disputed border, killing hundreds of Mexicans, and stealing their livestock. He achieved both goals, but he almost started a second Mexican War in doing so.

Those fifty-eight days were characteristic of his lifelong approach to problems: he employed action, vision, impatience, and leadership, along with strongly held views, curiosity, kindliness, personal fortitude, and courage. It had been thirty years since he was elected in 1823 as the first mayor of St. Louis, at the age of thirty-four. He had spent most of the intervening years in that city. He was reelected for eight one-year terms, appointed to another, served in the state legislature, worked as quartermaster general of Missouri, ran for US Congress, practiced medicine, traded real estate, started businesses, and raised a family. When he died in St. Louis in 1863, he had been married to Mary for forty-five years. His wife was shy, not as well educated, and could be difficult to live with. The loss of six of their eight children in childhood was devastating even in a period of high infant mortality. He had been born in Fayetteville in Southwestern Pennsylvania in 1789, the year Washington was first inaugurated, was an ardent supporter of slavery, damned Lincoln, and died in the winter the Emancipation Proclamation was issued.

The leadership, courage, and energy he displayed in New Mexico, were in evidence as a young man and, along with never-ending curiosity and restlessness, led him west during the War of 1812. He gave up a medical apprenticeship in Louisville to join an army brigade pursuing Tecumseh, chief of the Shawnee, in northern Indiana. Later, as surgeon's mate at Fort Belle Fontaine[3] north of St. Louis, Lane traveled hundreds of miles alone by canoe and on horseback through hostile Indian territory to military outposts in Illinois, Iowa, and Wisconsin. He had been appointed by President Madison.

Though few know his name today, he was highly respected by both contemporaries and historians writing of the period years later. John Darby, a leading Missouri citizen and another early mayor of St. Louis, wrote in 1880 after decades of dealing with him that

> Dr. William Carr Lane was not only a man of cultivated intellect, but he was also a man of the warmest heart, and governed by the most noble, laudable, and generous impulses that influence and govern the actions of true men. ... He was in truth and in fact, not only one of the great men of the city of St. Louis, but also of the State of Missouri.[4]

Richard Wade, in *The Urban Frontier*, concluded in 1959 after studying the development of Cincinnati, Louisville, Lexington (Kentucky), Pittsburgh, and St. Louis,

> No one better illustrated the new tendency (everywhere municipal affairs received closer scrutiny, administrations showed greater vision) than St. Louis's energetic and reflective mayor,

William Carr Lane. Elected five consecutive times to the highest office, he was the town's most popular and powerful figure. Carr Lane (as his constituents knew him) was not only a genial, warmhearted politician, but also the shrewdest observer of urban problems in the West. [5]

The Baltimore Sun reported in 1853 that "There is a bold and brave public servant in the administration of national interests at present in New Mexico."[6]

As I grew up in St. Louis in the 1930s and 1940s, I heard many stories about Lane; my grandmother was his granddaughter, and he was a family legend. My father, an English professor at Washington University and local historian, was particularly interested. Largely because of him, boxes of letters and papers of Wm. Carr Lane survived and are now preserved at the Missouri History Museum in St. Louis. [7] In this book, I have included Author's Notes ([AN]), which bring some of the individuals and events in Lane's life into the twentieth century. For example, I related my memories of racial relations in St. Louis in the 1930s and 1940s and my father's account of visiting Lane's daughter Anne prior to her death in 1904.

He wrote primarily to his wife. His letters remained in her family until they were found by his descendants in tin boxes in the attic of the house of one of her granddaughters in St. Louis when she died in 1938. Lane's other papers largely disappeared over the years, except for the journals of his travels over the Santa Fe Trail and actions in New Mexico. The first half of the journal was published in 1917 in New Mexico and the second in 1964 after a copy was discovered by my father at the University of Wisconsin. Less than twenty of the letters Mary wrote to him have been found, but it is clear from his regular remonstrations that she seldom wrote.

The hundreds of letters he wrote to Mary, his daughters, and his son-in-law provide a remarkable insight into his strong views and multiple interests, life on the American frontier as it moved west, and the life of his family. *He Moved West with America* includes long segments from the usually lengthy letters he wrote between 1819 and 1862 and his journals from 1852 and 1853. They are quoted as he wrote them, with his own peculiar abbreviations and grammar—he spread commas across a page like snowflakes and believed that a plus sign was proper shorthand for "and." That habit can be particularly confusing when followed by a dash.

After my wife and I moved to Santa Fe in 1992, I rewrote a fictional account of a twelve-year-old boy traveling over the Santa Fe Trail in 1852 to find his father. It was published as *Peter Becomes a Trail Man* in 2002. It, too, was based on Lane's New Mexico journal. I learned a great deal about him in the process and came to believe that he was a natural leader, with strong opinions and character traits, living through a significant period of American history.

Lane was affected by virtually every major movement and event that influenced the physical expansion of the country, the evolution of the American political system, and the changing culture from the Revolution to the Civil War. Slavery was an established institution and a cause of ever-increasing political conflict throughout this period. His family had owned slaves for generations, and he did so until the Civil War. There is no evidence that he mistreated his slaves or considered them as capital assets; they simply were a different class of people who were property that could be bought or sold. He believed Blacks should live under a different form of government. Similarly, while he did not support the massive Indian removals instituted by President Jackson, he believed they should live under a third and distinct form of government. Both Blacks and Indians would be under White control.

He was restless and adventuresome—and sometimes impetuous. Almost 70 percent of the seven million white people in the United States in 1810 were under twenty-five.[8] Tens of thousands of them moved west of the Alleghenies in the early nineteenth century to improve their lot, many doing so multiple times to obtain additional or more fertile land. Violence and alcoholism were endemic—it was a young, rough culture establishing itself.

Wm. Carr Lane was set apart by his pursuit of varied careers, not falling victim to alcohol, as did many members of his family, and always being recognized as a gentleman. He became a leader in every occupation he pursued but did not have the enormous personal ambition needed to seek a single path to power that characterized many contemporaries, such as Senator Thomas Hart Benton. Lane was a leader, but he was not ruthless.

Many men are remembered because of a military victory or loss. Others, such as Benton, are known because of their brilliant speeches and significant legislative achievements. Lane, in contrast, is not known, though his name and his effect on the daily efforts required to make a democracy succeed are often cited in Missouri and New Mexico history books. In *The Idea of America*, Gordon Wood wrote, "I have always emphasized the underlying importance of structural forces – demographic, economic, and social changes – in accounting for the various expression of ideas."[9] Though in a different sense and in a far different time and environment, Paul Volcker, former chairman of the Federal Reserve, expressed another belief in December 2012: "Grand policy and great strategy can't count for much without the skills needed for implementation and management."[10]

Wm. Carr Lane's life was affected by the social, economic, and expansionist movements of his era and by the political and military events that occurred while he established governmental structures and laws that had a significant affect in Missouri and, to a lesser extent, in New Mexico. He was a fascinating and important man living through a period of major and rapid change in the United States.

William C. Carson
Santa Fe, New Mexico

PART I

Pennsylvania to St. Louis:
Education, Military, and Medicine
1789–1819

BORN ON THE FRONTIER

Presley Carr Lane was twenty-four in 1788 when he and his nineteen-year-old wife, Sarah, traveled by coach from northern Virginia to settle sixty miles south of Pittsburgh in Fayette County. They followed an old Indian trail that led from northern Maryland to the Youghiogheny River. William Carr Lane, the second of their ten children, was born in December of the next year.

Sarah's grandparents, Onore and Richard Stephenson, had emigrated from Scotland and settled in the Shenandoah Valley near Winchester, in the northern tip of Virginia. The family was reasonably well off, but Sarah's father had died when she was very young. One of her uncles who knew the Lanes thought Presley, a dashing and wealthy young man, could be a good husband for Sarah while also providing some financial relief for his widowed sister. Several younger Stephensons had already left Virginia with others to settle in Shelby County, Kentucky, near Louisville. The matchmaking uncle arranged for Presley to stop in the

Shenandoah Valley and then go on to Kentucky. The marital strategy worked.

Two of Sarah's uncles were more adventurous and had left Virginia earlier for the frontier of Fayette County, where they became two of the earliest settlers, establishing communities while being forced to engage in ongoing and often brutal clashes with Indians. William Crawford, one of the uncles, met a grisly fate at the hands of the Delaware in 1782. He set out leading a detachment of five hundred men in early June of that year with the intent of surprising the Delaware along the Sandusky River in Ohio. However, the tribe had been joined by the Wyandotte and Shawnee as well as British rangers from Pittsburgh. After three days of fighting, the Americans retreated. Their commander was captured, stripped, tortured, and burned, perhaps broiled, at the stake with a fire burning in a circle two feet from the pole to which he was lashed—to prolong the agony. William's return to the army as a colonel at the age of fifty had been at the behest of General Washington, with whom he had served earlier. He had first met the future president when he stayed in the Stephensons' home while running surveying lines in 1749 and later assisted Washington in acquiring lands in Fayette County.

William's younger brother, Valentine, did not meet a similar end but did share the association with Washington and had to deal with other brutal clashes between the Indians and settlers. In 1774, while Valentine was overseeing Washington's lands and slaves in Pennsylvania, Dunsmore's War, named for Lord Dunsmore who led the Americans, broke out as a result of clashes between Indians and white settlers west of the Monongahela River. He reported to the then-Colonel Washington on May 16 that "but for this eruption, which, I believe, was as much the White people's fault as the Indians." "There were more than one thousand people [who] crossed the Monongahela in the day … I'm afraid I will be obliged to build a fort until this eruption is over."[11]

The first Lane to settle in America, Thomas, was brought from England by Lewis Burwell as a "headright" in 1648—almost a century before the Stephensons. The headright system provided fifty acres of farmland to anyone bringing a settler to Virginia, including himself, so Burwell received one hundred acres by default and an additional fifty acres for all other family members. Presumably Lane was then on his own. He established a solid foundation by raising tobacco. The family stayed in Virginia for five generations, first in Northumberland and Westmoreland counties between the Rappahannock and Potomac rivers and later west of Alexandria in Newgate, which is now Centreville.

The cultivation of tobacco ultimately led to the disappearance of Thomas Lane, probably at the hands of the British. In 1764, he sailed north 180 miles up Chesapeake Bay from Northumberland County and then traveled east twelve miles overland to sell his crop to the Dutch on Delaware Bay in New Amstel, which is now New Castle. He intended to avoid paying British taxes. He disappeared there, leaving no evidence as to what had happened.

Nevertheless, the family made steady financial progress and gained social respectability during the century following Thomas's disappearance, though they did not become members of the landed gentry. Thomas's son James did not advance the family fortunes in the second generation, for he died at the age of thirty-four, having been married twice. His second wife bore a son, William, before having an illegitimate son after James's death and disappearing into obscurity. Prosperity came with William, who was Presley's grandfather. He was apprenticed at the age of eleven because his family could not support him but later assembled a substantial amount of property through shrewdness, hard work, and marriage to Martha Carr, who came with one hundred acres of land as a dowry. During his lifetime, he gave his son, an earlier William Carr Lane, one hundred acres, and at his death he bequeathed another 570 acres, twelve Negroes, and assorted livestock to family members.

That William Carr Lane advanced even further during his short life of thirty-three years, becoming a man of wealth and respectability in the town of Newgate. He died of typhus. He and a brother had established the town with a tavern, gristmill, shops, and a yard in which slaves were bought and sold and prisoners were sent to indenture. Presley, the second of his three children, was only six when his father died in 1770. Nevertheless, he was off to a good start, for despite his young age, his father bequeathed him the family residence, the tavern, a substantial amount of land, and five slaves.[12]

Presley was sent away to school at age twelve but at nineteen was living on his own with no need to support himself. He traveled in Virginia, went to Kentucky to visit friends, and loitered at the Newgate Tavern, drinking and gambling. He soon got this life of leisure out of his system. Within five years, he had married Sarah, was managing the Newgate properties, and had left for the Pennsylvania frontier with his new family. There was much evidence of a fiery temper. He got into a bitter and public argument with the owner of a competing tavern about the morality of gambling; it flourished at the Newgate but was banned at the rival Black Horse. He printed an ad saying that "Joel Beach of Loudon County is a common liar and rascal," not exactly the action of a prudent man.

Though a grandson reported many years later that the second William Carr Lane was a man of even temper, he apparently inherited the hot temper, for he was challenged to duels at various times in his career—and issued challenges of his own as late as 1853. The temper, however, was spiced with humor and imagination, for once while serving as a surgeon's mate in the army, he was challenged to a duel. As the one challenged, he was able to select the weapon and chose a barrel of gunpowder. The scheme was to have both men sit atop the explosives as a burning fuse approached, and the first to run would lose. The duel was called off and the idea never tested.

Presley and Sarah acquired 209 acres on the Youghiogheny River north of present-day Connellsville when they arrived in Pennsylvania.[13] He was a farmer but retained ownership of the Newgate property in Virginia. He also became involved in the affairs of the community, was named the first county auditor in 1792, and then was elected to the state legislature seven years later, ultimately becoming speaker of the Pennsylvania Senate in 1814. He was one of the original trustees of the Uniontown Academy, which was established in 1808 "for the education of youth in the useful arts, sciences, and literature" and was described as "a man of culture and great gentleness of manner, and for those times quite wealthy."[14]

His education had a more permanent effect on him and his family than had the gambling and drinking. In addition to founding the school, he collected an extensive library. This included Plutarch's *Lives*, Gibbon's *Rome*, Hume's *England*, Jefferson's *Virginia*, Franklin's *Works*, Montaigne's *Essays*, a Latin dictionary, Seneca's *Morals*, Ferguson's *Astronomy*, a volume on algebra, a Methodist hymnal, maps, and a trunk of law books.[15] The books and Presley's political involvement undoubtedly were the foundation of William Carr Lane's education, curiosity, and understanding of people and institutions.

As was true of many during the American Revolution, fighting the British did not have much appeal to Presley. At the age of sixteen in 1780, he had paid the going rate of forty-five dollars, plus $355 for a wagon, driver, and supplies, for a substitute to join the Virginia militia in his place. There is some irony in the inclusion of his name on a plaque placed in Shelby County, Kentucky, by the Daughters of the American Revolution in 1940 to honor those from the county who fought in the Revolutionary War.

Though Presley was quartermaster of the Fayette County Militia in 1794, he was not called to act during the Whisky Rebellion. Fayette was one of four counties in which tax collectors were tarred and feathered by settlers as they tried to collect levies on whisky. President Washington finally sent thirteen thousand troops to quell the uprising.

The Lanes and Stephensons had owned slaves for generations, but beginning in 1782 the moves by Pennsylvania to abolish the practice became an increasing burden on Presley. In 1803 he was required to register as an owner. He finally decided in 1818 to join family members in Shelbyville, Kentucky – the loss of a reelection bid to the state senate had been the last straw. He died in Kentucky the following year, leaving slave girls to each of his three daughters.

Wm. Carr Lane greatly admired the character of George Washington, who seemed to loom over his entire life, perhaps initially because of the early associations with William and Valentine Crawford. Fayette County is the site of Washington's loss to the French in 1754; he also served with General Braddock at Fort Defiance in 1755 at the start of the French and Indian War, the North American branch of the worldwide conflict known as the Seven Years' War, which left Britain as the dominant power in North America. Presumably, he had direct contact with Washington, who stopped often at the Newgate Tavern on his way to Mount Vernon during the latter part of the eighteenth century.

Lane's admiration of Washington and love of Pennsylvania were lifelong. He was staying at the Girard House in Philadelphia on June 25, 1852, near the end of a long trip that continued to Washington, DC, and wrote his wife Mary at ten in the evening, "The world is ruled, more by <u>instinct</u>, than by <u>reason</u>, + that is proof of it, in my own sensations, this evening, when I put my foot, upon this soil of my native state, after an absence of near 20 years. There is not by any means as much reason for my leaving Pennsa, as Ken; & yet I feel deeper emotions, than I do when there; and I can ascribe this, to the <u>instincts</u>, associated with the land of my nativity, + to those instincts only; for all the association of my Boyhood are connected with the Western slope of Alleghenies, alone."[16]

He visited Mount Vernon and again wrote Mary eight days later, "when I put my foot upon my Father-land, after an absence of 31 years, I found I was still myself, - in spite of this long lapse of years, - with their ups and downs, their joys + their sorrows, - yea, their desolation – sorrows – my heart bounded, I cannot say with joy, but with deep emotions, of mingled pleasure + pain."[17] He had traveled from Washington with a group but was wandering alone through "the dilapidated Halls of his hoary mansion, in spite of myself I became abstracted + saddened."[18] The scenery was so beautiful that it reflected "great credit upon the judgment + taste of the great man, who selected it."[19] All of the grounds and buildings were as Washington had left them, "save only the Iron-tooth of time, is constantly doing its work of destruction."[20]

The evidence of the passage of time combined with the continued natural beauty brought him to think of the advances during the period through which he had lived and been part of – much of which he did not entirely approve. "I looked at the present, + I looked upon the past, – the heroic age of the Republic – before men (+ women too), gave so much time to the study of Arithmetic + paid so much devotion to the almighty Dollar."[21]

RESTLESS YEARS

Lane had led a turbulent life in St. Louis for decades prior to writing Mary from Philadelphia in June 1852 and then from Washington in July. He didn't know as he wrote that he would soon be appointed governor of the Territory of New Mexico, nor did he know that the next twenty-one months would be even more turbulent.

He was in the territory on a Sunday evening in June 1853, a year after he had written the letters from Philadelphia and Washington, when he again reflected on the influences on his life. He sat at a simple table in a bare room in the Palace of the Governors on the plaza in Santa Fe and wrote to his single, thirty-four-year-old daughter Anne. She, along with her mother, had refused to accompany him from St. Louis to New Mexico eleven months earlier. Mary had said in her usual cheerless way, "I will never see you again."[22] When he wrote that evening, he had already resigned as governor, knowing that as a Whig, he would soon be relieved of his duties by President Franklin Pierce, a Democrat who had taken office in March. He was considering running to be territorial representative in Congress but had not yet told his wife or family. They were expecting him back in St. Louis in less than two months.

It was not to be – he entered the race on August 9. As he expected, the election was conducted under highly questionable circumstances, with additional votes arriving from the Hispanic village of Mora two days late. His Hispanic opponent, who could not speak English and was a defrocked priest, was declared the official winner. Lane compiled the results independently and claimed victory.

He finally reached St. Louis on the evening of October 28 but was off to Washington in less than a month to press his claim of victory in the US House of Representatives – a result that would have required him not just to be in Washington, but also to return to New Mexico. He was still driven to keep moving by the need to confront challenges. He could not give up, despite his claim to be aging.

But on that June evening in 1853, the election was in the future. He wrote, "as folks advance far upon the march of life, year after year, the avenues of agreeable sensations, one by one are closed up forever; and they cling, with a firmer and firmer grasp to the sources of enjoyment that are left open to them – of these enjoyments, the pleasures, which flow from avarice – from ambition, and from the use of stimulants of all kinds, are, for the most part, coveted to the very last."[23]

He felt he was an old man at sixty-three who no longer cared of money or political distinction and even "less for all sorts of stimulants, than 40 years ago."[24] He dwelled on less salutary family traits to which he had not succumbed and was relieved that for the first time in his life he was not in danger of becoming "an inebriate."[25] He had worried about the addiction to alcohol that cursed both his mother's and father's families – perhaps the Newgate Tavern had more than one purpose. He described various family members. "Col. Jos. Lane destroyed himself by Brandy." "John was a sponge, always full and heavy." "No Horn was also a hard drinker." "His numerous family of gifted sons, were generally intemperate, and died young."[26]

"On my mother's side it was no better." "Richard Stephenson ended his days at an early age by the hardest kind of drinking." "The brothers of my Grandfather Stephenson were what are called Drunkards – many of their descendants drank hard, + kept going steadily down in the scale of respectability, until they attained the zero." "He was naturally weak minded, + when he became a drunkard, he was little else than an Idiot." "2 married men who became Drunkards, + a large number of my maternal cousins were drunkards."[27]

He was convinced, however, that his father had never overindulged and questioned those who claimed to have seen him drink brandy during his last year in the legislature. "Of my brothers, 1 died in infancy, 1 in early manhood + the rest, as you know, shortened their days, by hard drink."[28] He had six brothers but said nothing of his three sisters.

The destruction of so many of his family members was perhaps not unusual—alcoholism was rampant in America in the 1790s and the first three decades of the nineteenth century. Alcohol had been part of American life from its beginning. The *Mayflower* carried large quantities of beer and wine in 1621, and the *Arbella* in 1630 was loaded with three times as much beer as water and

10,000 gallons of wine when it set out for Boston in 1630.[29] Tastes had shifted by 1800 to hard spirits for those Americans who moved West. Liquor was readily distilled from grain crops, was cheaper, and could be used in trading—the Whiskey Rebellion of 1794 had shown how profitable the latter could be.

The per capita consumption of alcohol was probably higher from the early 1790s to the early 1830s than at any other time in American history. Such statistics are based largely on tax records but can hardly be precise and are probably on the low side. The annual per capita consumption of absolute alcohol by the drinking-age population, i.e. those over fifteen, in 1810 was 7.1 gallons, not including Blacks and presumably few women; in 1985 it was 2.5 gallons, including everybody.[30]

Heavy drinking was prevalent in the army, which until the mid-1830s issued a quart of whisky to every enlisted man each week.[31] More could easily be obtained from distributors who followed the troops. An officer complained that the men sought every occasion to drink and get drunk, but this habit was not confined to the enlisted men. In 1820, surgeon William Beaumont talked about "very strong symptoms of dissipation among the officers."[32]

There were stern warnings from many who were concerned about the future of the country because of the effect of alcohol and the frequent violence to which it led. James Madison was one. Another, the respected physician Benjamin Rush, published in 1784 An Inquiry into the Effect of Ardent Spirits on the Human Mind and Body.[33] The temperance movement, however, did not have a significant effect until it became a part of other broad social reforms, including abolition and women's suffrage, in the nineteenth century.

Wm. Carr Lane did not die at an early age as did his siblings, nor is there any evidence of personal drunkenness, though he spent many nights in inns and above barrooms while traveling during the long separations from Mary. He must have been in daily contact with heavy drinking while in the army. His admission that for the first time he was "not in danger of becoming an inebriate," coupled with the vivid memory of the end of so many relatives had obviously haunted him, and he feared that he, too, might suffer the same fate. He liked his wine, but his basic character kept him from succumbing to alcohol.

Lane's strength of character and adventurous spirit did not come from a single source. Little is known about his mother, but his father clearly had the ambition and sense of community to always take on more responsibility and accept new challenges while simultaneously managing his Pennsylvania farm and the Newgate businesses in Virginia.

By the time Lane was a boy in the 1790s, Fayette County was no longer on the edge of the frontier. It had been established as a legal entity in 1783. During the next few years, commissions were appointed and buildings constructed, including a courthouse, a school, and a jail. The threats from the Indians had moved farther to the west, where Sarah's uncle had died the year before the county was established. While daily dangers did not exist, the recent past could not have been far from the inhabitants' minds. Other settlers passed through Fayette County on their way west to Ohio and beyond to establish farms and settlements by taking Indian lands. Both sides suffered. The pressure was relentless and the movement unstoppable. Americans, including Thomas Jefferson, thought the Indians were not civilized and, thus, not ready to settle into an agricultural and peaceful life.[34]

Many years later Theodore Roosevelt summarized the views of the Western expansionist, and probably most of the country, during the first half of the nineteenth century. "Much maudlin nonsense has been written about the governmental treatment of the Indians, especially as regards taking their land. For the simple truth is that they had no possible title to most the lands we took, not even that of occupancy, and at the most were in possession merely by virtue of having butchered the previous inhabitants."[35] He did not say who had preceded the Indians. Roosevelt acknowledged that the Americans had sometimes been too harsh but also argued they were often too lenient. Legal ownership was dependent on Western law, not centuries of occupation. There was concern among many that the frontier environment would cause the Whites to behave as the Indians, particularly when "White savages" committed even more bloody atrocities than did the Indians.[36]

The land of Bullskin Township, in which Lane grew up, was rolling and contained many streams. It was quite fertile, though better known for the Connellsville coal mines than for the farms. It is probable that his father grew crops and vegetables for subsistence. Because of his family's history, it is hard to know if he distilled whisky. Large families were needed to provide extra hands. It is easy to imagine the second son feeding chickens, getting water, and chopping wood and early on showing his adventuresome spirit by roaming the hills and mountains and exploring the many streams with his younger siblings.

As a boy, Lane attended perhaps one of the first country schools in Bullskin Township, which was housed in a log cabin near the Baptist church. There is no evidence of the Lanes being very much involved in religious activities—or of when Wm. Carr acquired his strong and critical views of church dogma.

Early in his teens he was sent to Jefferson College in Washington, Pennsylvania.[37] He may have been the only one of the Lane children selected for such an education. The college had been founded in 1794 as an academy and then chartered as a four-year institution in 1802. Sixty-three years later it merged with a nearby rival to form Washington and Jefferson College, which still offers a liberal arts education.

At its founding, the college provided what would now be called a classical education. The courses, taught generally by ministers, included languages, geography, mathematics, natural and moral philosophy, rhetoric, logic, metaphysics, Roman and Greek antiquities, and history.[38] There was a strict set of rules and regulations governing student conduct. The trustees expounded their belief in a classic education when they decided to start a grammar school stipulating that the classics not be translated. The attendance must have been selective and the courses essentially tutorials, for only sixteen students graduated in 1805.

Lane spent three years at Jefferson College, but his name does not appear in the college graduation records of that period. His failure to complete the four-year course could have been caused by impatience with academic life, discomfort with rules, or the first evidence of the restlessness that led him throughout his lifetime to move on to a new challenge before completing his immediate work. The departure from Jefferson College led him back to the family farm, where he worked in the fields for two years, gaining an understanding of agriculture and presumably selecting books to read from his father's library. He was then sent to an academy in Fairfax County, Virginia, for two years.

At the age of twenty in 1809, he was back in Pennsylvania working for his older brother, Richard, who on January 1 of that year had been named the Prothonotary—first notary—of Fayette County, serving as chief clerk and record keeper. This work did not occupy Lane full time and must have been very dull, for he was also appointed the captain of a company of light infantry in the Pennsylvania militia. His father had avoided military service, but Lane embraced the inherent adventure. In the spring of 1810, he marched with Colonel John Collins to the Canadian border. The purpose was not recorded but had to have been related to disagreements with England prior to the War of 1812.

While the knowledge he gained of the details of legal filings in the office and his military experience would be of assistance in the future, he resigned both his office position and his captaincy in the summer and was off again, this time to enter Dickinson College in Carlisle, Pennsylvania. Dickinson had been founded in 1783 by Benjamin Rush, a signer of the Declaration of Independence, who believed that a strong country could be built only by an educated citizenry with a sense of civic duty. The plan of education included five languages, mathematics, geography, logic, moral philosophy, history, mythology, philology, and divinity.[39]

In 1810, Dickinson, despite the curriculum, was in the midst of a bitter fight between those who wanted it to be a school of theology and those who insisted on the introduction of science. As a result, the school closed in 1816 and did not reopen until 1821. Whether it was because of the turmoil, the academic environment, or the required evening prayers,[40] Lane was off again in 1811 to study medicine as an apprentice to a Dr. Collins in Louisville, a position undoubtedly arranged by members of his mother's family in nearby Shelbyville. Many of the shifts he made throughout his life were characterized by impulsiveness and a need to leave an intellectual atmosphere for one of action.

It is hard today to imagine qualifying to be a doctor through an apprenticeship, but the general state of medicine at that time was as primitive as its education. The title of a history of medicine on the frontier, *Bleed, Blister, and Purge*,[41] encapsulates the common treatments of the time. Anesthesia was not administered. A dentist in Hartford, Connecticut, is generally credited for the first use of ether in 1842. A second great advance introduced by Joseph Lister in 1862 was antiseptic surgery.[42] "Behind the general surgical principle at the beginning of the nineteenth century … injury cases which were invariably traumatic and infected or which it was impossible to keep from becoming infected."[43] The thrust of medical philosophy of the time was to rid the body of toxins, and any treatment that caused an evacuation of the upper or lower intestinal tract was considered sound therapy. The body was to be kept in balance, not cured of unknown diseases. Dosages containing mercury were thought to be particularly effective. Tartar emetic, a drug used to induce vomiting, was indispensable.[44]

Benjamin Rush was a doctor as well as an educator. In the 1790s, he was perhaps an extreme advocate of bleeding, believing that there was only one source of all diseases and illnesses—and the cure was purging and bleeding. He also believed that the average person had twelve quarts of blood, not six as we know today; so when he took five, recovery was often in doubt.[45] He also believed that the guilt arising from adultery always led to insanity. In this era, premarital pregnancies rose to a level not reached again until the 1960s.

By 1810 there was some recognition of the use of natural remedies but still virtually no acknowledgement that insects and unsanitary conditions were the sources of disease. Some sense of the state of medicine is reflected in a medical order General William Henry Harrison placed during the War of 1812.[46]

		Instruments	
Peruvian bark (in powder)	50 lb.		
Opium	10 lb.		
Camphor	10 lb.		
Calomel	5 lb.		
Corrosive sublimate	2 lb.		
Tartar emetic	2 lb.		
Gambage	2 lb.		
Jalap	10 lb.		
Ipecuanto	17 lb.	Instruments	
Rhubarb (in powder)	10 lb.	Amputation	3 sets
Kino	15 lb.	Trepanning	3 sets
Colombo (in powder)	20 lb.	Pocket	3 sets
Nitre crude	20 lb.	Cases scalpels (No. 6)	
Nitre sweet spirits	40 lb.	Lancets	3 doz.
Glaubers salts	50 lb.	Splints	12 sets

Prepared chalk	20 lb.	Sponge	7 lb.
Castor oil	12 gal.	Muslin	1,000 yd.
Olive oil	5 gal.	Wine	200 gal.
Gum Arabic	20 lb.	Brandy or rum	100 gal.
Allume	5 lb.	Vinegar	200 gal.
Acquous	20 lb.	Molasses	200 gal.
Adhesive plaster	20 lb.	Coffee	300 lb.
Barley	2 bbl.	Hyson tea	50 lb.
Chocolate	300 lb.	Rice	5 bbl.
Tapioca	50 lb.	Sugar	5 bbl.
Blistering ointment	20 lb.	Sago	50 lb.
Beeswax	20 lb.		
Muriated acid	4 lb.		
Sulphuric acid	4 lb.		
Nitric acid	4 lb.		
Vials	5 gross		

It is not clear how these remedies and instruments were to be used or what cures Dr. Collins passed on to Lane, for his apprenticeship was cut short in 1813 when he joined the Kentucky militia to pursue Indians in northern Indiana and, thus, start another chapter of his ever-changing life.

A MILITARY LIFE

Wm. Carr Lane was seeking adventure, not a military career, when he set out as a Kentucky militiaman in June of 1813. He had volunteered as a private and mounted rifleman with no pay or allowances to join an expedition that would stretch over a hundred miles. His decision to go west that summer under the command of a Colonel Runnel set the course of his life for the next five years and influenced it for the next forty-five. He was named quartermaster general of Missouri in 1822 and appointed by

Brigadier General Henry Atkinson as surgeon for the troops under his command in 1832 during the brief Indian uprising known as the Black Hawk War. The immediate goal in 1813, however, was the protection of northern Indiana from what had been frequent Indian raids.

Lane's journey west during the War of 1812 was a reaction to the ongoing efforts by the Indians, often encouraged by the British, seeking to protect their lands from the hordes of Americans moving west. The men controlling United States policy generally believed, as did the settlers, that the Indians had no claim to their native homelands. When treaties were signed, they were generally broken by the United States, increasing both the hostility and the savagery on both sides.

The settlers had sought protection as early as the 1780s. The government responded to those pleas by sending militia west to subdue the Indians, but they lost as many men as did the Indians. Finally, in 1791, General Arthur St. Claire, the governor of what was then the Northwest Territory and now would be considered part of the upper mid-west, decided he had to put an end to Indian resistance.

In November, an American army of over 1,400 regulars and an unknown number of militia moved one hundred miles north of present-day Cincinnati in pursuit of that objective, only to be overwhelmed. The Americans suffered over a thousand casualties, including more than six hundred dead—the worst defeat ever suffered by the US Army at the hands of the Native population.[47]

Nevertheless, as expansionist pressure continued, Secretary of War Henry Knox became even more determined to drive out the Indians who, despite their victory, had failed to establish an organized defense. Congress passed legislation with the long but explicit title *An Act for Making Further and More Effectual Provision for the Protection of the Frontiers of the United States*. President Washington selected a Revolutionary War hero who needed a job, Anthony Wayne, to lead the forces. "Mad" Anthony also had other problems, suffering attacks of gout two years later during his final campaign.

Wayne not only instituted strong discipline but, more importantly, abandoned the rigid army tactics in favor of flexible strategies better suited to attacking the Indians and their British supporters, who were not organized in traditional military formations. He set out with a force of two thousand troops, seven hundred mounted volunteers, and a hundred Chickasaw and Choctaw.[48] The decisive battle occurred on August 20, 1794, when over a thousand Indians were overcome and their British allies forced to retreat to their forts.

Through the terms of the subsequent Treaty of Greenville, the Indians ceded most of Ohio and parts of Indiana to the United States. The military was now well established, and more settlers poured in. Ohio was admitted as a state in 1803. The British had already agreed to leave American territory in a treaty negotiated by John Jay in 1794.

The Indians were broken. Many of their leaders were dead and their British supporters gone. In 1800, there were an estimated six hundred thousand Indians in the United States, most west of the Mississippi River. It is believed there were more than five million before the English and Spanish brought disease and displacement.[49]

The Treaty of Greenville did not, however, end the disputes as intended. Tecumseh, a Shawnee, and his one-eyed brother and mystic, The Prophet, were so outraged by the continued incursions by the Whites, despite the treaty, that he attempted to establish unity among the many tribes to ensure that no individual chief sold land to the Americans. They hoped to create an Indian nation that could deal from a position of strength and protect their lands. The most prominent of the many villages they established was Prophetstown, with over two hundred houses at the confluence of the Wabash and Tippecanoe Rivers a few miles northeast of present-day Lafayette, Indiana. The federation, however, did not achieve Tecumseh's goal. Individual tribes put their own financial well-being ahead of the vision of a single Indian federation. Governor William Henry Harrison, with the support of President Jefferson, took advantage of this fact and signed treaties in the early 1800s with various individual tribes to acquire vast amounts of land in Indiana, Illinois, Wisconsin, and Missouri for two and a half cents an acre.[50]

Most Americans believed the British were the source of Tecumseh's drive, not recognizing the Natives' goal of protecting their lands. Finally, Harrison, in defiance of the orders of President James Madison, goaded the Indians into attacking his troops camped near Prophetstown and then swooped in, burning the village, as the Indians fled west. This was the Battle of Tippecanoe in November 1811. Tecumseh and his followers then had little choice but to join the British as war fervor increased in the United States. Though the country was inadequately prepared, the growing disruption of commerce led to the declaration of war in June 1812. Ambitious plans to invade Canada failed on every front. Detroit fell to the British and their Indian allies in August. Harrison, the hero of Tippecanoe, was unable to recover from a humiliating loss or make any progress towards the recapture of Detroit. However, after almost a year of frustration, he was able to gather enough troops to attack Detroit, but only after the twenty-seven-year-old naval officer Oliver Hazard Perry defeated a British flotilla at the east end of Lake Erie on September 10, 1813. The victory has been stamped in history by his statement, "We have met the enemy and they are ours." It turned the tide of the war.

Harrison drove the British and the Indians from Detroit, pursued them eastward, and defeated them at the Battle of the Thames River at the eastern end of Lake Erie in Ontario on October 5. Tecumseh was killed and, some say, skinned by the Kentucky volunteers.

The British captured and burned Washington, DC, in August 1814 and occupied Baltimore in September but failed to seize Fort McHenry in its harbor. The "rockets' red glare" during the attack inspired the "Star Spangled Banner." In the same month, Thomas McDonough with a small fleet defeated the British decisively on Lake Champlain. The two defeats, coupled with the Duke of Wellington's belief that the British could not win unless they controlled the Great Lakes, resulted in the signing of a peace treaty on Christmas Eve 1814, with the conditions existing prior to the start of the war little changed.

Detroit was still held by the British when Lane volunteered in 1813, but by the time he and his fellow militiamen reached northern Indiana, the Indian threat had vanished. The troops returned in late July to Fort Harrison, on the Wabash River near Terre Haute, then commanded by Major Zachary Taylor. They were soon devastated by bilious fever, characterized by high fever and vomiting. Sixteen other varieties of fever were listed in *The Army Medical Department 1775-1818*, including putrid, camp, typhoid, malignant, and typhus, but there is no description of distinguishing symptoms or recommended treatments. It is not clear on what basis it was identified as 'bilious.' Regardless, Wm. Carr Lane, with his medical apprenticeship and natural leadership—he had been invited as a militiaman to join the officer's mess—was assigned to treat the victims. However, he, too, was soon stricken with the fever and unable to perform his official duties. This was to be only a short interruption, for as soon as he had gained sufficient strength, he rode alone over a hundred miles to Lexington, Kentucky, to buy medical books, which he would study when he returned to Fort Harrison.

He was acting as surgeon's mate as he performed his duties at Fort Harrison and later at Fort Knox near Vincennes, Indiana, though he did not receive a formal commission for several years. Again, in the fall of 1814, some combination of restlessness and a desire to gain additional medical knowledge led him to resign from the army to work with a physician in Vincennes and finally form a partnership with him. Lane was by then twenty-five.

Medical education and medical treatment were grounded in the then extremely limited knowledge of the causes of disease and infection, much less how to fight them. The great majority of doctors had served as apprentices in some form or were 'healers' who prescribed all kinds of cures, some adapted from the Indians and many others involving alcohol. Lane, however, recognized that being in partnership with a physician in Vincennes provided insufficient training. So, notwithstanding his failure to complete previous academic endeavors, he entered the University of Pennsylvania's medical school in Philadelphia in the fall of 1815. The school laid claim to being the first medical school established in the colonies, founded in 1765. It was larger than the rest of the university—in 1825 there were 484 enrolled in medicine and 49 in the arts.[51] That comparison may in an indirect way indicate the common presence of disease and frequent epidemics.

There is no information available as to the content of the courses, but the list of professors included those teaching anatomy, the practice of physic and clinical medicine, surgery, materia medica and pharmacy, chemistry, and midwifery.[52] A list from the 1811 University of the State of New York College of Physicians and Surgeons (now Columbia University) is similar but notably also includes mineralogy, botany, and zoology.[53] The graduation rate at both schools was about 25 percent. Not surprisingly, Lane was not one of the sixty-nine in his class to graduate.[54]

He had given 'US Army' as his address when he entered the university, and perhaps that, combined with a report of his earlier service as a surgeon's mate, resulted in the military entering his life again on January 20, 1816. President Madison appointed him with the "advice and consent" of the Senate as "garrison surgeon's mate."[55] The appointment opened with, "That reposing special trust and confidence in the patriotism, valor, fidelity, and abilities."[56] Specific medical training was not mentioned and apparently was less important than were military values. The effective date was over a year earlier—September 14, 1814. The delay must have been caused by slow communications and higher priorities related to the war. The date reflected his earlier service as a surgeon's mate.

Lane left the University of Pennsylvania and joined Morgan's rifle regiment in Vincennes and then proceeded to St. Louis on May 10. From there he went on to Fort Belle Fontaine, which had been founded in 1805 north of St. Louis at the mouth of Cold Water Creek, about ten miles from the confluence of the Missouri and Mississippi rivers. It had served as the point of return for the Lewis and Clark Expedition.

When Lane arrived, the fort was a starting point for Missouri River expeditions and the base for support of a series of distant military outposts intended to guard the frontier—Fort Armstrong at Rock Island, Illinois, on the Missouri River; Fort Crawford further up the river at Prairie du Chien in southern Wisconsin; Fort Edwards at Des Moines in central Iowa; and Fort Clark in central Illinois. Lane's assignment included providing care at these posts. He traveled hundreds of miles alone on horseback or in a canoe to reach them and was gone for months at a time.

The care he could provide on these infrequent visits had to be the most basic kind. The history of the Army Medical Department[57] of that period specifies the medical duties of a mate to be:

1. Visit patient with surgeon, take note of his prescriptions;
2. Keep case book;
3. Attend to carrying out of surgeon's prescriptions;
4. Dress all wounds;
5. Enforce discipline;

6. One mate at least, to remain on call;
7. Responsible for medicines and instruments.

Those assigned duties indicate more about the distance of Washington from the frontier outposts than the responsibilities Lane faced. He was on his own, relying on his basic good sense and training. He did not report how much he bled, blistered, and purged—if at all.

Even these trips could not overcome the boredom of life on an army base, though he apparently traveled the one hundred miles to visit Mary in Vincennes at various times. He tried to resign from the army but was denied. He was, however, granted a furlough to serve at Fort Harrison near Vincennes.

He expressed the underlying reasons in a letter to Mary after their marriage.[58]

> From what I have felt, + from what I have heretofore seen and lately heard, I begin to think the life of an officer, in a peace army, the most boisterous + unpleasant that can be imagined. It is a paradox but is no less a truth as it regards others, that war brings unity fellowship + quiet, + that peace is attended with ill-blood, strife + misery – It results in this inevitable conclusion, that a standing army is at war with the principles of our government, but of our nature.

The five changes made in his life between 1812 and 1817 while he was still in his mid-twenties reflected more than simple restlessness. There was a constant struggle between intellectual pursuits and action that was to intrude on the first year of his marriage and continue throughout his life.

AN ITINERANT MARRIAGE

The repeated changes in location and occupation in Lane's mid-twenties appeared to have come to an end when he married Mary Ewing in Vincennes on February 26, 1818, after discarding the idea of joining Simón Bolívar in his uprisings in South America. He had reportedly earlier rejected the idea of signing on with Mexican revolutionaries after meeting with a General Toledo, who was on a recruiting trip in the United States. In July 1811, Simón Bolívar, along with others of the Creole elite, had declared the independence of Venezuela; but within a year, the new state had collapsed. Bolívar continued his revolutionary activities for the next eight years and, in May 1814, succeeded in establishing an independent state comprising current-day Columbia, Venezuela, and Ecuador. Lane could easily have learned of Bolívar's attacks on Spain or attempts to attract foreign assistance during those eight years. Regardless of the source of his information, the opportunity for adventure while seeking justice would certainly have appealed to him.

His choice indicated more than his ideas about the seriousness of marriage, for he seemed to have decided to abandon his life of almost constant movement and changes of occupation. Mary was twenty-two, the eldest of the ten children of Nathaniel and Anne Breading Ewing, who had prospered since settling in Vincennes, Indiana, in 1804. Lane met Mary, and perhaps become infatuated, in 1814. Because of his future father-in-law's prominent position, he undoubtedly became acquainted with many of the leading citizens of Vincennes, but there is no record of who introduced them—nor, not surprisingly for the period, any reports of earlier relationships with women. They both had grown up in large families on farms on the edge of the frontier, but the similarities did not go beyond that basic background.

Vincennes had been founded sometime before 1732 by French

traders and in 1800 became the capital of the Indiana Territory, which included Indiana, Illinois, Michigan, and Wisconsin. William Henry Harrison was governor. President Thomas Jefferson appointed Ewing to the position of Receiver of Public Money in the Territorial Land Office, which divided territorial lands and issued deeds to buyers. Ewing also founded the Bank of Vincennes. As his financial position improved, he established a large farm and home north of the village. He also served in the Indiana legislature after the territory became a state in 1816. Unfortunately, the bank became overextended itself and failed during the Panic of 1819. The directors reportedly paid themselves a large dividend before declaring bankruptcy. The resulting lawsuits continued for decades. The Ewing family, however, lived quite comfortably on the farm.

There is no record of Mary's activities as she grew up, but it is likely that as a girl she received little education and was primarily involved in the chores and responsibilities that fell to women at that time, including taking care of her younger siblings. She not only did not share Lane's interests but was almost his opposite in temperament -- shy to the point of embarrassment and often extremely difficult. Despite these seemingly insurmountable differences, she was as devoted to Lane as he was to her. Nevertheless, she spent months at a time living with her family in Vincennes while her husband traveled and worked tirelessly at his many and varied responsibilities. The Ewing family home, Montclair, was certainly more comfortable and secure than the changing Lane homes in St. Louis. Moreover, the death of six of her eight children, one almost at birth and four before the age of two, must have compounded her inherent insecurity. The death of Victor Carr at the age of fifteen resulted in her sitting in a dark room for a year trying to read. Only the two eldest children, Anne and Sarah, survived and lived long lives.

Lane was on furlough at Fort Harrison in Indiana at the time of the marriage but under great pressure from Mary's family and friends to leave the army and practice medicine in Vincennes. To that end, he took a series of exams and on May 4, 1818, was certified by the resident and members of the Board of Physicians for the First Medical District in the State of Indiana to practice physic and surgery. In contrast to his earlier military appointment, this one cited proficiency in the healing art in addition to moral character as a qualification.[59] His marriage to Mary, however, did not alter his basic drives. The family pleadings to stay in Vincennes did not prevail, and in July he rejoined his comrades at Fort Belle Fontaine accompanied by Mary, who became pregnant in September. In March, he took her back to the Ewings and then returned to the military life, not to return to Vincennes until after Anne was born on May 4, 1819.

After leaving the seven-months-pregnant Mary with her family, he rode alone from Vincennes to St. Louis and the fort. In his first letter written on the evening of March 26, he complained that some roads were blocked by water. "I have no company + the roads are very bad, but I apprehend no difficulty – at least no serious difficulty from the creeks."[60]

The trip was not easy. Three days later he tried to ford the flooded Wabash but decided he would have to swim "half the distance from hill to hill"[61] and instead rode downriver until he found a boat to take him across. He had to deal with a hailstorm and then found the drunken proprietors at both the places he stayed to be a "great annoyance."[62] His illegible handwriting might be explained because he wrote "before sunup – in a house without windows – of course in the dark - + upon my knee into the bargain,"[63] but his script even under the best of conditions was often barely legible. He finally reached St. Louis on the evening of March 31 and settled into Pitzer's boarding house, promising to write soon.

He did write a long letter from Fort Belle Fontaine on April

17,[64] which included admonishments about her not writing: "I have not rec'd a sylabe from you My dearest Mary, nor heard a word from you, or any of the family, since I saw you last. Why will you serve me thus."

He commented on politics. "The formation of a State Government is the general subject; which is that we ought to be allowed to form a constitution at once, and without any restriction on slavery." He went into detail about four meetings and the personalities of their attendees. He outlined the situations of her women friends in some detail—"Miss B__ is much talked about but not in the strain she could wish." He told her that she would have two calves, but news from St. Louis was not all favorable: "There are 2 additional Doctors located in StL. … a plague take them."

He spent four days at the fort taking stock of the medical supplies and ordering replenishments. He enjoyed the company of the commander and friends but had little use for others who wasted his time. "The rest pass their time much after the manner of Sir Hildebrand's sons, - in birding, hunting – worming dogs, etc. etc. – pursuits about as useful to society, as edifying to themselves." He worried about a young wife who had no girl to do the washing and whose hands were raw. "Alas! The infatuation that induces girls to marry – not only beggars, but poor beggars."

He returned to St. Louis to concentrate on his nonmilitary affairs and wrote again on April 18. [65] "I have at Pitzers boarding-house, + have lodged sometimes there and sometimes at our old establishment." It is not clear to what "our" refers, unless they had acquired it while she accompanied him at Fort Belle Fontaine. He had purchased a lot, built a board fence, was cultivating potatoes, but was afraid to undertake constructing a house, though he had sought funds from the Ewings. "Like a trembling wretch, upon the brink of a yawning gulph into which he is doomed to plunge, I hesitate. It will cost at least 2000 Dolls to fix us in any degree of comfort."

Though he was able to take care of personal affairs and stay in St. Louis, Lane's regular military career was about to end. He wrote on April 21 that "The Surg. Genl. has continued me in my employment ... but a Rascally surgeon has just showed his hand." [66]

He again wrote on May 1, "I go to Belle Fontaine this evening, + and am notified that I am to be relieved of the duties of surgeon immediately by Dr. L. William H. Pierson." [67] His prediction had come true, and he was not pleased. "It would have been easy for this man to have left me in the undisturbed possession of my place." He did not like the move or the man. "I told him what I thot of him, + the little fellow seemed to acquiesce in the opinion; at least if he did not, he kept it to himself." He may have expected a challenge to a duel but assured Mary that "I despise the practice + love you too well." A few days later he refused to walk beside Pierson in a funeral procession of a Major Gantt.

His first child Anne was born three days later, and he rode to Vincennes and remained there until the middle of July. Now that he was no longer part of the military, he returned to St. Louis to become established and beseeched Mary to come with their baby.

He wrote a long letter concentrating on their personal life on August 3,[68] admonishing her and berating himself. "It is now 23 days my dear Mary since we parted, + I have not yet recd. A syllable from you, nor even heard a word from Vincennes." "I am however not entirely satisfied with the prospect – your discontent with the place (St. Louis), ... (not withstanding that I am conscious of being an unkind + unfeeling husband), gives me an uneasiness. When, my dear, will we be snugly seated upon a little domain of our own – our granaries, cellars + etc. stored with abundance, + our cabin filled with sensible, healthy smiling + beautiful little fellows."

His medical practice was sufficient to support him, and he was paid twenty-five dollars a month to attend to the recruiting party for the much publicized Yellowstone Expedition, which had been planned by the secretary of war to explore the Missouri River and awe the Indian and British traders. Only one of the five steamships that started up the Missouri River got even halfway to its destination.

He was disturbed by a potential medical partner and castigated him for his "haughtiness + sterness of my manners ... This little incident has affected me somewhat, I have thot of it 20 times since + really fear that there is something unfortunate + unpopular in my deportment." He was pleased, however, that his brother Dick was sending a slave named Lish, "for she is a first rate young woman."

When he wrote again, starting on August 14 and finishing on August 16, [69] he had received two letters from Mary, the only ones she wrote during their separation.

He again remonstrated her, "but your own feelings will inform you my dear, that I must become uneasy should I not receive letters from you at shorter intervals." Mary must have been a constant worrier, for he recounted the state of his health in every letter.

He saw the economic problems all around him resulting from the Panic of 1819. "Under the state of things it behooves a penniless character to pause + consider well, before he launches into Debts far beyond his means." He included many paragraphs about local politics, and commented on one of the frequent duels, "Whether the Ball (wh passed thro' him), went thro' his hips or buttacks + whether he is merely, badly, or is fatallay wounded, I have not been informed – This dueling is a poor business."

He teased her, "now who knows what this may do in the eyes of the ladies? But, I forebear, lest you be suffocated with jealousy."

In September, Mary was ready to join him but placed certain conditions on her travel. He assured her that the roads were safe and asked if she wanted to ride or travel in a coach. He wanted to meet her with a coach at the Wabash River; so he would only be absent from his growing medical practice for five or six days – not the three weeks required if he picked her up in Vincennes. He had leased a house for one year, postponing construction of their own home for economic reasons. The bad times had reduced the annual rent from $600 to $450, and he thought he could lease one of the two cellars to offset part of the rent. He had wisely decided not to go into debt to start construction. This cautious behavior would be abandoned in the future.

The long letters Wm. Carr Lane wrote during the seven months they were separated during the first year and a half of their marriage differed from those written in later years. Though the shift was not abrupt, it seemed to indicate a change in their relationship. The early letters included much about politics. He not only later omitted such accounts but on at least one occasion said he was doing so because she would not understand. His teasing and expressions of love also became less frequent as time passed and the length of their separations increased. Perhaps infatuation had led to his marriage to a person of such different character and interests, though he continued to write frequently and profess his devotion whenever they were separated during the next thirty-four years.

Finally in October, after all the years of changing course, he was settled with his wife and child in an important Western city. Lane was thirty. He thought there was great opportunity to succeed in the medical field despite the competition. It did not take long, however, for his energy and interests to lead him simultaneously in many directions, and Mary returned to Vincennes after a little over a year.

St. Louis

The St. Louis in which Wm. Carr Lane and Mary settled in the fall of 1819 had been created by a very different history from that of the towns and cities Lane had known during the first twenty-nine years of his life. The city didn't start as an English colony, nor was it founded as the result of Western expansion. Situated on the Mississippi River, St. Louis had been buffeted since its establishment in 1764 by struggles between the British, French, Spanish, and Americans for control of the Mississippi and the Louisiana Territory. Moreover, there were always hostile Indians. St. Louis was the key to the Upper Territory, as New Orleans was to the Lower. The purchase of all of the Louisiana Territory in 1803 by President Jefferson removed, or at least simplified, the governance question. The city was not much larger than a village when the Lanes arrived – it had grown to 3,500, then to 5,500 in 1821, including slaves, free Blacks, and mulattos.[70] It had been laid out in a rectangular pattern stretching two miles along the river but only a few blocks inland.[71] It was a river city.

The decades of uncertainty started in 1762, two years before the founding of St. Louis, when the King of France secretly transferred New Orleans and that portion of the Louisiana Territory west of the Mississippi River to Spain. In the same year, the French governor in New Orleans, not having been advised of the transfer and wanting to expand French power, granted the exclusive Indian trading rights in the territory to a company in which Pierre Laclede was a partner. Laclede and a party that included the fourteen-year-old Auguste Chouteau embarked on the seven-hundred-mile journey up the Mississippi in August 1763 and started construction of the first buildings of the future city on the banks of the river in February of the next year. Communications finally caught up with Laclede, and he learned of the 1762 transfer and the Treaty of Paris that had shifted the Illinois country east of the river from the French to the British. Laclede was not deterred. Soon after the buildings were constructed, he plied a tribe of Missouri Indians with gifts and persuaded them to return to their village rather than settle nearby. Later in the year, Americans in Illinois started crossing the river to avoid becoming British subjects.

Auguste Chouteau and his descendants would play a major role in St. Louis business and society for a century, but their influence and power had a scandalous origin. Marie Therese Bourgeois married Rene Auguste Chouteau in New Orleans and had one son, Auguste. She was, however, soon estranged from her husband, who died a penniless alcoholic.

Soon after Laclede arrived in New Orleans in 1755, he took up with Marie, and they then had four children. Because she was Catholic, divorce from her still living husband was impossible, and the children were all baptized as Rene Chouteau's. Soon after Laclede had founded St. Louis, he summoned Marie, who waited only until their fourth child was born before starting up the river with the newborn and the three others, aged six to sixteen. Laclede initially prospered but in 1776 was overwhelmed by debts incurred in buying out his partners and died in 1778 of "bilious colic"[72] while returning up the river from New Orleans. The young August Chouteau, who had also prospered, acquired most of the estate, including an extensive library and the great stone house. "Laclede was not his father, but no father could have had a more faithful son."[73]

The American Revolution did not directly affect St. Louis initially, because Spain took the side of the United States and allowed the fur trade to continue, seeing the potential for solidifying its hold on the Mississippi and Upper Louisiana. With the capture of Cahokia and Kaskaskia in 1778, the Americans under George Rogers Clark took control of the area east of the river from the British. Clark soon visited the Spanish governor in St. Louis, Don Fernando de Leyba, who had also arrived in the same year. With the support of Chouteau and others, he agreed to supply aid to the Americans. The assistance continued for over a year. The British retaliated by organizing a force of traders, servants, and Indians in early 1780 – estimated at 950–1500[74] – to attack what they believed to be the unprotected St. Louis. They were wrong, for

Governor Leyba had built fortifications and armed the population. The Indians were repulsed much to the fury of the British, who saw the collapse of their grand strategy of isolating both Clark in Illinois and the Spanish in St. Louis. The city suffered an estimated one hundred killed, captured, and wounded,[75] roughly 10 percent of the population of considerably less than a thousand. Leyba died less than a month after he had saved the city. The British continued to plot, and St. Louis was a hub of intrigue for the next twenty years.

Even after the end of the revolution, the British attempted to gain control of the river and the fur trade. At the same time, some Americans in Illinois wanted to conquer the Spanish territory, and Creoles in St. Louis dreamed of reestablishing French rule by taking Detroit. An expedition to achieve the latter started out with great confidence but soon suffered ignominious defeat and many casualties when ambushed by Indians allied with the British. The British threat grew. In January 1781, the Spanish governor, Francisco Cruzat, set out with sixty-five militiamen and an equal number of friendly Indians on a thirty-day, six-hundred-mile march to destroy the British Fort St. Joseph in southwestern Michigan. They succeeded without the loss of a life. At the same time, Indians were appealing to the British for protection from the Americans who were driving them from their land. Moreover, St. Louis struggled through intrigues and plots caused by the failure of Spain to develop its colony and the ambitions of the Americans in Illinois unhappy with their own government and looking covetously at the trading opportunities in St. Louis. In 1794, an elderly General George Rogers Clark, then in Ohio, sought to raise a force of 1,500 to liberate St. Louis and seize upper Louisiana from Spain – it came to naught.

Amidst this ongoing turmoil, St. Louis grew slowly to a population of 975 in 1796, including 42 free mulattos and Blacks and 282 slaves of the same races.[76] The inhabitants were not farmers, as was true of communities further east, but a mixture of wealthy French merchants, with the Chouteaus at the top; fur trappers, some of whom prospered; and the largest group, termed Creole, who had come from Canada, France, and New Orleans and continued to speak French. Slaves had accompanied the first settlers, but most were household help, not field hands as in the American South.

The Creoles would have been elated had they known of Napoleon's secret agreement in 1800 under which Spain returned Louisiana to France. However, the rumors of such an agreement in 1802 were of such concern to President Jefferson that he dispatched James Monroe to Paris. It was one thing to have the inefficient Spanish controlling New Orleans but quite another to have the French in possession. The sudden offer by Napoleon to sell all of the Louisiana Territory, nine hundred thousand square miles, for fifteen million dollars[77] was a shock to all, particularly those in St. Louis when they learned of it late in July 1804. The Creoles were appalled that their dreams had been shattered, and many Americans were equally unhappy, having come West during the previous decade to escape what they considered to be governmental incursions into their lives. Finally, on March 9, 1804, Upper Louisiana was transferred from Spain to France and the next morning from France to the United States. Whatever their preference, the citizens of St. Louis no longer had to wonder who governed them.

The forty years between the founding of St. Louis and the Louisiana Purchase were filled with uncertainty caused by Indian and British attacks, distant rule by Spain, and the indifference of France. The population was diverse both in background and occupation. There was a vast difference between the Chouteaus, with their associations in New York, Paris, and Montreal, and the fur trappers on whom the Chouteaus' fortune was built. French refinement came up the Mississippi from New Orleans, while rough frontiersmen came down the Missouri from the West.

Some sense of stability and growth came with American control, but there was little loss of intrigue. The most serious involved Aaron Burr's plot in 1806 to form an army, attack Mexico, and persuade Western states to secede from the Union. Burr's co-conspirator, General James Wilkinson, was both commanding officer of the US Army and governor of the Louisiana Territory. He had been described as "money hungry" and "with loyalties only to himself."[78] The latter trait led him to later betray Burr to President Jefferson. Burr was apprehended and tried for treason in 1807 but acquitted. While on bail waiting to face other charges, he fled to France, where he hoped to join Napoleon in further schemes.

As the population grew, the city began to organize itself. The Territorial Legislature allowed towns to incorporate and elect trustees, and St. Louis did so in 1809. The five trustees set about raising taxes—the first fiscal year produced $529.68.[79] By 1811, there were 176 taxpayers included in the population of 1,500.[80] The mixture of people and the rough nature of the river men and trappers—in contrast to the refinement of the Chouteaus and others—led to alcoholism and violence. The streets were strewn with garbage and dead animals. An 1811 ordinance stated that "whenever circumstances shall require," the chairman of the Board of Trustees could call out a patrol in which all men over eighteen were required to serve—a kind of standby posse.[81] St. Louis was struck by a December 11, 1811, earthquake centered in New Madrid, Missouri. It is still the strongest ever recorded in North America, according to current records, but there was little damage in the city.

Then came the War of 1812, which caused a growing fear of Indian attacks provoked by the British, particularly after their capture of Fort Dearborn (Chicago). It is unlikely that Lane knew of the panic in his future home as he rode to northern Indiana as a militiaman in futile pursuit of Indians. After the war ended, St. Louis continued to grow with the arrival of doctors, lawyers, preachers, and businessmen. Most citizens were armed. A Pittsburgh newspaper reported that families were afraid to go to St. Louis because everybody was armed and murders were commonplace.[82]

The landing of the first steamboat, the *Zebulon M. Pike*, in St. Louis in August 1817 while Lane was at Fort Belle Fontaine started the transformation of the city that would ultimately make St. Louis the busiest inland port in the country. By 1841, there were 1,928 landings made by 186 steamboats discharging 262,681 tons of freight.[83] Keelboats and rafts had required two to three months to travel from New Orleans to St. Louis; the steamboats took a short ten to twelve days.

Immediately after the arrival of the *Zebulon M. Pike*, growth was slow, but the revolutionary change not only bolstered the economy of the city but altered the character of the inhabitants. Businessmen and others continued to arrive, gradually replacing the heavy-drinking and often violent river men.

Wm. Carr Lane and Mary came to a French city that had been shaped by decades of uncertainty and violence. It was also in the early stages of rapid growth, despite the setbacks caused by the Panic of 1819 and the raging national controversy focused on whether Missouri should enter the Union as a free or slave state. St. Louis was almost a pawn.

A Fox and a Hedgehog

The many books describing political developments of the United States during the first half of the nineteenth century contain frequent and lengthy references to Thomas Hart Benton but none to Wm. Carr Lane, though he does appear prominently in St. Louis histories of that period and those of New Mexico in the mid-nineteenth century. These differences clearly reflect Benton's significant influence on crucial national issues, including the US Bank, nullification, Western expansion, and slavery. At the same time that Benton held positions of influence in Washington, Lane was cleaning up streets, founding institutions, establishing sound local governments, signing treaties with the Apache and Navajo, and forcing President Pierce to buy land from Mexico—the Gadsden Purchase.

The difference between their influences on the development of the United States was the difference between national policy and local development. It could be argued that it would take many Wm. Carr Lanes to match the effect of one Thomas Hart Benton, but it was the local development that made Benton's eloquent and effective speeches ultimately have meaning. Lane's inauguration addresses in both St. Louis and New Mexico were incisive, comprehensive, and explained clearly what was needed to develop the two entities; they were not bombastic, filled with senatorial rhetoric.

The two men's routes to careers of prominence in different spheres were determined by their basic character traits. Lane, a doctor, was perpetually curious and had a wide range of interests. But he was not driven to reach a single goal, never gaining great financial success or reaching a position of national influence. He accepted challenges. Benton, on the other hand, was a lawyer, fiercely ambitious, and ruthless in his attempts to attain political power.

They reached St. Louis at about the same time, though from very different backgrounds. Lane arrived over a period of years, as he associated with important St. Louis citizens while at Fort Belle Fontaine and then settled permanently with his family in 1819. Benton came to St. Louis in 1816, leaving Nashville in part because of the notorious fight he and his brother Jesse had with Andrew Jackson and General John Coffee. There was already bad blood between Jackson and Benton when they encountered each other in Nashville late in 1813. Jackson pulled a gun and advanced on Benton, saying, "Now, you damned rascal, I am going to punish you. Defend yourself."[84] Jesse Benton shot first and almost tore Jackson's arm off. General Coffee's shots missed Thomas Hart, who was then attacked with a knife. Everybody survived. Later, through a combination of political expediency and congruent beliefs, Benton became an ardent Jackson supporter in the Senate during Jackson's presidency. His support became so strong that when Martin Van Buren was inaugurated and Jackson left, Benton mourned the occasion as the crowd was "profoundly silent … It was the stillness and silence of reverence and attention; and there was no room for mistake as to whom this mute and impressive homage was paid."[85]

Benton was born in 1782 in North Carolina to a family immersed in scholarly learning. Though Lane changed direction often while growing up, there is no indication that he was ever asked to leave school, as was Benton when he was expelled from the University of North Carolina for threatening students with a gun and stealing their money.

When Benton arrived in St. Louis, he quickly went about becoming known to prominent men, establishing his law practice, and expressing his hostile views of the Creoles as editor of the *St. Louis Enquirer*. His developing political base, however, suffered a setback in 1817 in a duel with Charles Lucas, who at twenty-four was considered a rising star—Benton had lost an important case to him the previous year. In August at a polling place, Benton's referral to the young Lucas as a "puppy"[86] elicited a challenge to a duel. They stood thirty feet apart on Bloody Island and fired. Benton's shot went through his opponent's throat, while he suffered only a grazed knee. Benton demanded that Lucas "stand again,"[87] though that right was traditionally reserved for the challenger. Benton finally agreed to let Lucas lie bleeding, but only if they would meet again. Despite attempts by Lucas through intermediaries to seek reconciliation, Benton would only agree to shorten the distance in the next encounter to ten feet because Lucas was such a poor shot. When they next met, Benton shot him through the heart. In the same period, Lane rid himself of a duel by proposing the threat of an exploding powder barrel to settle a dispute.

While Benton had many supporters, he was widely detested. Judge William B. Napton had said earlier that "His passions were overpowering and malignant, and compromise and forgiveness was not in his nature; those who opposed him or seemed to stand in his way, he attempted to crush."[88]

There was another aspect of Benton's character that was vastly different from Lane's—influencing national policy for the benefit of his supporters. Bernard DeVeto describes it in his exhaustive history of the Western fur trade, *Across the Wide Missouri*. The *Company* to which he refers is John Jacob Astor's American Fur Company, which had taken over Chouteau's extensive St. Louis fur business. "A corporation like the Company could use inside information about the activities of its competitors, strict enforcement of government regulations against them, a liberal construction of these regulations in its own behalf, and a dependable means of circumventing the government's plain intent to deal justly with the Indians and equably with the traders." The company had employees all over the Western country in which beaver were trapped. In addition, "On the highest level it had such men as Thomas Hart Benton, who readily abandoned the egalitarian principles of the Jacksonian revolution when interests in fur were threatened, and Daniel Webster, whose notes and whose friends notes the Company held."[89]

Lane never attracted real enemies, despite his strong feelings and sometimes a quick temper. John Darby, a decades-long associate in St. Louis had said, "hence, everybody who was honored with his acquaintance and friendship became warmly attached to him."[90] Calvin Horn wrote of his short time in New Mexico, "His kindness, mature understanding and appreciation for things New Mexican won friendship and respect for the Governor's office."[91]

Not surprisingly, their personality differences extended to their family relationships, most noticeably with their daughters Anne and Sarah Lane and Jessie Benton. Lane was solicitous of the health and well-being of both daughters, particularly Anne, who never married and lived with her mother and father much of her life. He had the highest regard for Sarah's husband, William Glasgow Jr., a member of a family of successful Santa Fe traders. They remained close during the Civil War, though on opposite sides.

Benton, however, doted on Jessie, the second of his six children, and attempted to impose his will on her. He objected to her marriage to John C. Fremont. But when he could not stop it, he tried to advance the career of her husband until he ran for president in 1856 as the first candidate of the Republican Party. Benton then stayed true to the Democratic Party and voted for Buchanan, even though he didn't like him. Jessie worked tirelessly for her husband. Fremont was controversial throughout his life and remains so.[92] At least three facts are clear about Fremont: one, he was court-martialed on January 31, 1848, for disobeying orders of General Kearney during the Mexican War—President Polk granted clemency; two, he lost his bid for the presidency in 1856 in a vicious campaign centered on slavery—he was opposed; and three, his presumptions as commander of the Armies of the West in St. Louis caused him to be replaced by President Lincoln in 1861 after one hundred days – among other things, he had placed St. Louis under martial law and ordered the houses and possessions of Southern sympathizers seized. Still, many considered him as The Pathfinder because of his earlier expeditions in the West, flamboyant manner, and the influence of the even more ambitious Jessie.

Benton reached elected office first when he was selected by

the Missouri legislature in 1820 to represent the state as one of two senators in the United States Congress. He had to wait to be seated until 1821 when Missouri was finally admitted as a state. He was so disliked in his home city that only three of the twenty-seven votes he received came from St. Louis.[93] The deciding vote was cast by Daniel Ralls, who was carried on his deathbed to the legislative chamber to vote for Benton and died shortly after being carried back to his room.

Lane was elected mayor in April 1823 with more votes than his two opponents, one of whom was the elderly Auguste Chouteau. In 1826, he was elected to the State House of Representatives as a Jackson Democrat. He was reportedly offered the opportunity to run against Benton who was seeking a second term in the Senate, but turned the offer down, even though he was assured of victory. That one event may in itself summarize the differences in the two men.

The contrasts in character and motivation that governed their parallel careers over the next three decades can be interpreted in various ways but are well defined in the well-known phrase, "The fox knows many things, but the hedgehog knows one big thing."[94]

Lane was a fox --Benton a hedgehog.

Part II

St. Louis: A Complex Life

1820-1846

The First Mayor

Wm. Carr Lane's restlessness had not been dampened during the first year and a half of his marriage, but it again seemed likely that it would be when he, Mary, and the five-month-old Anne settled in St. Louis. The city was still on the urban frontier, with a mixed and often violent population prone to barroom fights amongst river men and duels between lawyers.

It was also in the midst of the economic hardship resulting from the Panic of 1819, which had overwhelmed the entire country and is generally considered to be America's first depression. Since then, economic ups and downs have continued at not infrequent intervals for almost two hundred years. The causes would now be familiar --, the bursting of a land-price bubble, a fall in the price of export commodities, and the contraction of bank credit initiated by the Second Bank of the United States, which had forced local banks to follow suit and ultimately fail, including some in St. Louis. Many blamed the profligate living of gamblers and the greed of speculators, but the banks, with good reason, bore the brunt

43

of the attacks. Thomas Hart Benton railed against them, "all the flourishing cities of the west are mortgaged to this money power. They may be devoured at any moment. They are in the jaws of a monster."[95] The crisis continued until 1823, the year Lane was elected mayor. By that time, the proliferation of business failures had caused the city's population to drop by 35 percent.[96]

Lane must have believed that he had finally settled down, but it was not to be. In a little over a year, Mary, again pregnant, was back with her family in Vincennes. Lane stayed in St. Louis for over three months lamenting their separation but did get to Vincennes before the birth of their second daughter, Sarah, on March 19, 1821.

When the one-year lease on their house expired, he and a friend, William Pettis, moved to a boarding house—"We pay $4.50 per week + are well fed + civilly treated."[97] He was lonely. "I have lived in boarding-houses, taverns + such like places, for at least 13 out of the last 17 years of my life, of course I do not feel strange in them, but be assured there is no place like one's home – provided always that the Husband's bosom warms at the very sight of his wife."[98]

The separation took its toll—or at least caused some doubts. He defended himself against questions Mary raised, "If there is ought in it (a letter from Pettis) impeaching my steadiness or constancy, recollect that I am entitled to a hearing before judgment is pronounced – About those ladies who you say 'do not love their husbands better than they do a certain Doctor,' pray be easy."[99] He goes on to accuse her of running away to the arms of an old beau and leaving him to freeze, though he had said in earlier letters that it was entirely his decision for her to return to her family. It is a little hard to imagine any young woman eight months pregnant and with a daughter not yet two falling into the arms of an old beau, much less Mary.

Lane was beset with financial concerns because of the number of doctors moving to St. Louis. He occupied his shop and moved back to the house, which had not been re-let, to save the cost of living in the boarding house. Even though he formed a partnership with a younger doctor from Virginia, he vacillated between going to Vincennes and staying in St. Louis and in the process wrote of the motivations that had governed his life. "In this conflict between <u>inclination</u> and prudential considerations – I may say <u>duty</u>, what am I to do? Shall I upon this occasion persist in what I have done all my life (to my unutterable sorrow) – obey the dictates of <u>feeling</u> and of <u>passion</u>, or shall I for once listen to my old + faithful but slighted monitor prudence, + remain at my business until it becomes indispensably necessary to go to you?"[100] "Prudence," which he seemed to ignore while single, won out now, and he stayed in St. Louis.

There were other reasons for his pleading financial stress. He was building a house and worried about both the workmen, who often failed to appear, and the shortages of material, but agreed to look after the two children of a widow who appeared to be dying. One eventually joined the Lane household. He also contemplated a way of life in the new house and explained to his mother in Kentucky how to send two slaves to St. Louis, assuming it were legal, when the family was reunited. The two would be sufficient to provide household help and look after his horse.

While he fretted about his daily financial problems and planned a new way of life, he described the Panic of 1819 at the local level. "I know not who is rich in this community besides Mullanphy, who is seizing upon every wreck that offers. Easton is sold out of house + home – literally – property will not bring anything – 3 lots upon the hill, (one of wh. had been contracted to be sold for $1,000 last spring only), the other day sold for $140. God preserve the land from total ruin, but I can see no help for those who are much in debt, because their property will not command anything."[101] He was frugal enough to avoid going into debt and built their new house on his doctor's fees.

Despite his strong feelings, contending with daily problems apparently precluded him from taking part in or commenting on the great debate raging in Washington over slavery, which forty years later would isolate Lane while tearing the country apart. It was not of great concern to people in St. Louis, who not surprisingly were concentrating on their economic survival and simply considered slavery a part of life. The uproar was started by James Tallmadge, a New York congressman who offered an amendment to the 1819 "enabling act," which would have made Missouri a state. His proposal, which was similar to one enacted in his state, contained several provisions which would have led gradually to emancipation by prohibiting the importation of slaves after statehood was granted and requiring that children of slaves already residing in Missouri become free when they reached the age of twenty-five.

This proposal unleashed tensions that had been smoldering since the War of 1812. There was always the underlying concern that the balance between free and slave states would be upset when a new state was admitted. Of greater importance, however, was the introduction of cotton in the South, which had made slaves even more valuable. The price of a first-rate field hand had increased from four or five hundred dollars in 1814 to eight to eleven hundred in 1819.[102] Moreover, a woman giving birth to male children provided another source of long-term capital gain. On top of the political and economic concerns, the Southerners saw in the amendment both the first steps towards emancipation and the loss of the opportunity to extend slavery to the west.

The initial debate ended in March 1819 with no resolution but started again when a new Congress convened. The Missouri Compromise, for which Henry Clay was given much credit, consisted of a series of bills passed early in 1820. The compromise eliminated the Tallmadge provisions, allowed Maine to enter as a free state, and prohibited slavery in the Louisiana Territory north of 36° 30', the southern boundary of Missouri, except for that state. It seemed to be over. Missouri with ten thousand slaves, about 15 percent of the population, would become a state.[103] But it was not over. The Missouri Constitutional Convention included a clause in the proposed constitution that required the state legislature to enact a law that would bar free Negroes or mulattos from living in the state. This clause caused another uproar, and Missouri was not admitted until August 1821 after a way was found around the conflict with the US Constitution that had been created by the Missouri Constitution.

Lane was in Vincennes for the birth of Sarah on March 19, 1821,but stayed only a few weeks. Sometime early in May he took Mary, the newborn Sarah, and Anne who had just turned two, to stay with his mother in Shelbyville. Presumably, there was a road suitable for a carriage—the trip was over a hundred miles. About a month later he set off on horseback on another journey of over four hundred miles to Fayette County, Pennsylvania, to take care of business both there and en route. He was accompanied by "Jane," who may have been Mary's niece and wanted to return to her family in Pennsylvania. "Miss Jane got into a good humor at my mothers + continued so generally throughout the journey, of course she was very little trouble to me."[104] They had made nine stops along the way, taking care of business for Mary's father in Frankfort, Kentucky; tending to Lane's unspecified business in Chillicothe, Ohio; and managing his land speculation near Columbus, Ohio. On at least three days they were delayed by rain, so when they were free to ride without hindrance, they must have traveled at least forty miles a day.

The feelings he expressed on again seeing the land of his boyhood were not the musings of an old man about the land of his birth—those came decades later. He wrote Mary on this trip, "I leave you to imagine the strong but mingled emotions which took possession of my mind upon again beholding the bold + romantic land of my birth + the home of my boyhood,"[105] but he did not express any regret at leaving.

He rode alone back to his family in Shelbyville, arriving sometime in late June or early July, gathered them up in a coach, and returned to St. Louis, undoubtedly stopping in Vincennes. Because of a three-year gap in his letters to Mary, it appears that they settled in their new house while he went about his varied occupations. During this period, their third daughter, Julia Gratiot, was born in October 1822.

Whatever the date of their arrival in St. Louis in the fall of 1821, Lane had to get busy again with his medical practice and tend to family and household duties. He and Mary attended many parties and cotillions with the upper levels of St. Louis society. In the same year, shortly after Missouri became a state, he was appointed aide-de-camp with the rank of colonel to Governor Alexander McNair of the Missouri militia. Early in the next year, he was made quartermaster general, a position that required him to travel about the state with large amounts of cash to pay members of the militia. Because of the constant threat of robbery, he carried the funds in an old, dirty sack, which he threw in the corner of his room in the rural inns and taverns in which he stayed. There is no indication of the length or duration of his trips, but the ruse apparently worked. It was similar to his earlier ventures from Fort Belle Fontaine, but now with a different rank and carrying cash rather than medical supplies.

He was clearly an established and respected person who had become acquainted with a wide range of prominent citizens. Lane was not a lawyer or politician seeking power but a professional man with military and business experience. He also cared enormously about his family. He simply commanded respect; joining the officers' mess during the War of 1812 while an unpaid militiaman had been an early example.

He could not, however, turn down a challenge or opportunity

to employ his experience and judgment in new fields. His stated tendency toward "inclination over prudence" was dominant.

He was elected the first mayor of St. Louis in April 1823 with more votes than the combined total of his two opponents, the city's most prominent citizens, the seventy-three-year old Auguste Chouteau, and another elderly, long-time resident, Marie Philippe Leduc. The nine elected aldermen were young businessmen from Pennsylvania and Virginia.[106] The election, however, almost did not take place, for in the previous month the vote to incorporate the city had won by only 17 of the 197 votes cast. Only taxpayers could cast ballots, and the Panic of 1819 had substantially reduced their number.[107]

The election was a further sign of the change from the dominance of the old families. In 1811 almost two-thirds of the total tax assessments were held by six men.[108] In 1818, two-thirds of the population was still French and their language dominated the community. However, between that time and the election, as in other frontier cities, there was an influx of businessmen, doctors, lawyers, and even theatrical companies. St. Louis remained primarily a trading center, in contrast to Pittsburgh and Cincinnati, where manufacturing flourished. The fur trade had been dominant for decades, but lead mined in Wisconsin and Missouri now grew in importance. The city sold raw material originating in the west to consumers in the east, while manufactured goods from the east moved through St. Louis to be sold on the frontier. This exchange caused trade to grow substantially after 1821 with Mexico's Proclamation of Independence and the opening of the Santa Fe Trail by William Bicknell. St. Louis, by virtue of its location, was growing in importance as a center of commerce.

Term One and Getting Organized

The inauguration of the first mayor of St. Louis, Wm. Carr Lane, on April 14, 1823, was an historic event for the city and a milestone in his life. Missouri had been admitted to the Union as a state almost two years earlier, and now its largest and most important community was organized as a city. Until this date, Lane had devoted his life to medicine, business, the military, and for the previous five years his family. He would, for the next thirty years, also devote a major part of his time and energy to significant government positions.

The inauguration itself was carried out with an element of ceremony, if not pomp. The board of aldermen convened in response to a proclamation issued by the mayor. After they had been duly sworn in, they elected officers. They then established a committee of two to notify the mayor that a quorum had assembled. Mr. Gamble was designated to be one of the two committee members and the messenger. He left to inform the mayor, who was presumably waiting in an adjoining room. Mr. Gamble returned to report that he had delivered the message, and the mayor then appeared and spoke.

Lane was thirty-four and had received a classical education. His only responsibilities involving law or government had been during the short time he worked in his brother's prothonotary office recording deeds in Pennsylvania fourteen years earlier.

He was a natural and highly respected leader, but his understanding of the responsibilities of government and practicalities of reaching his goals had to have been based on his early and varied education, including instruction from the ministers at Jefferson College and the beliefs of Benjamin Rush embedded in the curriculum at Dickinson College. The formal training was augmented by reading his father's books.

When Lane appeared before the aldermen, he delivered an

address that revealed his remarkable understanding of the existing problems in St. Louis and the philosophy of the government that should lead the city in the future. He began with their current situation:

> In governments so essentially popular as that of this corporation, the will of the people must be specially consulted, before anything of magnitude is begun, if it is not, even when the measures are wise what is the result? Why, the next election produces an entire change of men and measures, and what had been begun is abandoned, and what had been expended may be lost.

The actions to be undertaken were limited, but should not be isolated:

> As we came into office with a Treasury literally empty, and as heavy taxes cannot, at the present time, be easily borne, our undertakings must be limited to those of the first necessity only; but let whatever is undertaken, be done according to some general plan …

He spoke of the past and the future:

> A few years since this place was the encamping ground of the solitary Indian trader; soon it became the depot and residence of many traders, under the organization of a village and now you see it rearing its crest in the attitude of an aspiring city. The regulations adopted in the first stage, did not suit the second, and those of the second, are

in their turn out of date ... The fortunes of the inhabitants may fluctuate; you and I may sink into oblivion, and even our families become extinct, but the progressive rise of our city is morally certain.

He raised the problem of streets that were not in a rectangular pattern but knew correcting that was a long-term project. Health, however, required immediate attention:

I recommend the appointment of a Board of Health to be selected from the body of the citizens, with ample powers to search out and remove nuisances, and to do whatever else may conduce to general health. ...

An authority to the register to employ a carter, with one or more attendant labourers, to be immediately employed in removing nuisances, making drains and doing the occasional jobs of the town would, I think, be an economical and useful arrangement.

He was always worried about education:

I will hazard the broad assertion, that a free school is more needed here than in any town of the same magnitude in the Union.

He concluded:

Gentlemen – We have assumed heavy tasks and high responsibilities, let us not hope to give universal satisfaction; many enlightened Boards have sat heretofore, and perhaps none ever escaped censure. How could it be otherwise? Our citizens are assembled from every part of Europe and America; ... Let us pursue our course with cautious moderation, with steadiness and unity; and let our motto be, impartiality, industry and economy.

St. Louis, April 14, 1823. Will. Carr Lane.[109]

His second inaugural address delivered a year later continued many of these themes, but the third laid out what he believed to be the foundation of government. His subsequent addresses were devoted largely to immediate concerns. He had already established the foundation for an effective city government.

NEVER A HEDGEHOG

The newly elected mayor and aldermen were well acquainted with each other; nevertheless, it had to have taken months to organize a government that could achieve even the short-term goals Lane had set out. The aldermen and the mayor, whose annual salary was three hundred dollars, were all part-time.

It would have been out of character had he not thrown himself into the task of governing by first getting rid of the dead animals on the levee. Practical matters, however, had not eliminated symbolism. Ordinance No. 1 was approved on April 22: "prescribing the emblem and devices of the Common Seal of the City of St. Louis, – a steamboat carrying the United States flag. The seal was to be circular and no more than one and a half inches in diameter." Dogs must have been a problem, because Ordinance No. 2 imposed a tax on dogs of two dollars each. Any dog found without a collar and no evidence of the tax having been paid could be lawfully shot with the killer paid a bounty of one dollar.

At the same time he was dealing with carcasses and untended dogs, he was engaged in many other pursuits, as he would be with seemingly unending energy until 1846, when he was stricken with malaria and the death of his son Ralph. During the intervening twenty-three years, he was occupied with a variety of medical positions, business enterprises, and military assignments while at the same time serving as mayor for nine years and a member of the Missouri legislature for six.

He was a physician who was ready to respond to a call at any time of the day or night. "Between my business + my practice, I am always employed, - + I must add, - annoyed also – accidents are continually happening around us of late + claiming a portion of my attention – A boy + a man, was each run over by carts – another man was buried some 5 feet under ground, - he standing nearly erect, by the falling of a Bank of earth. We dug him out + he will live – Another man got his skull fractured, + I trepanned him – removing about 3 square inches of skull bone - + he does well – all these were the occurrences of yesterday + just at hand."[110]

Aside from this mention of the trepanning, Lane rarely commented on the treatments he utilized. From 1841 to 1844, he was Chairman of Obstetrics and Diseases of Women and Children at Kemper College. He bought and sold real estate, often involving the Ewing and Glasgow families. His business ventures met with varying degrees of success and one dramatic disaster. The Eagle Powder Works and adjoining magazine, which he owned, exploded in 1836, causing great devastation but apparently no deaths. It was located on twenty acres and produced six hundred pounds of powder a day.[111]

He was part of the political power structure of Missouri but did not seek national power. He apparently had declined the offer of a Senate seat but in 1827–1828 announced his candidacy for the Democratic nomination to the US House of Representatives. He withdrew later because of the party's fear that his and Spencer

Pettis's dual candidacy would split the Democrats and result in the election of a Whig. Shortly thereafter, he became dissatisfied with Jackson's policies and switched to the Whig Party.

During all this activity there was ongoing violence, often between Creoles and newcomers. Prior to the mayoral election, a group of men established the Regulations to hold midnight courts to punish by whipping and banishment those guilty of financial fraud and gambling. In 1820, the St. Louis Guards were established to replace the Regulations. "A whipping post was built where male and female criminals received the standard thirty-nine lashes, administered by a sheriff who was sworn to lay them on without 'fear, favor or affection.'"[112]

In the 1820s, the county sheriff had two sets of stocks constructed. Murders continued to take place in broad daylight. In 1826, a young lawyer killed another attorney in midmorning but escaped. A year later, a young man killed a soldier while drunk. He did not get away and was hanged publicly. Among the more prominent citizens, dueling continued on Bloody Island until 1856.[113] The most infamous of all the duels had occurred in 1817 when Thomas Hart Benton killed Charles Lucas to seek revenge, not honor.

In 1835, Lane included in a letter to Anne and Sarah, who were then in school in Philadelphia, a description of a duel on the street between two Spaniards with knives. They both died. He also described two Italian musicians getting into a knife fight. One died, and the other went to prison. In 1842, he wrote of the killing of a man who had been refused admittance to a ball. Several days later, accompanied by a friend and armed with pistols, he sought out the doorkeeper, who shot first. Lane considered it "justifiable homicide."

Constant concern for his family and a wife who retreated to her family's home in Vincennes for months at a time was combined with all these activities. Mary is remembered as being morose and irritable, not a pleasant combination. But life then was not easy. During the seventeen years between May 1819 and May 1836, she bore eight children. She was pregnant over a third of that time. Only the two first born, Sarah and Anne, lived into adulthood, Anne dying in 1904. Of the remaining six, five died before their fourth birthday. Except for a period of three months in 1836, there were never more than three living at one time.

Mary seemed to worship her husband but refused to have any part of his professional life. She and her husband were very different, both physically and emotionally. "He was a tall, heavy-set man with an ebullient, gregarious disposition and an explosive temper. She was short, and, as she was then described, 'fleshy.'"[114]

TERM TWO

Because St. Louis was a trading hub rather than a manufacturing center, it recovered from the national financial crisis of 1819 rather quickly and, in fact, never suffered as deeply as did other frontier cities such as Pittsburgh. Those individuals whose personal financial disasters had been described by Lane would not have agreed.

The two main elements of the St. Louis economy were fur trading and shipping lead, both of which were well established when Lane became mayor but expanded rapidly during the following decade. The fur trade grew to a large extent because of the breakup of the so-called "factor system," which had placed the government in control of key trapping sites on western streams. The government monopoly was broken in 1822 under pressure from Thomas Hart Benton.[115] Within six months, one thousand men went up the Missouri, and five hundred started operating on the Mississippi.[116] The lead trade continued to grow, as did St. Louis. More of the goods shipped over the Santa Fe Trail were made in St. Louis, rather than back east. In 1821, a city register listed a tannery, three soap and candle factories, two brickyards, three stone cutters, fourteen bricklayers and plasterers, twenty-eight carpenters, ten painters, a nail factory, four coopers, four bakers, a comb maker, a bell factory, and two potteries.

This listing may not have been very impressive, but during the next decade, hundreds of businesses started and thrived with the new western trade. In addition, St. Louis provided much of the equipment required by the wagon trains. Joseph Murphy completed his apprenticeship in 1825 and opened a shop that, in the coming years, became a factory that manufactured thousands of wagons. Jacob Hawkin started making guns in 1821; the blacksmiths flourished.

The mayoral term was one year, but Lane and the aldermen were easily reelected. He delivered his second message to the opening session on May 3, 1824, again reminding them of the heavy responsibilities placed on them and emphasizing the importance of determining the limits of their responsibilities. All the frontier cities were struggling to convert the sometimes vague clauses in their charters to the practical definitions needed to establish enduring institutions.

There was much business left over from the prior session, and Lane quickly turned to the straightening and paving of roads that had been started by assessing owners of property adjacent to the street. The owners were now seeking refunds. Lane thought this method was basically unfair, because the general public benefited from the improvements. He believed, however, that property owners should be assessed for the sidewalk, because they could build a cellar under it that would be for their sole use. Lane, therefore, devised a financing scheme that allowed property owners to be assessed, but at the same time gave them a tax credit of an equal amount. The city would in effect borrow the money from its citizens. He justified the nonpayment of interest because of the increase in value of the property.

He believed that taxes overall should be lowered to a level

adequate for the normal expenses of operating the city but not used for capital improvements, such as water works and streets. Borrowing from the citizens for those purposes was a temporary measure to be employed only until funds could be borrowed from those whom he termed "capitalists."

His strong views about public markets, which offered a variety of goods, showed a basic understanding of the functions of free enterprise and competition. There were a number of markets open to the public on different days. He advocated for a single one operating on an established schedule to assure real competition and lower prices.

The Lanes' third daughter, Julie Gratiot, died at the age of one year, nine months on July 24, seventy-eight days after he spoke to the aldermen. There was never an explanation of the illnesses to which the children succumbed or of how long they had been ill. Mary soon departed for Vincennes, taking Sarah and Anne with her. Both he and Mary were deeply depressed when he wrote her on August 21 showing his deep feelings and at the same time revealing his inability to remain idle. "You went away on Sunday, it was a heavy day to me … I know not how it was, but I felt an indefinable sensation of loss and desolation, which made all places alike worrisome + gloomy."[117] He had to go to the country and passed the "hallowed spot"[118] where Julie Gratiot was buried. Two days earlier another child, Isabelle Cabanne, had also been interred there. He visited the Cabannes but returned home and attended to business, "which made me forget all things, save those that were before me."[119]

Death was always present. "Mrs. Dorsay's child is dead – Miss Ames at Shockford's is dead."[120] Accidental deaths continued to occur on a regular basis: "one of an extra ordinary kind – a drunken Irish-man careening on the Hill in late very dark night, encountered the shaft of a one-horse Dearborne which he met without seeing – the shock was so great that the shaft entered and posted up along the muscles, + ran deep into his body – what made the affair the more remarkable was that the Dearborne contained Leonard + his second on their way to fight a duel with Taylor Berry."[121] The event that caused the duel had occurred earlier, after Major Berry had assaulted Leonard in a courtroom. The major asked for a two-month delay because of pressing business. Both men had to go to New Orleans, so the duel took place on an island in the Mississippi near Cairo. Berry survived a shot in the chest but died two weeks later of pneumonia. The letter was also concerned with larger issues – he was pleased that Frederick Bates had been elected governor.

He soon wrote again, saying Mary's first obligation was to her parents but asked her not to neglect the girls. He was, understandably, concerned about their health and education. "I am in too much dread of sickness to consent to Anne's going to school until after frost – but the growing up so rapidly in total ignorance is a source of disquiet."[122]

His mind switched constantly. In a postscript he asked, "What does your Father think of my scheme for raising sheep? and Pray what sends the Hormonites away from Indiana?"[123] The Hormonites, a strict and communal sect, had been founded in Württemberg, Germany, in the eighteenth century. In 1803 some 250 moved to Pennsylvania, and then a few moved on to Indiana.

Mary did not write often, but she did so on September 19, 1824, a few weeks after arriving in Vincennes. Perhaps due to grief over the first death of one of her children, she wanted to return. Despite the warmth of her family and the comfort of the farm, she ended with, "never had a greater wish to see you, but will let you decide when I return – Fall – Winter – Spring.[124]

TERM THREE AND THE MARQUIS DE LAFAYETTE

Four days after Lane delivered his third address to the St. Louis aldermen on April 25, 1825, the city was overwhelmed by the arrival of the Marquis de Lafayette. The hero of the revolution was touring the country and had come up the Mississippi from New Orleans on the steamboat *Natchez*. It had tied up the night before at the village of Carondelet, five miles below the city.

St. Louis was able to organize an enthusiastic, if not elegant, welcome for the sixty-eight-year-old hero with a unique combination of the crude behavior common in a frontier town and the cultivated style of the prosperous and dominant French. Mary was not in St. Louis to participate in the festivities but rather in Vincennes, with her two daughters, where she would reside for much of the next six years.

The city did not have a wharf at the time and only two landings. The *Natchez* arrived at the Market Street landing at 9:00 AM with over half the population waiting on the levee. The band played *Hail to the Chief* until the general came ashore followed by his entourage, which included his son, George Washington Lafayette. The crowd surged forward as the mayor read his speech and Lafayette responded, "I have once more the satisfaction to see the descendants of France, and the descendants of my American contemporaries mingle in the blessings of republican institutions, and in a common sentiment of devotion to the confederate union; a union, Sir, so essential, not only to the fate of each member of the confederacy, but also to the general fate of mankind that the least breach of it would be hailed with barbarian joy, by a universal war whoop from European aristocracy and despotism."[125] His words were as fine as his leadership in the decisive battle at Yorktown, but the crowd was not listening, and the frontier St. Louis took control.

A butcher named Jacob Roth, wearing his usual greasy apron spattered with blood, slid from his horse, rushed through the crowd, and seized the startled general's hand, "Whooraw for liberty! Old fellow, just give us your hand. How are you!"[126] This assault was particularly galling to the crowd, for Roth was known to steal and butcher cows and then sell the meat back to the real owners. A drunken member of the reception committee intervened, and Lane ushered the general into the waiting barouche.

The barouche and two horses had been provided by Thomas Biddle, brother of Nicholas Biddle, president of the United States Bank. Judge Peck had also loaned two horses. The procession was led by Captain Archibald Gamble's light horse troop and followed by the crowd from the levee. The general, the mayor accompanied by a Revolutionary War veteran, and Colonel Auguste Chouteau all arrived safely at Chouteau's elegant mansion.

A band played "Auld Lang Syne" while the general was introduced. One Creole lady asked if this were his first trip to America. Another who came forward was Old Eleckzan, who had been with Lafayette during the revolution. Only after the soldier recounted an event that occurred on the ship carrying them from France did the general remember There was then combined embracing and weeping.

The rest of the day was occupied by a military review, a special meeting of the Masonic Lodge, and a visit to the general's old friend, William Clark. At four o'clock, an elegant dinner was served at the Chouteau mansion, followed by a ball. The finely dressed ladies and gentlemen of St. Louis danced late into the night, but Lafayette left after dinner to return to the *Natchez*, which departed early the next morning. The mayor remained until the general was out of sight.

Both the planned and unexpected events of the day illustrated the diffuse character of the city's population and again showed Lane's ability to act decisively. Prior to the visit, the aldermen were not sure that they could use city money for the welcome but hoped the state would provide funds for a grand reception. The capital was in St. Charles, but because there was no building, Governor Bates spent most of the time at his farm located beyond the capital. Lane rode the twenty miles to the farm, only to be turned down flat. Not only would the state not pay but Bates would not come nor be available if Lafayette traveled to St. Charles. The mayor and the aldermen decided to use city funds but agreed to repay them if the citizens objected. They did not, and the grand day cost the city thirty-seven dollars.

Less than two weeks elapsed between the time Lane made the futile forty-mile round trip to beseech the governor and the arrival of the *Natchez*. During that **period**, he had moved rapidly to organize Lafayette's reception with minimal funds, protected the general from a crude assault, and hosted him at an elegant dinner and ball. If Lane's actions related to the festivities demonstrated his ability to take charge and act, the address he delivered in the middle of this period revealed again his grasp of history, governance, and human nature.[127]

He began the message to the aldermen with reminders that they were all there to serve all the people: "let us wash our hands of all party and personal feelings, whether kind or unkind, before entering upon our duties, and act with an eye single to the good of the whole." He presented a sweeping view of the responsibilities and limitations of government.

He then took up the nature of "the law." He touched on the assumption that every citizen would understand legislation:

> Our institutions are built upon the flattering presumption that every citizen has the capacity to fulfill the expectations of his partial + indulgent friends + neighbours – in fact, that he is a competent legislator, whether he has any acquaintance with the first principles of law or morals, of state or municipal policy or not.

He argued that due consideration should be given to any proposed laws:

Nothing should be done passionately, or hastily. Passion deforms and defiles everything that it touches, + haste is, in all things, incompatible with excellence …

Experience is the best guide, in all human affairs, + from the aged we may reasonably expect lessons of experience. The records of other towns is another source from whence we expect to derive useful hints of the same kind.

He was concerned about overreaching laws that could encroach on individual freedom …

Many of the subjects on which you must legislate are in themselves contemptible, but it does not thence follow that an unstudied + (if I may speak), *contemptable* enactment will subserve your purpose therein the law in relation to it must be as minute + declaratory, as if you were legislating upon *High Treason*, with competent powers. A right of person or of property, even the most trifling, is dear to him who is in soul a Freeman; and if we are guilty of claiming the surrender or taking away a right however small, without the clearest necessity + the fullest power, we will deserve, not only the penalties of the law, but public obloquy.

He believed that laws could be effective and valuable to society only if they were understood:

The phraseology of our ordinance, in common with the state laws, seem to me unnecessarily verbose + repetitious. …

I would ask who knows the whole extent of his rights, or his duties, under the code of this state? Let us avoid an example so pernicious. The course is most unwise, for men are more 'guided and influenced by custom than by reason,' and if laws are not sanctified by age, + supported by custom + habit, they operate a feeble restraint, compared with their influence under opposite circumstances; and how can we become habituated to them, - how can they become venerable, if every new Legislature, or Board, makes new codes. ...

Publicity is essential to the obligations of an act or ordinance, to affirm to the contrary is to support the absurd presentation that the tyrant who engraved his edicts upon plates of brass, + nailed them upon pillars so high no one could read them, was right in punishing infractions of those edicts.

He believed the authority of government was limited:

The Charter is our Polar Star, + as far on our way as it lights our path we have an unerring + acceptable guide: beyond this point, however unwillingly we must some times go: + there we launch into a sea of trouble.

He then went on to propose ordinances and amendments dealing with issues ranging from taxes and the salaries of city employees to the urgent need for a wharf.

Again showing his depth of understanding, he raised the issue of public schools. "In vain does our Constitution declare equal rights to every citizen! For as long as schools are open to some

+ shut upon others, so long will the highway to usefulness, to distinction, to wealth + renown be impeded if wholly blocked up against some, whilst no impediments will like in the carrier of others, - the children of wealth."

Despite Lane's plan for simplicity in language, he did not apply that rule to his speeches. The inclusion in one address of his philosophy of government, civic duties, and specific proposals combined with his verbosity must have caused him to go on for well over forty-five minutes.

At the same time that he was tending to the aldermen and Lafayette, he was seeing patients and fending for himself with the aid of household slaves. Mary was in Vincennes; his mother had died in Shelbyville, Kentucky, in November. His father had died there five years earlier. Mary apparently did return to St. Louis sometime in the late spring or summer, but there is no record of the date or method of transportation. She was certainly there until November, for her father wrote Lane on the twenty-fifth. His first concern was Anne's health, apparently the condition of her legs, for he offered to send some flannel he was making. Lane must have mentioned difficulty in collecting bills, for Ewing suggested he follow the practice of Vincennes physicians, who withheld bills until the patient died. It is not clear why Nathaniel thought the heirs would be glad to pay. He had heard a report that Lane had invested in a steam mill. Such a mill had ruined the Bank of Vincennes six years earlier. "You had better sell it ... I hate the very name of steam."[128]

Slavery continued as a part of life in St. Louis, but slaves were essentially household servants, and owners often owned more than were required for such duties. It was common, therefore, for owners to contract them out, frequently to work in factories. This not only provided income and removed them from the owner's property and supervision but at the same time created a sense of freedom in the contractees that concerned many in St. Louis. At times they became free Blacks—another matter of concern.

Lane shared these concerns and attempted to do something about them amidst his other activities. He convened a group of citizens to form an auxiliary of the American Colonization Society, which had come into being as a means of reducing the risk that free Blacks might live in the United States. The movement had started more than ten years earlier. Ten state legislatures had adopted it, and in 1819, President Monroe provided federal support. Former President Madison headed it. Following the British example of establishing Sierra Leone on the west coast of Africa as a home for Blacks leaving England, the society with the help of the US Government purchased adjacent land and established Liberia, with its capital, Monrovia, named after President Monroe. By the time of the Civil War, almost fifteen thousand Blacks had emigrated. But the basic idea never had a major effect, nor is there evidence that anyone from St. Louis was included.

TERM FOUR AND POLITICS BEYOND ST. LOUIS

Lane was reelected easily to a fourth one-year term in 1826, but his opening message on April 28 to the aldermen was vastly different both in content and length than the previous ones. Gone were the lectures on responsibility and philosophy of the law. He was not even in attendance but was in Vincennes with Mary, as one of their daughters was seriously ill.

His message opened with assurances that his absence meant no disrespect and that he would be gone no more than twenty days. The recommendations were confined to a proposed twelve-month budget, several appointments and leaves of absence, an accounting by the acting harbor master, and amendments to an ordinance dealing with paving streets. All were approved. An order that required members of the board to pay the fines they had incurred for nonattendance at scheduled meetings was introduced, but no vote was taken.

His basic character traits never changed – Lane was always a fox. He had said of himself that he followed the dictates of feelings and passion, both of which were driven by his always-present restlessness and curiosity. He was in his fourth term as mayor, dealing with the continuing problems of an expanding and changing city, maintaining a medical practice, dealing in real estate, managing a house and slaves, and looking out for himself because Mary was in Vincennes with Anne and Sarah. He traveled to Vincennes at least once, probably more frequently, for Julia Carr was conceived there in September.

Nevertheless, he decided to run as a Jackson Democrat for the Missouri legislature and was elected easily, becoming one of the three representatives from St. Louis County.

He also associated with members of the Missouri congressional delegation in Washington, and the letters he wrote during the rest of his life frequently showed a deep interest in national affairs and personalities, usually accompanied by his strong opinions. The two senators from Missouri, Thomas Hart Benton and David Barton, had been elected by the Missouri legislature in 1820 in accordance with the national method of choosing senators in anticipation of Missouri becoming a state as a result of the Missouri Compromise. However, Missouri did not become a state until 1821. Thus, when the two senators' terms expired in 1826, they had served only five years of their six-year terms. Though the opportunity to replace Benton was reported with some certainty by a personal friend, Lane had rejected the offer.[129]

Gordon Wood describes in *The Idea of America* the belief of many of the founding fathers in the need for "disinterestedness" on the part of public servants. They used the word in its true sense, not in the modern corruption, which makes it a synonym of "uninterest." Jefferson said, "The whole art of government consists of being honest." Samuel Johnson, the renowned English lexicographer of the eighteenth century, defined "disinterested" as being "superior to regard of private advantage; not influenced by private profit."[130]

Lane certainly had many private interests while he held public office, but there is no indication that he ever used these positions for personal gain. One can only speculate about what the effect on Congress and perhaps history would have been if the ascendancy of self-interest in American politics and Benton's subsequent fiery rhetoric dealing with Western expansion and the national bank had been replaced by Lane's speeches on the law and responsibility.

Lane had to make many preparations before leaving in mid-November for Jefferson City, which in 1822 had been designated as the state capital, including making arrangements for his medical practice, presumably seeing that all was in order in the mayor's office, and completing the purchase of a lot he had bought from a William Schlatte. However, it was personal matters he described when he wrote Mary at eleven at night on November 14. He had found places for four of the six slaves, Elise was soon to be located elsewhere and Lish was to stay at the house with the pigs and a dog named Pepper. "Almost all the moveables are stowed away in the garret, on acct. of the greater security of that place – Wm. (a slave under the temporary charge of a friend) will take the keys, - will sleep in the house every night."[131] Finally, at one thirty, he added a postscript describing his dinner with Cox. Lish was out doing the laundry at Chouteau's Pond, so the meal was prepared by substitutes. "The dinner neither looked nor eat so very well – there was not one drop of gravy or sauce – but I have no time for either facts or fun."[132]

Chouteau's Pond was adjacent to the city. Though located on Chouteau's land, it was treated as public property by the citizens of St. Louis, who used it for bathing, boating, sailing, and apparently laundry. The tone of the postscript to the letter describing the evening meal, "they had made a great sputter over dinner," reflected either the late hour or perhaps the consumption of wine, which he did not want to admit to.

Lane did as he had said and set out riding for the capital, which was located on the banks of the Missouri River a little over a hundred miles west and a little south of St. Louis. His journey, however, spanned 150 miles as he rode along the south side of the river – "people poor and accommodations bad."[133] He described the capital as "A cluster of short steep hills, on the Missouri river, with wide ravines, - over a wide extent of which are scattered 3 Brick buildings (one of wh. is the Governor's house + contains for the present both Government Legislature, + and the other two, Half finished taverns."[134]

The accommodations for legislators were in keeping with the town's development. He was housed in a cabin with four others and three beds. There was a kind of central dining arrangement feeding forty or fifty people with a well-supplied table.

He wrote Mary on Christmas Eve after all his roommates had gone to bed and added a postscript on Christmas morning.[135]

> The Egg-Knog is all drank up – the festive salutations of the day have been exchanged – Breakfast is over – the mail hour is at hand – the hour for the house to meet is near. And now my wife, remember that upon New Year the difficulties, the collisions + the heart burning of the year are to be forgotten – remember this my wife, + that I now kiss my hand to you, in anticipation of that day.

The legislature finished on January 2, but it is unlikely that they accomplished much on Christmas and probably less on New Year's Day.

Term Five and Seeking National Office

Lane gained a fifth term as mayor in 1827, easily overcoming minimal, though bitter, opposition. Again, he did not appear before the aldermen to deliver the annual message but sent a long report dated June 4. He was clearly gaining experience and did not feel it necessary to review the bases of laws but reported what had been learned and accomplished during his first four terms.[136]

> Many enlightened citizens have given aid, during the last four years, to build up a municipal code, suited to our condition; but much yet remains to be essayed, and much that has been done requires amendment. In truth, the whole body of our ordinances, presents a sort of patchwork, and calls for revision, amendment and consolidation.

He was not sure if the aldermen would want to take up such a complex task but felt it his duty to make a wide range of specific recommendations, including those related to administration (changing meeting duties); finances (there was no auditing of city expenditures); safety measures (increasing the fine for runaway horses and allowing chimneys to be burned out if the roof were wet); health (the establishment of a hospital and the location of privies); behavior (the prohibition of bawdy houses); basic finance (the simplification and equalization of a complex set of city, county, and state taxes); and a change in the method of financing capital improvements from operating funds to debt. He continued his plans to settle the question about refunds of assessments for the paving of streets, the establishment of a single marketplace, and the construction of wharves, perhaps floating ones similar to those in Cincinnati. The aldermen ordered fifty copies of his report to be printed.

He apparently was in Vincennes with Mary in April when their fourth daughter, Julia Carr, was born, almost three years after Julia Gratiot had died in St. Louis. Julia Carr lived to the age of three years and eight months, two years longer than her namesake. Prior to April, however, there had been a rather remarkable and revealing exchange of letters. Mary wrote Lane on January 1, 1827, apparently in response to a very critical letter he had written sometime in the fall. That letter has not survived, and it would seem likely that she destroyed it. She was so concerned that somebody other than Lane would open her letter that she posted it to Jefferson City. He left for St. Louis on the fourth, so he probably had not received it before his departure, and his long letter written from St. Louis on the ninth does not acknowledge it. It may never have caught up with him, or he may have decided that there was nothing to be gained by prolonging the bitterness.

Mary started her letter, "Dear Husband, your letter found us in great grief and you may well suffice it was not calculated to soothe my feelings. I therefore delayed answering it until I could do so with more propriety than I would have done at the moment."

Her distress was focused on her brother William, who had been dispatched to live in the Lane household some months earlier. She also acknowledged her own ill temper and seeming dependence on her husband. "I know I have many faults and much temper but even at this distance of time I see nothing to fault myself with. With regard to last summer disturbing you I knew you could not do otherwise than make a Brother welcome for a visit – but still you cannot know the difficulties I had to contend with and your letter convinces me there would be a repetition of them was our family composed of the same individuals. The presence is sufficient to destroy the peace of our house. I want no other evidence than it causing you to write the first unkind letter in your life whether he does it by insinuations or by making you view everything on the dark side the effect is the same and it is for you to say whether your children are to be sacrificed for a man who cares for no human being but self."[137] It would appear that William's behavior in St. Louis had set off Lane's temper and caused him to write the "only unkind" letter.

In contrast, Lane wrote a very favorable report of William on January 9, "James is doing well in business – he makes a very favourable report of Wm. – who is also pleased with his situation – but Wm.'s Education is incomplete – he must recommence school before long – the fact is, after all is said and done Wm. is a promising youth – I really do anticipate his becoming an ornament to his family – It is remarkable that in a Town of such vicious habits, the he shd. be, as he really is, free from all kinds of vice ‑ me thinks I now hear you compliment yourself, for the hard hand you have held upon him – But alas! here we differ in opinion."[138] It is only possible to speculate, but it is at least plausible that it was the atmosphere in the Ewing household that caused William's behavior.

Mary had continued on January 1, "I read your letter of a previous date with double the satisfaction I ever read one in my life there you are the quiet man and affectionate husband."[139] She then wrote of family members before ending, "I feel there is an apology due you for the commencement of this letter but as you appeared to think every person perfection but me ..."

She then reminded him that she had not complained when his brother Richard had come to live with them and upset their household. She ended almost with desperation, "Whatever course you may think proper to pursue toward me I submit to. I have no other home than your house. I cannot write anymore. May you and the children be happy whatever becomes of Mary Lane."[140]

Lane began his January 9 letter with a description of his return to St. Louis and his disappointment at finding that Mary was still in Vincennes. He had returned on the north side of the Missouri River riding Judy. He had encountered ice but did not indicate where he had slept. He had hoped to find her in St. Louis but was not surprised that she had not returned, though, "I saw that the weather was settled, + the roads good beyond example. I knew that an excellent line of stages, with good + careful driver ran through twice a week."[141]

He was sorry to find his brother Richard and hoped he would soon move on. "I changed my plan of going into a Boarding-house, + made a third one in the mess – (Richard – Wm. Ewing + myself) – our bill of fare is simple enough God knows - + as for my usual potation of wine it is utterly denied, + nothing is seen but whiskey, which you know I abominate – I will let things continue thus, until I learn your determination as to the time that you purpose returning – which I desire to know as soon as convenient."[142]

He was not sure that the "cabin" in which they were living would be large enough, but he was hopeful that court proceedings would allow him to get possession of the "other house" in the spring.

He described at great length the activities of their friends, describing deaths and gossip. He had not attended either of two grand balls, one at Jefferson Barracks and the other at a Mr. Barber's mansion. He wondered if he should slaughter her pigs and reported that her potatoes were "rich and safe" with "80-100 cabbage heads alongside." He was worried about the steam mill.

He finally ended the long letter, "To sum up all things in relation to myself – I am neither happy nor miserable – neither plenty nor scarce of cash (Note – This is a slip of the pen – I am scarce + fear I always will be so -) surrounded by secret + open enemies, but not at open war with any – nobody sick."[143]

Managing his personal affairs required a great deal of time even as he carried out the duties of the mayor. In addition, he maintained some kind of medical practice. Paul Gerbert, a thirty-two-year-old French physician, died the previous November while Lane was in Jefferson City. "When dying I understand he recommended me as the honestest man + safest physician in Town, but this cannot avail me much with the French – I have stood too much in the way of the ambition of their Patriarchs – They will never forgive me."[144] His defeat of the seventy-three-year-old Auguste Chouteau, the city's most prominent citizen, in the first mayoral election had not been forgotten.

Sometime in the spring or summer he decided to change course once again and run for the US House of Representatives in 1828. His decision not to challenge Benton for the Senate seat and to run for the House may have been prompted in part by the fact that Missouri had two senators and only one representative, so he might have had a greater voice as a representative. At least, he did not run again for the State House. He apparently did not discuss this potentially life-changing decision with Mary.

He ran as a Jackson Democrat, but it is not clear if he did so because of Democratic policies or because his background was in some ways similar to Jackson's. If nothing else, Lane was attracted to certain aspects of military life and had said that the Patriarchs would never forgive him.

He did not write of any direct contact with General Jackson, who was wary of Missouri at the time because of the vote of the single Missouri representative in the presidential election of 1824, which was thrown into the House because none of the four candidates had won a majority. Jackson had won a plurality of both electoral and popular votes – Jackson 42.5 percent of the latter, John Quincy Adams 31.5, William Crawford 13, and Henry Clay 13. Crawford withdrew because he did not have enough electoral votes to qualify and was in ill health.[145]

Clay realized he could not prevail but could not bring himself to align with Jackson, who he feared would become a military dictator. He delivered Kentucky, Ohio, and Missouri to Adams to give him the electoral votes needed to become the sixth president of the United States—and deepen his enmity with Jackson. Benton changed alliances twice as he tried to decide where his fortunes lay, starting as a supporter of Clay before changing to Crawford and finally to Jackson, which became of great significance when Jackson was elected president four years later and Benton had become a power in the Senate.

Lane stayed in St. Louis, occupied with his many responsibilities and preparing for his Congressional campaign, while Mary and her three daughters remained in Vincennes.

TERM SIX AND BETRAYAL BY BENTON

Lane, as usual, threw both time and endless energy into the campaign for the US House. Mary was in St. Louis in June 1828 when he wrote her from Fredericktown almost a hundred miles south of St. Louis, or "not more than some two + and a half days ride from home ... - But I have traveled much further in reaching here."[146] He left the next morning for Greenville, about fifty miles further south, and expected to get there that night after a "hard ride."[147] From there he intended to ride another sixty miles to New Madrid but found "the swamp to be impassable, + that I must return to Jackson in Cape Girardeau (county), + gather from that point."[148] He did not say that the detour added over forty miles to his trip. He could not refrain from being somewhat dismissive of Mary. "But it is needless to make these details of you, who knows little of the Geography of the country – To make a long story short – I will return home as soon as such as I possibly can, + 'you must not look for me until you see me.'"[149]

His business pursuits and medical activities were not put aside as he prepared for the campaign trip. Nine days before he wrote Mary from Fredericktown, he had sold six slaves, including two children, to Russel Farnham for $1,700. He had received five of the individuals three years earlier from Wilson P. Hunt as security for a debt of unknown amount, which was not repaid.

- William, 43, dark yellow complexion
- Lack, 20, yellow complexion
- Delia, 18
- Lydia, 10, yellow complexion, daughter of William
- George, 28, husband of Delia
- Molly, daughter of Delia (born since conveyance of slaves to Lane)

The deed concluded "the same slaves above mentioned and described. To have and to hold the said several slaves and their offspring, as slaves for life unto the said Russel Farnham, his heirs, executors, administrators, and assigns forever."[150] There was no more emotion involved with the sale of human beings who had been part of his household than there would have been with the sale of a horse. Like most of his contemporaries, it is doubtful that Lane thought of his slaves as human beings.

It was not the first contract between Lane, Hunt, and Farnham. Hunt had borrowed two thousand dollars from Farnham and on August 30, 1827, by a quick claim deed had assigned a substantial amount of property, including horses, oxen, cattle, hogs, sheep, wagons, and other equipment, to Lane to hold until the debt was satisfied.

No two individuals in the diverse population of St. Louis could have had more adventuresome and arduous backgrounds than Russel Farnham and Wilson P. Hunt, both of whom trusted Lane explicitly in their business dealings. Years earlier, they had been in the employ of John Jacob Astor, who built his fortune in the fur trade with a shrewd mind and an uncanny ability to predict the future. It is hard to imagine now that not only wealth in St. Louis but fortunes in New York were based on beaver pelts. Beyond leading to personal success and failure, the trade was the basis of ongoing disputes in American-Canadian relations.

Astor had prospered for years because of the fur trade in the

Great Lakes, but during the War of 1812 he aimed also to take over the trade in the West. In April 1811, he dispatched Hunt up the Missouri River to establish a trading post at the mouth of the Columbia River in Washington. At about the same time, he sent Farnham on a ship that was to go around Cape Horn and up the Pacific coast to Washington. At some point, the ship was wrecked. Hunt, however, reached the Pacific coast by the Missouri River route in February 1812 and established a post appropriately named Astoria. It is not clear when Farnham arrived, but by the time he did, the British Northwest Company had taken over Astoria while Hunt was away on an expedition in Canada. When he returned, the British forced him to accept forty thousand dollars for Astor's furs, which were reported to be worth double that amount.

Farnham was assigned the job of transporting the cash to New York. He chose to travel up the Pacific coast, across the ice in the Bering Sea to the Kamchatka Peninsula, across Siberia to St. Petersburg, hence to Paris and New York. He delivered the money to Astor two years later. It was obviously an arduous and a seemingly impossible trip by a single man. He had started out with a few provisions and ultimately had to eat his shoe tops. The only possible explanation for choosing the improbable route was fear of the British in Canada and of the Indians or the American government on the Missouri River.

Farnham eventually arrived in St. Louis in 1826 after overseeing Astor's fur interests in the Great Lakes region. But he died almost penniless at the age of forty-eight, a victim of the 1832 cholera epidemic. Hunt had arrived about 1820, settling down as a farmer and mill owner, but was plagued by financial problems until his death in 1842.

Lane's political ambition and campaign came to naught, not because of electoral defeat but because of backroom dealing. The incumbent, Edward Bates, was a Whig whom Benton and the Democrats were determined to defeat. Unfortunately, in addition to Lane, Spencer Pettis was also running as a Democrat. There was no primary, so the quandary over a split Democratic vote was referred to Thomas Hart Benton representing Lane and John M. Bass representing Pettis. The usually persuasive Benton capitulated, because he was determined to defeat Bates and apparently thought Pettis the better candidate. While Secretary of State, Pettis had ended every piece of official communication with the words, "Please say that I am a candidate for Congress."[151] It was simply a cold political calculation. He was trying to strengthen the Jackson forces. Lane was from St. Louis, where Benton had little support, and he did not think Pettis would withdraw under any circumstances. Lane later shifted to the Whig party, with which he remained the rest of his life. The change may well have been caused by a combination of gradual disillusionment with Jackson and a personal sense of betrayal.

The defeated Bates returned to St. Louis with his wife and large family. They had seventeen children, eight of whom survived to adulthood. As a judge, he was highly respected and prosperous but gradually withdrew from public life. However, he was later persuaded to seek the Republican nomination for president in opposition to William Seward, Salmon Chase, and Abraham Lincoln. Lincoln named him attorney-general after the election, and he became one of the influential Team of Rivals in the president's cabinet.[152]

Pettis's career in Washington was, however, not to be lengthy. He was reelected in 1830 and ran again in 1832. His opponent in the latter campaign was an aging David Barton, a strong supporter of the National Bank and, therefore, of its president, Nicholas Biddle. Pettis's attacks on Barton and the bank so angered Major Thomas Biddle, paymaster of the United States Army and a director of the St. Louis branch of his brother's National Bank, that he physically attacked Pettis as he lay ill in a hotel room. Benton, who lived next to the hotel, intervened. He persuaded

Pettis not to issue an immediate challenge to a duel but to have Biddle arrested and wait until after the election. He did not want to risk the addition of another voice in Congress in favor of the bank. Pettis bided his time until he won, but within weeks of his resounding victory, he challenged Major Biddle to a duel at three in the afternoon on August 26, 1831 on Bloody Island. Biddle, as challenger, selected pistols at a distance of five feet. The long barrels clinked as they hit at the same time the triggers were pulled. Both men died.

National recognition of the Whigs as a second political party occurred on the fourteenth of April 1834 with a speech in the Senate by Henry Clay. The name "Whig" was used because of the comparison of Jackson with British monarchs. "A denomination, which according to the analogy of all history, is strictly correct. It deserves to be spread throughout the whole country." Only an American Whig party could, Clay said, rescue the nation "from a chief magistrate who is endeavoring to concentrate in his own person the whole powers of the government."[153] The immediate cause of Clay's wrath was Jackson's transfer of federal funds from the National Bank to state banks.

Jackson shared the public's suspicion of banks, particularly the Second National Bank, which had been chartered in 1816 along the lines of Hamilton's First National Bank. Despite the fact that the bank was "the arbiter of the nation's money supply, the bestower or withholder of property,"[154] the US government held only 20 percent of the stock, and the president appointed only five of the twenty-five directors.[155]

Nicholas Biddle, a man of great ego and ambition, became the bank's president in 1823 and simultaneously a bitter adversary of Andrew Jackson. He was bolstered by the Supreme Court's ruling that the bank was constitutional and saw no conflict in a private entity holding such power over the national economy.

He immediately set about making Philadelphia the financial

center of the country by consolidating the bank's power and constructing marble headquarters on Chestnut Street. The disagreements between Jackson and Biddle grew but did not reach the crisis point until 1832 with Jackson's bid for reelection. The bank's charter ran until 1836, but Biddle decided to assure its and his future by seeking in 1832 to have the charter extended for fifteen years past 1836. Congress passed the bill.

But on July 10, 1832, Andrew Jackson issued "the most important presidential veto in American history."[156] The president spoke eloquently about the average person. "The rich and the powerful too often bend the acts of government to their selfish purposes ... to make the rich richer and the patent members more powerful, the humble members of society – the farmers, mechanics, and laborers – who have neither time nor the means of securing like favors to themselves have a right to complain to their government."[157]

In a letter to Mary four years later, Lane wrote, "Clay has tried my patience exceeding, - he is nearly as egotistical + as overbearing as Old Hickory himself. I will bet something handsome that they are blood kin if they could trace their lineage, + that they were both born in Ireland."[158] He had no use for men who maneuvered and were ruthless in reaching their political objectives.

He decided not to run for a seventh term as mayor in 1829 and was out of the legislature because of his run for the US Congress. He did not hold public office until he was reelected to the state legislature in 1830.

OUT OF OFFICE AND INDIAN REMOVALS

Lane had just turned forty in 1830 when a new decade began. He held no public office for the first time in seven years. Mary must have been in St. Louis, for the last letter to Vincennes had been written in October of the previous year, and there were no more until November 1830. At the time, they had three living children. The youngest, Julia Carr, died in mid-December at the age of three years, eight months, leaving only Anne and Sarah.

Andrew Jackson had won the presidency in 1828 in a campaign featuring outlandish claims. Jackson's people had accused John Quincy Adams of providing a woman for the czar of Russia, and the Adams campaign in turn claimed Jackson's wife was a bigamist and his mother a whore.[159]

Early in 1830, Congress started work on legislation that would enable Jackson to achieve one of his primary goals -- the removal of all Indians to the west of the Mississippi River. The Senate Indian Affairs Committee in February reported out a bill entitled "The Bill for an Exchange of Lands with the Indians Residing in Any of the States or Territories, and for Their Removal West of the Mississippi." The bill not only authorized the actions indicated by the title but abrogated all existing treaties with Indian tribes.

Thus was set in motion a policy that ultimately drove almost one hundred thousand Indians from the South.[160] Some apologists believed that Jackson thought this best for the Indians, who would otherwise be removed by the arbitrary actions of individual states. Shortly after Jackson's election, Georgia had moved against the Cherokee. While the law was aimed primarily against southern Indians, it was also used as justification for the Black Hawk War against the Sauk in 1832, which essentially completed the removal of all Indians from Ohio, Indiana, Illinois, and Wisconsin. The Western tribes would continue to fight on.

That war, however, had greater significance than its length would imply. Early in the year, Black Hawk, chief of the Sauk Nation of six thousand who lived in settled villages, led his tribe and members of the Fox across the Mississippi to occupy lands in Illinois that had been taken from them by force and dishonesty. They were at the same time being pushed east by increasing attacks from the west carried out by the Sioux.

The tribes' movement was in violation of the removal legislation which Jackson had worked so hard to establish. The president was determined to pursue the policy and dispatched federal troops to force the Indians back across the Mississippi. However, those troops, along with Illinois militia, suffered embarrassing defeats. Even worse, they had killed Sauks who had tried to arrange a treaty.

The War Department then ordered General Henry Atkinson to proceed from Jefferson Barracks south of St. Louis with federal troops, meet and federalize the militia, and move north. He did so, winning a number of battles and finally in early August overwhelming the Indians. The militia slaughtered men, women, and children—and collected scalps. The Indians who managed to get back across the Mississippi were set upon by the Sioux.

Black Hawk and other elderly chiefs had abandoned their people to establish a home east of Bad Axe in Illinois, but they were discovered. In late August, he and his band surrendered at Fort Crawford near Prairie du Chien, Wisconsin, on the Mississippi River due west of Madison. Black Hawk was taken to Jefferson Barracks, where he was put on display. Later, he was carried around the country to be exhibited until his death in 1838.

Wm. Carr Lane had been appointed chief surgeon by General Atkinson as soon as he received his order to move north. It is probable that Lane accompanied the troops, but there is no record that he did so. If he did, he would have been back at Fort Crawford, which he had traveled to as a surgeon's mate years earlier while stationed at Fort Belle Fontaine.

The duplicity of the government's southern removal was clear. The Five Civilized Tribes—Cherokee, Creek, Choctaw, Chickasaw, and Seminole—had followed the lead of the Americans after signing the Treaty of Holston in 1791, engaging in agriculture, establishing governments, and creating a written Cherokee language. They published a newspaper, the *Cherokee Phoenix*, with columns in both English and Cherokee.[161]

Sadly, despite often high-flown language and the protests of many, including Harriet Beecher Stowe, two underlying forces prevailed. The first was simply White supremacy over Blacks and Indians. The second was economic greed for the Indian lands, especially in the South, where cotton could be grown and tended by slaves. Speculators and opportunists were always present—a combination that created rampant corruption. In the end, it was imperialism. Jackson obtained one hundred million acres, including farmland, in exchange for thirty million acres in Oklahoma and Kansas. The Indians received little of the promised compensation of seventy million dollars.[162]

Lane did not comment on the removals in his letters but revealed his feelings about Indians—and Blacks—in a report he presented as a member of the Santa Fe Trail Committee to the Missouri Legislature on December 21, 1830.[163] While the writer of the eight-page document is not identified, it is clear from both the style and the insight that Lane was its author. The report made specific recommendations concerning the protection of traders traveling over the Santa Fe Trail but went much further to deal with the general policy towards Indians, which

> ought perhaps be left to the General Government, to choose between the evils which are presented to her, upon this subject, – evils necessarily growing out of the anomalous, temporizing and unwise legislation heretofore adopted, in relation to the Indians.
>
> What then is the true state of the evils in question, what then is the true state of the fact? Why, no less than an immense portion of the population, subject to this mighty republic, is permitted by government, to remain with little or no responsibility to the law. ... all manner of

outrage is continually committed, with impunity, amongst themselves, and against their neighbors.

The report then established the number east of the Mississippi as 100,000 and west as 300,000 prior to the recent migration. It then makes a crucial point that the government policies ignored.

But one thing common amongst them, and that is a similarity of colour; the habits of life and grades of civilization, amongst the different portions of them, being as dissimilar and as distinct, as are the extremes of civilized and savage life.

These people so respectable in numbers, being an appendage, and of course a subordinate part of the republic, have, as such, undoubted rights, amongst which we may name, the right to claim a form of government, suitable to the state of society, amongst those to be governed.

The report excoriates the United States government.

by throwing them into one great mass, under the enormous denomination of savages, and by continuing an absurd and anomalous system of bastard diplomacy, it has, in half a century, witnessed the annihilation of the almost entire population; over a space of nearly a thousand miles from East to West.

The report came to a definition of government.

Government is at the same time a want + a right, in the people of every clime, and under every

variety of circumstances; and the only choice left
to the lawgiver, is to adopt his civil regulations, to
the actual condition and wants of those, who are
to be governed. The white portion of our country
has its own code of laws; the black portion could
not be well managed without a code adapted to
their peculiar condition; and why may not the
red man have a code also, suited to his condition,
which is different than either of the other two.

This view must have been developed from Lane's experience
and education. It shows much deeper thought—reflective of his
early addresses to the St. Louis aldermen—than simply labeling an
individual as Black or Savage. He believed slavery was appropriate
for Blacks and that a range of institutions would be suitable for
Indians depending on their status as barbarian or civilized. This
broad conclusion was reinforced by his views of at least one Indian
leader, Tecumseh, whom he referred to as "the celebrated Indian
warrior, was much of a gentleman, (as your Mother can attest, who
knew him) – altho' he lived with wild barbarians."[164] Apparently,
Tecumseh visited the Ewings in Vincennes when Mary was a
child. In 1813, Lane had set out with the Kentucky militia in
pursuit of Tecumseh's barbarians.

It is not clear what relationship Lane had with Jackson, but he
believed he could write the president directly and did so on May
5, 1830, concerning the removal of his brother, Henry Lane, from
the position of Receiver of Public Monies in Palmyra, Missouri.

I am slow to believe that Col. Benton and Mr.
Pettis have lent their official influence to effect an
object so unnecessary for the public good. If the
individual merit of the officer, and his popularity
in this District were considerations that had no

weight with these Gentlemen, it might reasonably have been expected that both of them ought to have felt sufficient delicacy, if not personal obligation to me, when I ask nothing at their hands or from the government, to have insured justice at the very least, to my brother.

Apparently, there was no reversal of the decision.

St. Louis was enjoying a period of prosperity as the decade began. The city had attracted a variety of people from the East as well as from Europe, particularly Irish and German immigrants, both of which groups would play important roles in the culture and politics of the city in the future.

Missouri expanded at an even more rapid rate as farmers occupied its fertile land. The population of St. Louis had increased to five thousand during the prior decade, 27 percent, while the number of people in the state had more than doubled to over 140,000.[165] Ten years later, the population was 384,000, 90 percent of whom were farmers.[166]

St. Louis became an increasingly important transportation hub, receiving goods from the east through New Orleans and Ohio River cities and re-shipping them on steamboats with shallower drafts up the Mississippi, Missouri, and Illinois rivers and in wagons going southwest over the Santa Fe Trail. In turn, Missouri farmers could ship their harvests east on a competitive basis, as could Astor with his furs. In 1836, 186 steamboats made 1,928 landings and unloaded 263,000 tons of goods. Almost half of the ships were owned locally.[167] This growth attracted more people—the city's population was 35,000 in 1845.[168]

Wm. Carr Lane was a key leader during these years of rapid growth and development, which he had predicted in his early inaugural addresses. During the first half of 1830, he was in St. Louis with his family, practicing medicine and engaging in the always present business and real estate activities, e.g. promising to pay Wilson P. Hunt $196.35 on February 5. It is hard to imagine him mulling over the direction of his career at the age of forty.

These activities, however, were not sufficient – he was reelected to the legislature and was back in Jefferson City by the end of the year.

MISSOURI LEGISLATURE AND DOUBT

While Lane was serving in the Missouri Legislature from November 1830 until mid-January of the following year, he wrote eleven letters to Mary in St. Louis and one to Sarah. He struggled during this period between his sense of responsibility to civic duties and his emotional attachment to his family, particularly on learning of the death of Julia Carr on December 18. He was not happy and expressed doubt about his life, but as usual, his need for action and sense of duty prevailed.[169]

The means of transportation to Jefferson City had improved; he traveled four days in a carriage, not alone on a horse as he had done four years earlier. He said the trip of over 120 miles was uneventful, except when the carriage broke down and turned over. "Upset after dark – I fell upon Miss Ann Dillon – nobody hurt – nobody even frightened – a hearty laff afterwards."

On December 1, he responded to a letter from Mary that had taken a week to reach him. The legislature had elected a US senator, Alexander Buckner, whom Mary did not like. "Kiss my children – my anxieties are continued about Julia – please give her a bit to buy something." On Saturday evening he was in his room on the second floor of Ramasey's boarding house, having moved from a garret. He had forgone the new Senator Buckner's wine party and wished he were at home. "Perhaps this feeling is not stronger than any other member, except Dr. Merry, + I dare say he will not stay out more than half the Session." Lane stayed after the session had ended.

Eleven days later, he started a letter during a House discussion "of the driest possible character, + which has been greatly protracted." Late in the evening he was alone in his room after a committee meeting – his roommate had gone out. He described the day, despite the "dry discussion," as being one of "noise, the bustle, the arguing, the listening, the brain puzzling, the managing + being managed, the intriguing + the defending against intrigue, the eating and drinking + the 1000 other actions and doings of the day." He wished that there were no such place as Jefferson City) upon Earth; he had lost weight and "had 2 fangs extracted."

He was again in a good humor on December 17, writing about adjournment dates and the mass of business still coming in, including "applications for Divorces by the dozen." "Shall I put in an application for you?" He suggested the names of three of their friends who might desire "a state of single Blessedness." If divorce were not routine, it was not uncommon.

He had been enormously pleased to receive a letter from the nine-year-old Sarah and in return sent her five dollars as partial repayment of the ten dollars the girl had loaned him. He admonished her to consult a number of adults before spending it and be "deferential to your ma, - kind to your sisters, - respectful to Uncle + Cousin + obliging to the Servants." The next day he read the report of the Santa Fe Trail Committee, which, in addition to his explanations of government, resolved:

> That for the protection of the Trade to Mexico, and the defense of the frontiers of this State, the Congress of the United States be memorialized to authorize the raising of *a corps of Rangers*, to be kept in constant service, at the expense of the United States. That a protest be made, against the location of any more Indians in our neighborhood, unless a more efficient means of protection against their encroachments be afforded to us.

That the present Indian Department be re-organized, and that civil government be extended over the Indians, upon our immediate frontier, under suitable modifications.

The Indian Removal Policy had started to affect the west, and the resolution was agreed to unanimously.

On the twenty-third, Lane received the "fatal letter" containing the news of the death of Julia. He did not respond until Christmas evening. Though he was crushed, he kept at the legislative business. "Well the blow is struck; + what could we do but beat it as we best could – we have had other shocks my wife, but was not this altogether the heaviest? I was engaged in writing out a long document – the Revenue bill of the State, being Chairman of the Committee of Ways + Means, + the House was waiting for it."

He kept writing to distract himself. "I felt as if my heart would actually break." It did not until nightfall, when "my bosom began to feel tight, my breath short, my head became dizzy – my ears rung – I became cold all over – I thought myself dying." That evening "Merry was at my bedside – my hands were chafed – hot applications were made to my shivery feet – hot coffee – toddy –laudanum – camphor + hartshorn were poured down." Laudanum was a source of opium and hartshorn of ammonia.

He survived both the attack and the treatment and by Christmas evening had decided he would not return to St. Louis and that Mary should not take a coach to Jefferson City. He thought of moving from St. Louis but concluded they would "make more money and property" by remaining.

Mary pleaded with him to return, but on January 3 he said he could not, though "Grief falls upon me like a dreadful overwhelming storm, + then passes away + I become calm." "There are many subjects of vital interest to St. Louis now pending."

"It would be wrong for me to leave here unless your situation made it imperative." One of these was a bill to establish a public hospital, which passed. The legislature also "destroyed some new Amendments to the Constitution, of a very mischievous nature."

The legislature adjourned on January 18, but he remained because he had been appointed to a committee "charged with the defacing of an immense amount of State paper, (about $190,000) which has been redeemed." No method of destruction was mentioned, but they may have burned the "paper" while keeping an accurate accounting.

The legislature had dealt with issues large and small. "Some good has been effected, during this session some harm has been averted; but I am not, by any means sure that we have not done many things wrong in themselves – Time will tell – for good or evil."

Lane returned to Mary and his two young daughters in St. Louis to pursue his many activities and, perhaps, lead a more stable life. His letters of the previous two months brought out the internal struggles with which he seemed to deal most of the time. He was devoted and loyal to Mary, but they simply could not communicate, although it is not entirely clear why.

St. Louis was changing as Lane pursued his various activities, and he and Mary, shy as she was, participated in a variety of social functions. One sign was his membership in a "committee of managers" to plan the social season—four single and four married men. It is not surprising that there were no women, but it was significant that the Creoles who had dominated St. Louis society were not included. The first event was a ball at the Missouri Hotel costing five dollars per person, including a carriage. It was a considerable sum for a party at the time.

Interest in religion was also growing, though the Creoles and Irish were fighting within the Catholic church. A volunteer militia, known as the St. Louis Greys, was formed in 1832 and soon became the city's most socially prominent group. In the spring of 1831, Mormon Saints passed through St. Louis on their way to establish the Independence Colony in Jackson County, Missouri.

The arrival that spring of four northwest Indians, three Nez Perce and one Flathead, again showed in a strange way that St. Louis was not far from the west. The Indians, who could communicate with Americans only by sign language and not very well at that, believed that their conversion to American religion would be rewarded with guns and ammunition for their tribes. Two died in St. Louis, bewildered by Catholic instruction; another died at the mouth of the Yellowstone while returning up the Missouri; the fourth was killed by a Blackfoot.

Lane never mentioned Freemasonry or his membership in his letters or journals until 1853. However, in 1813, he had sought membership in Vincennes Lodge 15, chartered by the Grand Lodge of Kentucky, giving his occupation as army surgeon's mate. Forty-one years later, he and a Hugh N. Smith were commissioned by the Grand Lodge of Missouri to convene Montezuma Lodge 109 and look into charges that had been made against certain members. This was two years before a scandal involving charges against Masons, including murder, erupted in Canandaigua, New York, fifteen miles southwest of Rochester.

Freemasonry came to America with the colonists. The first lodges were established in Pennsylvania in the 1730s. George Washington, Benjamin Franklin, and other framers of the constitution were members. Lane could well have been influenced by his admiration for Washington, but his beliefs, character, and political positions were completely in line with those of the Masons. Though its membership was known to the public, the Masons functioned as a secret organization based on a set of formalized rituals. The primary membership requirements were belief in a system of being, with the form left to the individual, freeborn status, good morals and reputation, and, of course, being male. Membership had grown rapidly among the influential men in the country. Andrew Jackson was a Mason. They were not all in the east—Kit Carson became a member of Montezuma Lodge 109 in Santa Fe in 1854.

In 1826 the unsolved murder in New York of William Morgan, who had been denied membership and then threatened to reveal Masonic secrets, became a national scandal. Masons were accused both of the crime and attempting to cover it up. New York Governor Clinton was a Mason. It all became the focus of widespread suspicion of Freemasonry as a secret government. Masons did, in fact, often view themselves as special leaders of the community. Anti-Masonry became a major influence in national politics based on the nationally publicized New York scandal and widespread suspicions of the Masons' actions.[170]

CHOLERA

Throughout the spring and summer of 1832, the people of St. Louis awaited with increasing dread the arrival of Asiatic Cholera, which had broken out in Europe and then been transmitted to America. It was approaching the city down the Ohio River from Pittsburgh and Cincinnati and up the Mississippi from New Orleans. It would be only a matter of time. Indeed, on September 1, cholera was reported in Jefferson Barracks south of the city.

The dread was well founded, for the cause of the disease was not known and no treatments had proved effective. Death was excruciating and quick—often a matter of hours. The symptoms included severe abdominal cramps, diarrhea, and a massive loss of fluids. Though filth was suspected as the source, it would be fifty years before the bacterium was isolated in human waste and the epidemics were eliminated in the United States and Europe.

St. Louis had tried to prepare. In August a public meeting had been held to seek ways to protect the population. The group settled on a day of resolution and prayer. A few individuals advocated that the filth and garbage be cleaned up. They added that physicians had recommended "frequent bathing in order to maintain personal cleanliness" but concluded that "the hope of escaping the malady is vain and dangerous."[171]

On the night of the report from Jefferson Barracks, another public meeting was called and a committee of ten with Wm. Carr Lane as chairman was appointed to make recommendations. When published, the report included the prohibition of the sale of fresh pork, watermelons, green corn, cucumbers, and other vegetables prejudicial to health. Regular inspection of those foods was instituted. The city remained filthy. The concern about cucumbers was common in Europe and the United States, not a result of St. Louis imagination. The 1848 edition of *Buchan's Domestic Medicine*, as reported by the Victoria and Albert Museum in London, reported that "Cholera was said to be caused by rancid or putrid food, by cold fruits such as cucumbers and melons, and by passionate fear or rage."

Two months later, twenty people were dying every day in St. Louis. An estimated three hundred perished before the committee declared the epidemic over, but nobody really knew, because many of the six thousand residents had fled the city. In November, the *Missouri Republican* said that people who had fled the city could return in safety.

The same paper, however, became nervous again the next spring. Mayor Page signed an ordinance quarantining steamboats carrying diseased people. The disease reappeared in May and then disappeared but was back in July. The city purchased an old house on an island in the Mississippi in which to quarantine infected people. It was soon filled. A yellow flag flew above it.

The search by physicians and others for causes and cures continued. The *Republican* noted that the disease struck "improvident and uncleanly people and those who ate green fruit, corn and those abominations of the land, cucumbers." A few weeks later, the paper decided cholera struck everybody. Doctors continued to work long hours bleeding, purging, trying a variety of drugs, including opium and black pepper, and applying tourniquets to restrict circulation.

The *Republican* reported in August that "the atmosphere is so strongly impregnated with the disease that you may literally smell death in the streets." There is no clear record of the number who died, but existing cemeteries were filled and new ones had to be opened. The final spurt occurred in August, with the arrival of 150 German immigrants, and then it was gone.

Lane was in St. Louis with Mary, Anne, Sarah, and the toddler Victor. He had been chairman of the committee in 1832 and presumably continued to care for a large number of patients, though there is no record of the treatments he employed. While the source of the disease had yet to be identified, newspapers, politicians, and some citizens made repeated pleas to clean up ditches, sink holes, and flooded basements. Little was done, however, until 1849 when cholera again struck. Lane was not active in the fight against this outbreak.

The statistics and descriptions of the 1849 epidemic were horrendous.[172] The city was still filthy at the beginning of the year—there were no sewers and few gutters. That lack was compounded by the practice of dumping garbage twelve blocks west of the river. Surface runoff filled basements, and sinkholes became cesspools. All of this bred swarms of flies. Terrible smells were compounded by slaughterhouses. Packs of rats sometimes attacked children.

Enough deaths occurred during the first five months of the year to cause hundreds to again leave the city and almost stop business activity, except for the continuing need to establish new cemeteries. By the end of June, as many as one hundred people were dying every day. In July, 722 died in one week. Late in July, the Committee of Health announced that the epidemic was over—8,423 deaths had been recorded. This figure is probably understated but still amounted to roughly 13 percent of the city's population. While there is no accurate count, it is believed at least 150,000 people died of cholera in the United States between 1832 and 1849.

Five St. Louis doctors died. Volunteers, many of whom also succumbed, worked tirelessly to ease the suffering. Then there were others who profited from such concoctions, as Davis Pain Killer, Dolly's + Oconnell's Magic Pain Extractor, Orin Green's Portable Shower Bath, and Anti-Cholera Bottled Soda. Imagination and greed existed simultaneously with care and sacrifice. Throughout the epidemic, the city continued to establish more quarantine buildings and intercept steamships—and finally to start planning sewers. They also banned the ringing of church bells as too depressing.

There were 883 cholera deaths in 1850 and a slightly lower number in 1851. Cholera did not reappear in epidemic proportions until after the Civil War, when 3,527 died in 1866. While it would be impossible to speculate on the ultimate effect of cholera on St. Louis, there can be no doubt that it disrupted and at times almost destroyed economic activity and social relations.

SLAVERY

Wm. Carr Lane was born in the eighteenth century and grew up in a family and culture in which the enslavement of Blacks was the normal way of life. The Lanes had owned slaves since at least 1700. His father, Presley Carr Lane, had moved from Pennsylvania to Kentucky in 1818 to escape limitations on slavery imposed by the state. Though Lane was only ten when George Washington died, he considered him to be the greatest of men—and Washington owned slaves. His wife's uncle had overseen the general's slaves in Pennsylvania.

There is no evidence that Lane mistreated any of his slaves;

nevertheless, they were property to be bought and sold. In his report to the Missouri Legislature in December 1830 he had said, "The white portion of our country has its code of laws; the black portion could not be well managed, without a code adopted to their peculiar condition."

He resisted anti-slavery actions until his death in 1863. He wrote his daughter Sarah in 1862, "After a visit from the most unscrupulous demagogue – traitor + knave Frank Blair + especially after a reverse to the federal arms, the screws are uniformly tightened on all of us Missourians who do not sing peons to the administration of 'honest old Abe,' which my Judgment, my conscience + my sympathies alike forbid." The Frank Blair of whom he spoke was Francis Preston Blair Jr., who had helped organize the Republican Party in Missouri and later prevented the St. Louis Arsenal from falling into Confederate hands.[173]

Lane's views of slavery were not changed when he abandoned Jackson and the Democrats to become a Whig. He maintained his position as the party evolved into pro-slavery and abolitionist factions. In the mid-1830s, the Whigs believed that their fights against government power assured Southern rights and, thus, slavery. During the following years, however, the northern Whigs split into pro- and anti-slavery groups. Abraham Lincoln was a Whig and minority leader of the Illinois Legislature during the legislative session of 1836–1837. He remained one until the establishment of the Republican party in the mid-1850s. The second Whig president, Zachary Taylor, was elected in 1849 but died in July 1850 after gorging himself at a Fourth of July celebration. He was succeeded by his vice-president, Millard Fillmore. There was always a pro-slavery place with the Whigs for Lane until the party disintegrated in the 1850s because of the north-south split. By that time, party affiliation would have made little difference to him.

Even while Lane was deeply involved in St. Louis and Missouri politics, there is little record of his opinions relating to specific national issues, e.g. the Missouri Compromise of 1820–1821; the so-called Compromise of 1850, which again held the Union together by balancing free and slave states; or the Dred Scott case. The apparent lack of interest in the latter is surprising, for the case started in St. Louis and became a major national, political, and judicial issue prior to the Civil War.

Dred Scott, then known as Sam, had been a slave on a plantation in Virginia in the late 1700s. His master and family left Virginia and arrived in St. Louis in 1830. By that time, Scott had a wife and two children. His first marriage had been destroyed when his wife was sold. In April 1846, Dred and Harriet Scott petitioned for their freedom based on the fact that they had twice been brought into free territory, first Illinois and then Wisconsin. The petition was granted.

The case ultimately reached the US Supreme Court after going through the circuit court, the Missouri Supreme Court, and the Federal Court of Appeals. Scott's ownership changed, and key witnesses died. But more importantly, the case attracted increasing political interest. In March 1857, Supreme Court Chief Justice Taney ruled that the authors of the Constitution did not intend Blacks to be free and that the Missouri Compromise was unconstitutional. However, when the Constitution was ratified, free Blacks were allowed to vote in all but three states.[174]

Lincoln attacked the logic on which the decision was based. Southerners extolled it, while Northerners attacked it on moral, legal, and logical grounds. Taney had shattered another bond holding the country together by embroiling the Supreme Court in the slavery issue. Dred Scott was sold to a Taylor Blow, who freed him immediately. He died in less than a year.

Lane may well not have commented in his letters to Mary on the national debates regarding slavery, because he thought she would neither be interested nor understand. In St. Louis, however, he was very much involved in events affecting slavery.

During his third term as mayor in 1825, he had organized an auxiliary of the American Colonization Society to ship Blacks to Liberia, a new African country. It is unlikely, however, that he participated in or condoned the mob activities that engulfed St. Louis ten years later.

In October, two men believed to have freed seven slaves were taken outside the city by sixty prominent men, tied to a tree, and lashed until almost dead. They were then dumped on the Illinois side of the Mississippi and threatened with death if they returned. One was later found to have had nothing to do with the freeing of the slaves. Within a week, Lane formed a Vigilance and Superintendence Committee to report people advocating abolition and recommended various legal actions, such as preventing free Blacks from moving to Missouri and limiting Blacks from assembling, even in churches. These actions were entirely at odds with Lane's speeches to the aldermen but consistent with the beliefs he expressed to the Missouri Legislature.

An even more explosive event occurred on April 26, 1836. A free Black, Franeith McIntosh from Pittsburgh, working as a cook on a steamship tied up at the levee and was arrested for helping two dockhands escape. On the way to the jail, he broke free, killing the sheriff and seriously wounding a deputy. Within an hour, the leaders of a mob with a crowd of hundreds had broken into the jail where McIntosh had finally been taken, dragged him to a tree, and burned him to death while he sang hymns and pleaded to be shot.

The mood in the city, which was already uneasy, was further enflamed by Elijah Lovejoy's articles in his paper, the *St. Louis Observer*. He had arrived in St. Louis at the age of twenty-four in 1826.[175] Four years later, he became a partner and editor of the *St. Louis Times*. He soon went on to what is now the Princeton Theological Seminary, returning as a minister and editor of a new *St. Louis Observer*. He soon attacked the Catholic church, urging priests "to see and renounce the dangerous and deadly errors of their religious creed." He was, thus, to say the least, controversial when he entered the slavery fight with vehemence.

After a mob destroyed Lovejoy's presses in St. Louis in 1836, he moved to Alton, Illinois, twenty miles north of the city. Another set of presses was destroyed there, as was a replacement set stored in a warehouse. Finally, a fourth set arrived in November 1837 and was placed in a massive storage facility surrounded by dozens of guards. The anti-Lovejoy mob again appeared, the guards disappeared, and Lovejoy was murdered – he was thirty-five.

Lovejoy had by that time become an ardent abolitionist with close ties in the east. His death, the first of an abolitionist leader, infuriated abolitionists. It was now clear that efforts to silence them were an attack on free speech.

Mob activity, which had become the expression of working-class fears and prejudice, was further fueled by the fear of job loss. In 1834, mobs in New York City rioted for three days, burning over sixty buildings belonging to Blacks and their sympathizers. At times the violence was directed at Catholics or Irish. In the years 1834–1836, eighty-nine riots were reported in various areas of the country, but that figure was thought to be a third of the actual number.[176]

The most significant expression of Wm. Carr Lane's beliefs about Blacks was contained in his 1831 message to the Missouri Legislature. He simply believed them to be different and, thus, in need of a different kind of governance. That belief, however, would not have embraced cruelty or mob rule.[AN-1]

FAMILY

Mary and Wm. Carr Lane were married almost forty-five years. Their relationship was complex and unusual, and it remains somewhat of an enigma. They expressed deep devotion in their letters, but the basic differences in education, intellect, and interests made them somewhat of a mystery to each other. These differences may not have been so unusual at that time, but Mary's frequent retreats to her family in Vincennes for extended periods could not have been common.

They were devoted to their children and devastated when one of them died, particularly "Ralph'" Anne was much like her father, strong willed and independent -- and never married. The younger Sarah was more docile and occupied with her family. The Lanes doted on their grandchildren.

Lane wrote frequently to Anne and Sarah, sometimes jointly. He gave them advice on almost every subject a father might think important. Anne was devastated when Sarah married and her attention switched to her husband and children. When Lane died, Sarah was in Germany with five of her children. Mary was in St. Louis; however, all members of the family pulled together to support each other's needs.

The first letter relating to the sisters was written in the fall of 1828 to Mary in Vincennes. The girls were with their father in St. Louis, attending the school Madame Philippine Duchesne of the Order of the Sacred Heart had opened the previous year. The reports of progress and deportment at the end of the quarter were mixed: "everything was well as it related to Anne but Sarah recd. no compliments – the list began with 'bad,' + ended pretty much the same way – But I still have hopes of poor said - she has a benevolent heart if she hasn't the clearest head –"[177] Lane also believed that Madame Duchesne was meddling with his children's faith.

Almost a year later, Anne was in Vincennes while the rest of the family was in St. Louis. Lane wrote his daughter, who was then ten, about the birth of her brother and matters of philosophy and trade. "Say to your Grand-Mother that your Ma was confined to bed, only a few days, + that both she + your little Brother – I ought rather to say your little big brother, are extremely well."[178] He speculated on names but thought "Victor" was particularly appropriate because of its connotation. "It might remind him perpetually that if he could seek honorable distinction in anyway, in his day, that he must begin by gaining <u>victory</u> over himself, - must vanquish, + school into obedience, all his idle + evil propensities. Depend on it my dear Anne that no rule of conduct is more sound than this."[179] Lane appears to have been a Victorian before there were Victorians.

The name did not have the opportunity to carry out its intended purpose, for Victor died on October 2, thirty-two days after his birth. Julia Carr, who was then two and a half, had insisted on calling him "Henry Hough." She, too, would die a year later.

He instructed Anne to negotiate with her grandfather Ewing for a pair of matched or unmatched young horses. He reminded her that he was short of cash and to bargain hard. He must have been smiling as he wrote this, for each negotiator would seem to have had their own particular advantage.

Lane traveled to Philadelphia in September 1834 to find an appropriate school for his daughters. While there, he felt compelled to write to them about their apparent distress with their mother.

He introduced the subject in a general way. "Parents have very different ways of manifesting their attachment to their children; + such is the peculiarity of some persons, from neglected education + badly formed habits, that the in best + kindest efforts are totally misunderstood, + are placed, by the children, to a different account – to caprice – ill-humour + a wish to annoy."

He then directed his attention to Anne. "Anne, especially, will please take notice of my last remark, for I have fancied that she did not always understand her mother. This is not wonderful, for she has spent a large portion of her life absent from her mother, who rarely writes letters, and it is by no means surprising, if, under such circumstances, she should be somewhat ignorant of her mother's true character."

Surprisingly, he himself admitted that he himself did not know Mary well when they were married. "Your mother has some striking peculiarities, + her true character is not very readily seen. I had known her well, as I supposed, some five years, before we were married, + yet I made a great mistake, after we were married, in making of my judgment of her. So odd was she in her ways, + so different from those whom I had known that I really thought her vastly indifferent to me, + this opinion was not altogether removed, until I found myself upon the brink of eternity, + saw clearly that she loved me, better than she did herself."

Finally, he pleaded with them to accept her as she was. "No, my dear children, the very same is true, with respect to you. I know it, + high Heaven can attest it, - she loves you, not withstanding her manner, now + then, better than she loves her own life. Treasure up this undeniable truth deep in your bosoms, + receive all her admonitions + all her reproofs, + bear with all her ways, with becoming respect, submission + forbearance, whether you may think, or even whether she be, <u>right</u> or <u>wrong</u>."[180]

He described some of the schoolmistresses he had interviewed in scathing terms, which he admonished his daughters not to repeat. A Mrs. Sarazin, who presided over what was considered the finest girls' school in Philadelphia, was "cold as an iceberg." He thought better of Miss Hawkes, but "not by any means the model for Female manner, which I could fancy." Mrs. Hughes' school, despite its fine reputation, "was out of the question." He did not think it worthwhile to visit Madame Segoine but would try to see Madame Greland, Miss Smith, and Miss Mandeville, among others. He went on to make a broad judgment about education in the City of Brotherly Love, which was ahead of St. Louis in "the means of instruction, but the expense, is greatly disportioned to the advantages; + to my judgment, the people hereabouts are not ahead of the folks of our region, in personal accomplishments, + the essentials of good breeding."[181]

Whatever factors affected his final decision, Anne[AN-2] at age sixteen and Sarah two years her junior were off in the fall of 1835 to attend the school that he had not thought worth visiting the year before, Madame Segoine's. Though it is not clear how long the girls were in Philadelphia, they were back in St. Louis some time in 1838. Their mother was in Vincennes.

Lane wrote constantly to them while they were in school, and they apparently responded frequently, though their letters have not survived. They did not, however, honor his request that they send diaries, though he sent them an example of one. His letters not only show perhaps an overly concerned father, but also reveal important aspects of his beliefs and business activities that seemed to have been largely controlled by crises. All of the quotations below come from these letters, which were dispatched by the postal service or carried by friends traveling to Philadelphia. The latter was preferred because it usually took less time. Mary visited once and Lane probably several times, as did Sarah's future husband, William Glasgow.

Lane had very definite opinions about education, industry, and inherited skills. "It therefore must be admitted that people 'educate themselves.' Websters advantages were perhaps not greater than mine – Clays were not the tenth part as great. You may think genius has done everything for them – that is not quite so – It is true that education will not make a great man or woman without genius, but is no less true that unassisted genius will not avail, without the aids of education. By education I mean – the store of knowledge, + the habits of thinking + of acting, which the individual acquires. Depend upon it, method, order + industry, have more to do with it than genius; and where genius exists, + and the professor will consent to labour, with method + patient industry, then assuredly, sooner or later, distinction, if not renown, will be the reward."

Lane's views of religion were perhaps even stronger. "You have been brought up in the Episcopal church, + I, as your natural + lawful guardian, desire that you will there remain until you are grown up – until you are married, - and then you can decide for yourselves – In the meantime, entertain that just measure of respect and toleration, for all Christian sects, which <u>charity</u>, the very basis of Christianity, teaches and enjoins."

He urged them to visit Protestant and Catholic churches and Jewish synagogues, but he had no respect for the Mormons. He warned them about being subservient to any doctrine. "You will have too much sense, to believe in the infallibility of the Pope – of the infallibility of any <u>man</u>, under the sun. You cannot believe that <u>wine</u>, at the pleasure of any man, or by possibility made into <u>Blood</u>; or <u>Bread</u> into <u>Flesh</u>. You must understand Chemistry, and the ordinary modes of common sound reasoning, too well, to admit such preposterous proposition."

He expanded on his basic religious belief with a discussion of "charity." "A lady in Phila. once asked me seriously if all our Missouri ladies did not wear Dirks; I graveled and 'certainly + some of them Pistols also' - of all things, my children, avoid the vulgar and common error of mankind, in drawing general conclusions from single facts; + in making of your estimate of individuals always look at them personally, + not thro' the medium of the general character of their nation, or race."

Not all of his instructions bore on issues of character. He gave advice on punctuation and spelling: "never send a letter with a misspelled word." He didn't say if his often excessive use of commas and unique abbreviations were to serve as examples.

He suggested that they copy passages from great books, leaving out any punctuation, and then put in their own commas and periods and compare it to the original. He urged visits to libraries and bookstores but told them not to read Byron until they were older.

All of the letters were full of accounts of the activities of family and friends. It is often hard to know who they were, for he had in his households not only members of his immediate family but various relatives, wards in his charge, slaves, and sometimes paid servants.

The letter of August 22, 1836, was written with deep sadness.

> My children – The Hearse + mourning carriages are at the front door, and your poor Mother + I are left to mourn over the irreparable loss of your dear little sister – the beautiful image of Sarah. Meet this dispensation of providence with becoming resignation, + take more especial care of yourselves, as the chief hope of happiness for your parents, during the few declining years that are left to them rest upon you + your little brother.
>
> It is the wish of your mother that you should not put on mourning.
>
> Adieu dearest daughters Wm. Carr Lane

Ellen was only three months old. This left only the two girls in Philadelphia and Victor, then five, at home. Lane had commented on Ellen's health several times but frequently mentioned Victor's growth, appearance, and well-being.

As would be expected, he gave Sarah and Anne advice on the means of selecting doctors and dentists. Despite his attendance at the University of Pennsylvania Medical School years earlier, he did not seem to be acquainted with local physicians. He was outraged that a Dr. Meigs had said Anne's spine was not straight. Her spine had not been straight in earlier years; so at age nine she was sent to Lexington, Kentucky, to be under the care of a renowned Dr. Benjamin Dudley while staying with her grandmother Lane. That treatment required her to crawl for two years rather than walk, but the recovery had been considered complete.

Lane's reports about finances, allowances, and gifts were far from consistent. He apologized for his inability to buy them anything other than inexpensive gifts, such as coral pins of which Mary disapproved, but paid the tuition regularly and sent their allowances of ten or twenty dollars on a steady basis. He once promised to give them each five thousand dollars or more when they graduated.

BUSINESS AND FINANCE

It would have seemed that after Lane had completed his third term in the legislature and settled his daughters in Philadelphia, he might have relaxed a bit, but that was not to be the case. It is not possible to follow with any degree of accuracy the myriad business, real estate, and slave transactions in which he was involved, either because the record is imperfect or because by nature he was going in so many directions at once. Within a matter of days, he would complain of a state of almost destitution and then spend large sums on his daughters and embark on new ventures. In one letter, there is a reference to his going to Cuba and in another a statement that a friend was returning from Cuba. It is not even clear where he, Mary, Victor, and Ellen, during her three-month lifetime, lived. At least four years were spent in a boarding house, which he apparently owned. Despite all these activities, he wrote long and frequent letters to Philadelphia, usually late at night and often adding postscripts in the morning.

He wrote Sarah on March 12, 1836, complaining about constant distractions. "My practice always beginning – never ended. Pray will I have repose, when I get into my grave? – at least, I will not be troubled with practicing Physic; nor will I have Notes to pay, in Bank by a given moment; nor will there be danger from such an animal as a <u>sheriff</u>. I have all my life been hard-run for money – perhaps my poor management makes it so and, at this time, my necessities for that 'root of all evil,' are pretty considerable."

There is some reference to consulting with an expert in Philadelphia about his powder mill, but it is not clear whether he bought it or built it. Regardless, his reporting of its destruction on April 11, 1836, highlights the magnitude and complexity of his affairs.

> My good children –
>
> Last night our town, + the country around us, was shocked by the most tremendous convulsion ever felt in this region, + and you may well imagine that the cause could be nothing less than the explosion of the Powder-mill + magazine attached to it, containing some 15000# + upwards of G. Powder. Fortunately, no lives were lost +, strange to tell, the cause of the accident has not been ascertained. The desolation is awful, the whole establishment having been utterly annihilated. The loss of property is very great, + the load of debt (which falls on me alone, is enormous). But, my dear children, I am by no means dismayed nor dispirited. My exertions must be redoubled, + I am full of hope for the future. The rise in price of property has been great, + will, I hope, enable me to pay off all I owe, + leave a clear surplus. But, to make assurances more sure, I have conveyed the Boarding-house to Ann, + the house adjoining to Sarah + Victor – some other dispositions have been made in my pecuniary affairs, but I need not detail them now.[182]

Mary urged him to bring the girls home to ease his burdens, but he refused, saying that he had many resources for raising money. He was resilient and optimistic.

He also paid close attention to details and small sums, writing to his friend John Darby, the mayor, that a judgment that had been brought against him by the city for $8.33 was "against the principles of law and justice." The cause of the judgment was the presence of one of his female servants on the streets at night without a pass.[183]

Though Lane owed $30,000 because of the powder mill either to banks or individuals, he had some reason to be optimistic. The city's economy was booming, with house and land prices rising rapidly. He did complain that not a single relative had come to his aid and that it had "been a sore summer upon me – I have felt the want of money, every day of the week except Sunday, which made Sunday more acceptable to me than it ever has been before."

In May of the following year, he advised Anne and Sarah that their mother was boarding the *Robt. Morris* for Pittsburgh on her way to Philadelphia and to be sure to have adequate accommodations for her when she got there. He kept calculating, "the Misses Stremcki will soon surrender their boarding house – rents advance apace – the House will rent next year for more than a $1000, - + and the adjoining one for $400 – the old House for 5 or 600 – In all I shall have upwards of $3000. rent per annum … servant wages are enormous – Fred lives at present for 480+ a year." [184] Not engaging Fred did not seem to be a consideration.

Sometime in 1838, he wrote to Mary in Vincennes about the financial transactions he had completed or had planned to extricate himself from his indebtedness. It is not clear whether she returned to St. Louis after her Philadelphia visit or went straight to her family. She either owned or co-owned some of the property, for her signature was required on some of the deeds. While he seemed to be involving her in some business matters, he really was informing her what he was doing.

> I have paid off Evans' claim, on the corner lot - $1375 with a years Interest superadded. I availed my self of your suggestion + used the note of Betts for process of the <u>Texians</u> – and what is still better, I this day executed a Deed for the powder mill tract – 20 *arpens* [an *arpen* was a French measure of about .85 acres] – (including Langhams House + 2 cottages, but leaving out the House on the Road to Vide Poche) the price $10,000 – which pays of Papins + Reels liens, + leaves the best end of a $1000. for a surplus."
>
> I am much in the spirit of selling, + be not surprised, if you should find Deeds to another $10,000 – ready for your signature, when you arrive – this would set me on my legs again after being in Purgatory for 2½ years.

While Lane sought to resolve his financial problems, the economic environment in the country—and St. Louis—went from boom in 1836 to bust in 1837. The Panic of 1837 came in full force in March of that year, with the collapse of inflated prices and the failure of banks. The effect in St. Louis was devastating, but somehow Lane seemed able to manage his way through it. He had described the high real estate prices in 1836 and may have had the foresight to position himself favorably. Lane also acquired approximately five hundred acres of farmland on the river about fifteen miles north of the city piece by piece, apparently starting as early as 1828 and continuing through his financial problems of the 1830s.[AN-3]

Mayor Again

John Darby, a friend of Lane's, resigned his position as mayor during his third term in 1837. Lane was immediately elected to take his place and then reelected in 1838 and 1839; Darby returned in 1840. The two had served as mayor in nine of the first twelve years of city government—Lane eight and a half. Lane's popularity was apparent from the election results, but there were detractors. Probably the most vocal was Beriah Cleland, a carpenter and self-proclaimed "Bard of the West." "Wm. Car Lane was chosen our first mayor, and served six years, but awful and horror sickening was his reign. ... - he was not only Lord Mayor of the city, but Lord God of the people, for his will was the law of the city." In one election, Cleland was selected as a candidate as a joke—and almost won. He had a favorable opinion of Darby, but "that monster Car Lane was elected."[185]

Lane could not suffer fools. He stopped writing his daughters after May of 1837, presumably because of his return to political life. He also did not write Mary until late in the following year when she was in Vincennes.

When he took over as mayor in 1837, he was dealing with his own problems, and both the city and the county were in a deep financial crisis. Martin Van Buren, Jackson's vice president, had been inaugurated as president in the spring of that year shortly before economic turmoil struck.

For many years prior to that time, the main channel of the Mississippi River had shifted toward the Illinois side and, thus, choked the St. Louis harbor with sand and hindered commerce. Mayor Darby had petitioned members of Congress to appropriate funds to alleviate the problem, but Thomas Hart Benton, as a Democrat and Jackson loyalist, could not support it because both his party and the president were opposed to the federal government paying for internal improvements. Nevertheless, an appropriation of $150,000 was made "for the improvement and protection of the harbor of St. Louis."[186] This action made St. Louis a port of entry under the direct supervision of the Army Engineers. The immediate effect was very favorable, though there was a downside in the near future when the funds were expended and the political climate in Washington changed.

General Charles Gratiot, a grandson of the grand dame of St. Louis, Madame Chouteau, was head of the Army Engineers. After visiting St. Louis to meet important citizens, presumably including Lane, and inspecting the river, he returned to Washington and assigned Robert E. Lee, then a thirty-year-old lieutenant, to design and construct the structures needed to solve the problem.

Lee arrived in the fall and, with the assistance of a St. Louis engineer, Henry Kayser, designed a series of underwater dikes projecting from the Illinois shore and down the western side of Bloody Island, which was north of the harbor. The solution was effective. By the time the funds were exhausted in the spring of 1839, the harbor had been cleared of sand. Lee endeared himself to St. Louis society as well as to those working under him. Darby was particularly impressed. "I saw him almost daily; he worked most indefatably, in that quiet, unobtrusive manner and with the modesty characteristic of the man." "He maintained and preserved under all circumstances his dignity and gentlemanly bearing, winning and commanding the esteem, regard, and respect of every one under him."[187]

St. Louis continued the work to secure the improvements under the direction of Kayser but was harassed by Illinois authorities. Lane, who by that time was mayor, was indicted in that state because of alleged damage to the eastern shore of the river.

In November, he wrote Kayser, "The state of the weather and the want of funds, make it, in my judgment, advisable (in the absence of any order from the City Council) that you should immediately discharge all your hands and discontinue your operations for the improvement of the Harbor."[188] He included instructions for returning property of the US government, paying claims, and returning other property to the city. The four-page inventory ranged from one steamship to twenty-eight shovels (six without handles) and twenty-two soupspoons. Further appropriations were not forthcoming from Washington. Kayser subsequently reported that Lee had turned the appropriate property over to him and requested five thousand dollars to secure some of the work already completed.

Failure to complete the plan resulted in the harbor again filling with sand, though Kayser kept it open through temporary measures. A Rivers and Harbors Bill was vetoed in 1847 by President Polk, and Illinois Senator Stephen A. Douglas blocked an attempt to override the veto. It was not until 1853 that the quarrel with Illinois was settled and Lee's work completed to assure St. Louis an open harbor.

Lane in his first address to the aldermen in 1823 had said, "I will hazard the broad assertion, that a free school is more needed here than in any town of the same magnitude in the Union." The first public schools did not open until fifteen years later when he was again mayor. "Public" may not have been an accurate description, for the schools charged tuition. Inspectors determined who could be admitted. The Lanes, as did other wealthy and prominent citizens, sent their children to private or church-based schools.

The public schools, however, were well financed because of the original plan of St. Louis laid out by Pierre Laclede in 1764 and the efforts of Col. Thomas E. Riddick forty-seven years later. Laclede's plan was based on a rectangular street grid, a public market and towpath, and a common field. In general, individuals were granted lots of 120 by 150 feet with title as long as they made specific improvements. All had access to the common lands to raise crops or pasture livestock. When originally established, these common lands encompassed nearly nine square miles.

The Treaty of Cessation of the Louisiana Territory stated that citizens would be "maintained and protected in the free enjoyment of their liberty, property, and the religion which they profess." Congress passed a series of laws attempting to settle property claims but achieved little. In 1811, Edward Hempstead was elected a congressional delegate from the Territory of Missouri. Though he could not vote, he prevailed upon Congress to pass a law that perfected the title to property of certain towns in Missouri and conveyed common land to the towns for the purpose of establishing schools. The school proposition was included at the urging of Col. Riddick, who rode alone to Washington from St. Louis to press his cause. Though the size of the St. Louis Commons had been reduced, it was still substantial. In 1876, the value of the land was $1,253,000.[189]

All controversies were not settled by the 1812 legislature. In 1838 Mayor Lane advised the aldermen, "I cannot approve an Ordnance securing Titles to secondary purchasers in the Common."[190] He then in his usual manner went on to explain how it could be modified to meet his objections.

Lane was not only acting on an opinion reached by his legal advisor but also his own practical objections, which could be alleviated "if a guard were placed so as to prevent the holder of the land from selling all the good portions and then forfeiting to the City all the bad portions." He later listed a series of ordinances and resolutions, which included paying for a fire engine that had been purchased the year before, appointment of a city marshal, establishment of an engineering department, and refunds of taxes that had been paid twice.

Riddick had not confined his efforts to schools. In 1819 he circulated a petition for the establishment of the first Episcopal church west of the Mississippi. Though Lane had just established permanent residency, he was one of the signatories, as was Thomas Hart Benton.

Lane as mayor in 1839 was struggling with both his own personal financial problems and with the economic stress continuing after the Panic of 1837. Banks failed throughout the country, and their paper money was worthless. In the spring, carpenters struck for a ten-hour day. Contractors ultimately capitulated after a long fight, but wages kept falling. Lane observed that, "Property is regarded as nothing, + human life is cheap."[191] It continued after Darby again became mayor in 1840, and Lane had to sell his own carriage and horses.

During his term as mayor in 1836, Darby convened a panel of four, including Wm. Carr Lane, to report on the feasibility of railroads in Missouri. Lane continued to support Darby in 1840 in his quest for railroads by lobbying the legislature. His involvement in both public and individual matters continued. During the same year, the editor of the *Argus* denounced an opponent on fiscal matters as "a jackass, toady and half-witted drone."[192] The recipient of these epithets avoided the editor but sought out the publisher, who was smaller, and struck his skull with a cane. The blow was fatal.

The controversy arose because of the conservative fiscal Democratic position of the *Argosy* and the softer approach of the Whigs. The assailant hired a Whig lawyer who, in turn, had three Whig physicians to testify that the publisher's death could have been caused by the holes bored in the man's head to relieve pressure, a process known as trephining. They admitted they might have performed the same procedure. Amidst all the confusion, the murderer was let off with a $500 fine for fourth-degree manslaughter.

A WEDDING NOT ATTENDED

Sarah Lane married William Glasgow Jr. in St. Louis on Thursday, April 16, 1840. She had just turned nineteen; he was in his twenties. Not only was her mother in Vincennes on the day of the wedding but she wrote to Lane in January and March without mentioning it. There is no explanation for her absence, other than that she was with her family. It is only possible to speculate. She could not always communicate effectively with her daughters but may have been unable to abide the thought of one moving out. She could hardly have objected to the Glasgows as a family, for they were prominent and successful.

Shortly after midnight on the day of the wedding, Lane wrote Mary, "It is over – and here am I in our chamber – 'solitary and alone,' with the exception of my sleeping companion Ralph, but I am indisposed to sleep myself."[193] He chided Mary about her absences.

He then described the ceremony and the people who had come and not come. He said Ralph had behaved well but oddly did not mention Anne, who was devoted to her sister. He may have simply forgotten to mention her, or she may have stayed away because she was jealous of Glasgow. He was pleased with the event, "the rooms looked well + everything was well done, or at least it seemed so to me." The ceremony was in the Lane home, and a Mrs. Hough took care of the arrangements that would normally have been made by the bride's mother.

Lane, however, did not let a wedding interfere with his other activities. During the day, he saw patients, many of whom were spitting up blood. He had spent much of the previous night with an infant whom he did not expect to survive. He did note that Dr. Merry, who was assisting him, had not gotten drunk at the wedding. Lane fell asleep before he could complete the letter but did so on Saturday.

He wrote that "We are well and all happy, + I am the happiest of all – indeed I am now ready to die." The bride and groom were ready to set out for the east on the next boat. Lane had considered accompanying them as far as Evansville, Indiana, on the Ohio

River but decided not to do so. He may also have intended to ride the fifty miles to Vincennes but thought it not worth the time. He was out all of Friday tending to patients and business; he also attended a lecture in the evening but "slept more than I listened." He had been to the theater several days earlier "to see Madame Lecompt + co. but was not much pleased – they kicked up their heels scandalously." Lane's criticism was not shared by all. A review at the time said the Madame was aged but reported that the beautiful M'lle Desjardins was a great favorite: "the ballet was repeated many times; the shawl dance and trial dance being particularly applauded."[194]

The infant he had tended to had succumbed, but all his other patients had survived. He pleaded with Mary to decide when she would return.

William Glasgow Jr. was a cousin of Edward James Glasgow and William Henry Glasgow, whose acumen and boldness had resulted in their becoming very successful traders. Their father, another William, had arrived in St. Louis in 1816 at the age of twenty-nine, three years before Wm. Carr Lane and Mary settled in the city. He soon became involved in commerce and married the sixteen-year-old Sarah Mitchell in Belleville, Illinois. They moved about, setting up stores in towns in Illinois and Missouri, having children, and returning to St. Louis in 1827 where Glasgow entered into a series of partnerships whose members changed over the years as individual fortunes rose and fell. One of the partners had substantial experience in trading in Mexico as well as mining gold and silver.

By the time the Glasgows returned to St. Louis, the Santa Fe Trail had opened, and the partners provided goods to be carried to Chihuahua. The sons went to school in St. Louis and then attended St. Louis University. A disadvantage of shipping over the was the double tariff. The goods they shipped that had come from Europe through eastern ports and had been taxed and would be levied again by the Mexicans when they reached Santa Fe. However, the import duty on European goods was refunded if they were reshipped by sea.

William Glasgow decided to overcome the advantage enjoyed by sea shipment, though he did not anticipate the complications that would make the venture of short duration. In 1840, as his cousin William Jr. was being married, the other William's son, twenty-year-old Edward James, and two partners were dispatched to Mexico from New York with two ships, one of which alone carried 189 tons of freight. After forty-two days, the ships landed at Vera Cruz on Mexico's eastern coast. The ships then set sail around Cape Horn while the partners hired a coach to take them partway to Mazatlan on the west coast. They had to purchase mules to ride the last 150 miles of the 800-mile trip through the Sierra Madre Mountains. Edward and the partner with the Mexican experience, Valois, then went over 300 miles north to Guaymas to determine if that would be a suitable spot to establish a business. Edward discovered to his dismay that Valois's vaunted experience included a $40,000 debt. Glasgow had to force him out of the partnership. When the two ships arrived two months after leaving Vera Cruz, the two remaining partners established their business at Mazatlan.

Not surprisingly, the venture would encounter further obstacles. A continuing one was the return of specie to St. Louis to pay the loans that had been obtained to buy the merchandise. One of the ships, the *California,* departed on the return trip in March, presumably with funds to help pay the $89,000 due in July. The partners then became alarmed by a revolution in Mexico led by Santa Ana. Though it was over quickly, Edward, who had remained, was afraid that the *California's* cargo would be seized when it arrived in Mazatlan. He, therefore, had the goods delivered to Valparaiso, Chile. The ship then returned to Mazatlan to load wood and $40,000 worth of bullion. Edward was on board for the five-and-a-half-month return trip, including a stop in Valparaiso to close the business there. While in Valparaiso, he wrote Sarah Lane Glasgow telling her of all the beautiful girls.[195]

By 1842, the senior Glasgow and his partners had decided trading in Mexico was too uncertain; so Edward's younger brother, another William, was dispatched to Mazatlan to close the business and return via Chihuahua and Santa Fe with silver specie. Edward made an additional four trips over the Santa Fe Trail prior to 1846. In that year, he was accompanied by his brother. The total amount of goods carried by the many traders in that year was estimated to have had a value of over one million dollars.[196]

Over 150 wagons, including those of the brothers, were delayed in 1846 by the start of the Mexican War but finally followed General Stephen Watts Kearney to Bent's Fort, where they waited for him to invade New Mexico. Though Santa Fe was conquered without a fight, their troubles were far from over, for there was little market for their goods in New Mexico. They had to travel on to Chihuahua while a war raged. The Glasgows were gone for two years but managed to return to St. Louis with a profit.

The two brothers combined their efforts and prospered in the 1850s, being listed in St. Louis in 1859 as "Wholesale Grocers, And Commission Merchants, Dealers in Sugar, Coffee, Molasses and Rice." Over three thousand steamboats arrived in St. Louis in 1852.[197] Their business continued to expand and diversify for years but ultimately failed in 1879, perhaps because of changes in commodity prices. The town of Glasgow still exists about two hundred miles west of St. Louis on the Missouri River, where the family had established a business in 1819.

William Glasgow Jr. was not engaged directly in the trading businesses but had similar enterprising characteristics, which led him to succeed both financially and in society. Prior to his marriage to Sarah Lane, his sister had married a wealthy St. Louis businessman, Thomas Larkin. William Jr. was initially associated with Larkin in a mercantile partnership but became interested in real estate and the culture of grapes. He founded the American Wine Company and began producing champagne but sold the company two years later.[AN-4] At the same time, he became associated with Dr. Greenleaf Eliot, a Unitarian minister who had been brought to St. Louis in 1834 by Christopher Rhodes, one of the first Unitarians to settle there. Through this contact, Glasgow served on the boards of the Church of the Messiah, the first school board, and the original board of Washington University. Eliot also persuaded him to support the Union cause in opposition to other Glasgows and all the Lanes.

Eliot came from a prominent and intellectual New England family. He had just graduated from divinity school when he came to St. Louis. Despite having few intellectual equals in St. Louis, he was at ease with all levels of society. He fought slavery, ignorance, and poverty in a quiet but effective way.

He gained support for institutions directed at those needs. His Unitarian church founded the Mission Free School for poor, homeless children in 1856. On his own, he founded the nonsectarian Washington University in 1853, Smith Academy for boys in 1854, and the Mary Institute for girls in 1859.[198] The schools were started at least in part to offset the dominance of Catholic institutions. St. Louis University had its origins in 1818, and there were various Catholic boys and girls schools. The Lane girls had attended a Catholic school.[AN-5]

Wm. Carr Lane must have welcomed the addition of an intelligent son-in-law who was engaged in many activities, for Sarah and her new husband were still on their honeymoon when Lane started writing him about political and other matters. He always seemed to have Glasgow on his mind. In 1853 while Lane was on his way with an armed escort to negotiate a peace treaty with Apache Indians in the Mimbres Mountains in New Mexico, he noted a new variety of grape and got out of his coach to collect clippings to send to his son-in-law.

WHIGS RISE AND FALL

On July 23, 1840, Lane wrote his new son-in-law, who was in Philadelphia with his wife after visiting New York. Lane was confident that the Whig candidate for president, William Henry Harrison, would defeat the Democrat, Martin Van Buren, who had neither the personal power nor the popularity of Jackson. "The Election near at hand, + excitement + noise increase: this is inconvenient, but if we want to enjoy the present enlarged liberty of this land, we must bear with its concomitant evils. The Whigs will carry this country, triumphantly, and will gain much throughout the state, but it is feared they cannot yet carry the state. I myself am more a spectator than an actor in the strife, - being engaged in professional dutys."[199]

He had written Sarah earlier to describe various events in St. Louis and report on family news. Mary had returned to St. Louis, but only for a short period. By the time he wrote Glasgow, she was back in Indiana with Anne, "and James has, at least for the present given his passions, for the Vickler shaw to the winds – By the way, if a lady should so far forget herself as to read Don Juan, she ought to exercise more discretion than the Widow did, + keep her reading a secret." He did not identify the people about whom he wrote. He had just seen a Madame Von Phul to deliver her thirteenth child. Ralph, now nine, was in a Jesuit school.

The Whigs held their first national convention in Harrisburg, Pennsylvania, in December 1839. Henry Clay expected to get the nomination but was dragged down by his association with the Masons and a speech he had made in the Senate, which placated Southerners but offended abolitionists in the North. He started, "I am no friend of slavery," and then spoke of feelings of the heart: "every pulsation of mine beats high and strong in the cause of civil liberty." He went on, "But I prefer the liberty of my own country to that of any other people, and the liberty of my own race to that of any other race. The liberty of the descendants of Africa in the United States is incompatible with the safety and liberty of the European descendants."[200]

William Henry Harrison had the support of the anti-Masons and gained the backing of Northerners suspicious of Clay. General Wenfield Scott was a possible alternative, but on the third ballot, Harrison won with 148 votes; 90 went for Clay and 16 for Scott.[201] Harrison offered the vice-presidency to Clay or one of his supporters but was spurned in what may well be one of the greatest ironies in the history of presidential nominations. With Clay's rejection, Harrison turned to John Tyler of Virginia, a choice that would prove disastrous for the Whig party.

Martin Van Buren had finally reached his long-sought goal when he had been elected president four years earlier. He was no longer under the shadow of Jackson and predicted that the prosperity of the early 1830s would continue. Unfortunately for him and the country, he was soon faced with the economic collapse of 1837 and the banking policies of Jackson, which had destroyed the US Bank and then required that sales of government land be paid for with specie, not paper money issued by state banks. These actions created the shortage of money of which Wm. Carr Lane complained. Van Buren's refusal to intervene in the banking system, combined with the continuing speculation in the west, caused the financial crisis to continue.

The Whigs ran under the slogan of "Tippecanoe and Tyler too."[202] The Democrats' attack on Harrison as both a drinker of hard cider and a rube backfired. The Whigs displayed pictures of a log cabin with a barrel of cider in front to show he was a man of the people. The Whigs updated the attacks on Van Buren as a dissipated man of the aristocracy who ruined the common man, using the slogan "Harrison and Prosperity or Van Buren and Ruin."[203]

Harrison won 53 percent of the popular vote and overwhelmed

Van Buren in the electoral college 234 to 60 --80 percent of the three million eligible voters voted.[204]

The Whig triumph, however, was to be short-lived. Harrison delivered his hour-and-a-half inaugural address without a coat on a cold, snowy day in March. He intended to offset the charges of old age that had beset him, but he died a month later – the first president to die in office.

Prior to his death, Harrison had called a special session of Congress to meet in May to repeal Van Buren's financial measures and establish a third US Bank. Tyler, despite his party affiliation, did not share its monetary views and vetoed the legislation. The next year, Lane added a postscript to a letter to Mary, "The 19th veto has come – puts people out of temper – I wish they would impeach Tyler for a Fool, or try him under the 2d Section + hang him."[205]

Lane had continued to write Sarah and William on their wedding trip in the east describing the health of family members, now including the Glasgows and the Larkins. William's sister Susan had married a Larkin. In a letter to Sarah late in July 1840, he wrote of the large number of deaths, "but they have happened for the most part amongst strangers, who are not missed from amongst us. This measure of mortality must be expected to continue until cold weather, as the number of unacclimated persons, amongst us, was never so great as now."[206] The death rate was apparently high in the largely German and Irish immigrant community.

Mary and the newlyweds were in St. Louis during the latter half of 1840 and all of 1841, for Lane did not start writing again until January of 1842. In that letter, however, he implied that Mary had been gone a long time, for he said they had finally gotten a letter from her. Though she still did not write often, he referred to her letters more frequently during this period than during any of her other long absences.

He wrote Mary again on Thursday, May 5, 1842, of the agony

that Sarah had suffered in the last days of her pregnancy caused in large part because "the ass of an apothecary had sent her Calomel rather than Magnesia." A baby girl was born Tuesday evening but did not live twenty-four hours.

The Glasgows had ten additional children, including two sets of twins. Seven lived to be adults. There is no indication that Mary was not in St. Louis at the time of the birth of her first grandchild because of a specific need to be in Indiana or if her absence was part of her basic character.[AN-6]

FINANCIAL DISTRESS

The lack of money and resulting financial distress caused by President Tyler's policies struck hard in St. Louis, wiping out many prominent citizens. Wm. Carr Lane would have suffered a similar fate had it not been for Mary's family. She was in Vincennes all of 1842. Lane wrote her regularly from May through December, describing both family health and the deepening financial crisis. His life was complicated further by Illinois's continued legal pursuit of him related to the Mississippi River project started by Robert E. Lee. The following quotations are from his letters of that period.

"They have abandoned the old ground, taken in Madison County, of obstructing a navigable stream, + I am now <u>Indicted</u>, in St. Clair County, for <u>an unlawful assembly</u>, + have been demanded and surrendered as a <u>fugitive from justice</u>. Was there ever such a mockery? Edward Guy + Elliot Lee are also in custody – On Monday next we will be conveyed to Belleville." "I was taken by the Barbary powers, on Monday last (with Lee + Ed Guy) to Belleville, (instead of Edwardsville) – in consequence of an error in the warrant of the Gov. of Illinois – This mistake caused our liberation." Though the case against Lane apparently was not pursued further, the controversy between St. Louis and Illinois was not settled until 1851 when Lee's planned construction was completed.

None of these activities diminished his engaging in additional political and medical ventures. He rarely mentioned sheriffs without adding an abusive description, such as "barbarians." Nevertheless, he decided to run for county sheriff. He first had to be nominated by the Whig convention. They "nominated Gordon for Shff. Now is it not strange that conventions and caucuses always decide against me, + when I run, the people – their masters, always decide in my favor." He still did not maneuver as Benton did.

He had been appointed chair of Obstetrics and Diseases of Women and Children at Kemper College the previous year. He wanted to resign in 1842 but did not do so and delivered his opening lecture in November to a class of forty, "which shows better material than last year." He continued in the Kemper position until 1844. As a leading citizen, he was included in the receptions for visiting dignitaries but did not always behave as others might have wished. Former president Martin Van Buren visited in June during his early campaign to regain the presidency. "But I took no pleasure in the man, + declined to be introduced to him. Perhaps, I was wrong, but I could not overcome my repugnance to him, as a mischief-making demagogue."

Charles Dickens and his wife arrived in April as part of their grand tour of the United States. "Altho' appointed to be one of his 'keepers' – I did not see him – I do not approve of the modern mode of showing off 'Lions' – and I will not participate in it. Those who saw him – including Ralph, expressed themselves pleased with him – his wife was both ugly + plain – God bless them – I suppose they will make a Book + inform distant places what asses we are."

Lane not only commented on the health of relatives and friends but reported on his own situation, which undoubtedly reflected his age. He was now in his fifties -- rheumatism was a recurring problem. In April, he wrote, "My second attack of Rhumatism was much less violent than the first, + did not confine me more than half as long ... My children were incessant in their attention, + nearly killed me with overkindness." Mary's father apparently suffered in the same manner. "Tell your Father his practice in <u>Rhumatism</u>, according to my judgment, is good, but as to his reasoning upon it, I cannot speak so confidently."

By May when he was seeking to become sheriff and being taken to Illinois for trial, he wrote, "The Rhumatic affection has left my limbs + located in my back, but not bad – I go about, but am not pained." In April he had changed his eating habits. "I eschew animal food in all its forms – even soup – eggs – milk – butter + cheese – also coffee – spts. – wine – malt liquors + hard cider." The change did not last long, for two months later he reported that "By the way, I have gotten back to meats, + perhaps once a fortnight, to a glass of wine." He frequently ate dinner with the Glasgows.

As he reported on the health of family members and the death of friends, he offered advice and commented on various aspects of life. He objected to his brother John's plan to leave Kentucky for Iowa, which had been described as "<u>Heaven</u> for <u>Men</u> + Horses, but <u>Hell</u> for <u>women</u> + <u>oxen</u>."

The once dominant Madame Chouteau died in August. She had been preceded in death by two other elderly citizens, Mr. Le Duc and a friend named Chenier. "What surprises me most, is the indifference, which seems to pervade the public at large on these occasions … yet a mere Padd or Mrs. Paddy, without any character or usefulness, has been followed to the grave, by ten times as many people, as followed the remains of LeDuc + Mme. C. – Pray what causes this growing indifference? Is it because the Americans are daily losing their respect for <u>age</u>? – is it the lamentable truth, that old people are often thought to be <u>in the way</u>? If so, God help the heartless rising generation."

To Mary, he wrote, "If you should ever be a widow, be careful whom you marry. Msr. Geo. Bullet's husband, turns out to be a penitentiary Bird, from Georgia, + a divorced man, from

Kentucky – where he took in another <u>widow</u> – he is now charged with forgery, + will soon visit our penitentiary."

Lane's affection for Ralph, now in his early teens, was obvious. "Ralph improves in good conduct, as he advances in years. He is not very studious." "Your son is of course asleep, - with the clothes half kicked-off, so as to show his shape, and really it required a second glance, at his long legs to assure me that it was not some <u>young man</u> who had crept into my bed." He often referred with some pleasure to the letters Ralph wrote to his mother. "I send you Ralph's last Bulletin, + refer you to him, for an account of his <u>Honors</u>, at the Examination … one thing is certain – he does not rise in the morning as early, as heretofore, nor is he as studious as he used to be." Ralph visited his mother in Vincennes in September.

Lane not only had frequent meals with Sarah but often tea or coffee. He worried about her husband's health. Anne traveled more now that Glasgow was in the family. Lane continued to practice medicine, frequently describing being called out in the middle of the night to attend to a birth or death.

However, the lack of money and resulting financial disasters were the overriding themes of his letters in the final eight months of 1842, growing in severity as the year progressed. In April, "One favorable sign however encourages us – our landing is crowded with Boats, carrying away Surplus products, + <u>returning empty</u>! This is right – export more, from one end of the Union to the other, + import less, + curtail + economize in all things + we will do better – Doubtless, our Lawgivers must do something, but we must do the greatest share ourselves."

Three months later, however, the optimism had proved misplaced. "Our pecuniary crisis is frightful. You have heard of some of the failures, - of John Anderson's – Kingsland + Lightner, Sweregen, John + Wm. Smith + Mr. Pettus. – Trs said that Paine + Messalie Gratiot have gone down with Anderson's, + that Tatum

+ Billions will also follow." "The Glasgows are safe, as far as I can ascertain." "As for myself, I am about as hard pressed as I can possibly be – every body presses me, + about half of those who owe me cannot pay."

He commented on Mary's behavior. "You are far from being deficient in understanding, but you lack fortitude very strikingly, + your distress which is always so very apparent, adds greatly to my embarrassments." "There being no money amongst us, property has come down so, that it is scarcely possible to force a sale." "I have heretofore felt a deep feeling of degradation because of my having been so overreached + deceived, but since such men as Collier + OFallon are placed in the same category, am in better spirits – 'misery loves company.'" Still, Mary had assets of her own and, in spite of his admonishments, gave him permission to sell with Glasgow's assistance a house and lot she owned. Her husband promised to repay her.

He continued to comment on the behavior of people towards those who failed financially. "Since Candy has stopped payment, 19 out of every 20 persons speak of him in terms of unmitigated disrespect." "You know how dependent the Sograin family has been for 20 years, upon Mr. Vonphul, - and will you credit it that they are now essaying to ruin him." He was, however, heartened by the fate of doctors, "many of our Doctors are starving out + quitting – that is right – we could spare about 50 more."

Financial disaster finally struck in December. He was in a stage on his way to see Mary on the first when, "I received a hint, that a trap had been laid, to make the Sheriff liable for one of my debts, if I crossed the Miss'pi, I of course immediately abandoned my journey, to the discomfiture of the enemy."

"On the 21st Ult., the mass of my Real-estate was sold by the Sheriff. The property comprised the ½ square at our old House – 50 feet on the River, in the next square below, – 100 lots in St. George, - 32 arpens in the common + 7 acres (beside that which is covered by the Pond), on Choteau Avenue. Upon all this Mrs. Berthold's lien-lies. And besides this, there was sold, the Massey Farm – 900 arpens, - some 12 or 15 acres of sand bar, or rather permanent alluvial deposit -, at St. George, all my Vide poche lots, and my Life-estate in your Pond property – upon all of which there remains no lien of which we have any knowledge."

"Wm. Ewing bought the whole of it for a song."[AN-7] Ewing was the thirty-two-year-old brother of Mary whom she had disparaged fifteen years earlier.

Three Years in St. Louis

Wm. Carr Lane's multitude of activities during 1842 are hard to contemplate. It would be impossible to imagine an ordinary day in his life. It is equally hard to imagine the constant buying and selling of real estate that must have occurred. That part of his financial distress was settled in December, but not all of his personal financial problems disappeared.

"My horse and Buggy will be sold ... and as far as my Library + the few articles of Household furniture which remain, I will have them levied upon, under one of the Judgments which Wm. Ewing has bought up, + which remain unsatisfied." "My person is all that can be reached, - + this must not be touched." Presumably all his slaves had been sold prior to his sharing a room with Ralph.

Nevertheless, he wrote in December, "let me assure you that I am freer from deep and abiding anxiety, than I have been for a long time, - since the 21st I have had the welcome assurance, that you + my children will have the means of a decent support, come what will, happen what may, to me." Despite the recurring financial disasters and often present anxiety, Lane always seemed to have the means to live well and travel. Title to property was transferred between family members, Mary's brother had bought most of Lane's real estate, and the Glasgows provided a sense of stability that did not exist with Lane. He also had income from his medical practice and other positions, including Kemper College.

Mary did not come back from Vincennes until at least August 1843. Prior to her return, Lane wrote on a variety of subjects, frequently about their grandson Jim who died at an early age. "Indeed the town goes ahead, despite the hardness of the times, will you believe that upwards of 600 Houses went up, the past season? And as there are not many Tenements, it must follow that our population is on the increase."

He would not attend a party at Mrs. Larkin's. "I do not go – being determined to attend no public or private party, until I see you once more." It would be more than six months. "I cannot say I am unhappy, for my weight yesterday was 199 – but I am restless – I constantly feel as if I should like to go away somewhere, I know not where. But one thing is fixed – all of my future movements will be regulated according to your wishes." Ten years later he would leave for New Mexico in the face of her violent objections.

He reported on a "justifiable homicide." A man named Farr had been refused admittance to a ball, because of his bad character. A few days later he sought out the doorman, who shot him before he could fire his own pistol.

Lane kept working harder. "The practice of Physic is exceedingly laborious but the labor is bearable, by any one as strong as I am, but the loss of patients is scarcely tolerable." Though he often mentioned individuals, he never described his treatments.

In February he described family weight. "You will find both Ann + Sarah much fleshier, than they were, when you saw them last – Ralph grows like a cottonwood sapling; +, since Dec. last, I think I have gained flesh daily." They seemed to eat well despite their financial woes.

He wrote regularly during the next four months, urging her to come home while reporting on family affairs. "I am exceedingly tired of my present condition, + I am not sure that all the rest are not quite as anxious to see you again as I am. Ralph remarked the other night – 'it was high time that mother should return.'" Mary responded at least once.

In late March, he wrote, "My present purpose is to set out for you myself during the first week of April," but said later in the same letter, "I confess I do not yet see how I can get off." He never did, in large part because the obstetrical portion of his practice had expanded, undoubtedly because of his position at Kemper College. "I cannot settle upon any plan of living, until I see you – It will be, I presume, housekeeping … but a suitable House – one with office + stable attached with reasonable rent is hard to get, in a central situation." "Write to me upon receipt of this, + apprise me of your intended movement – also what sum of money will be necessary to discharge all your bills." There is no way of knowing if his medical practice had eased his financial situation or if he also had other businesses.

Plans were finally made in April. His brother, Presley, Anne, and Sarah would travel on riverboats, though, as was often the case, Anne objected and argued for a stagecoach. His last letter was written in June, as was Ralph's. Mary and Anne were back in St. Louis in August, but Sarah and her husband were in Philadelphia.

Lane and Mary appear to have remained in St. Louis for the next two years while Ralph attended school, Anne traveled, and Sarah and William raised children. Presumably Lane maintained his medical practice and engaged in other activities, but he held no public office. He was now in his mid-fifties.

St. Louis grew at an explosive rate: the population was 16,469 in 1840 and 77,860 in 1850.[207] Along with the growth came increasing attention to the theater, balls, a variety of celebrations, the construction of a luxurious hotel, the Planter's House, and visitors from all over the world. It was known variously as the

"Queen of the West," the "Paris of the Plains and Mountains," and the future "Great City of America." The Lanes and Glasgows certainly were part of this St. Louis. There was, however, another party of the city that was characterized by drinking, violence, prostitution, and crime. Much of this involved the Irish, who immigrated with little money and few skills and often lived in slums growing on the outskirts of the city.

The prosperity in St. Louis depended largely on the Mississippi. Ownership of a steamboat could be very profitable, though the life expectancy of a Mississippi side-wheeler was four years and a riverboat on the Missouri three.[208] Danger was created by exploding boilers, hitting submerged snags, and adventuresome captains. The banks of the river were lined with wrecks. As some in St. Louis grew richer, the popularity of luxurious excursions grew. Boilers burst often. Those passengers in the cabins on top of side-wheelers fared better than those below, who were often drenched with scalding water. When the *John Adams* hit a snag in 1851, 84 of 100 cabin passengers survived, as did all 11 officers, 7 of 31 crew members, but only 5 of 87 deck passengers; in total, 222 died.[209]

The presidential campaign of 1844 was already underway. Lane had refused to shake Van Buren's hand. The Democratic convention met in May of 1843. Calhoun and Van Buren were bitter rivals, reflecting the North-South split. Neither could prevail on the first eight ballots; so the convention nominated the first dark horse candidate, James Polk, who had hoped to be vice president on a Van Buren ticket. Tyler had abandoned the Whigs but was rebuffed by the Democrats and started his own party.

The Whigs several weeks earlier had nominated Henry Clay unanimously. The election was extraordinarily close. Though Polk led Clay in the electoral college 170 to 105, his plurality in the popular vote was a slim 38,000 of 2,700,000 votes cast. An abolitionist candidate obtained 62,000 votes and may, along with

Democratic fraud, have cost Clay his long-sought presidency.[210] The election of Polk would have a profound effect on the course of the country in the next twenty years—and on the remainder of Wm. Carr Lane's life.

PART III

Everywhere: An Unusual Interlude

1847–1851

THE DEATH OF RALPH AND DESPAIR

Lane was overcome with grief on the afternoon of August 19, 1846, because of the death of his beloved son Victor Carr, affectionately called "Ralph," the previous day in Lexington, Kentucky. He felt compelled to write his son-in-law who was ill in St. Louis. "The memory of the past is all that remains ... my poor boy will repose near the remains of my own Father – the best of men and the best of boys."[211]

It was almost too much. The only other son born to Mary, also named Victor, had died seventeen years earlier at the age of one month. Ralph had been born two years later, and now he, too, was gone. The cause of his death is not known.

The next day, Lane, with Mary and Sarah, started in an old coach for Vincennes and St. Louis. Mary's father had died twelve days earlier, and her mother was not expected to survive the summer. Frank was left to bring the luggage up the river by steamboat.

It took three days to travel the 130 miles to Vincennes on a rough road through a steady rain and then waiting another three days in Vincennes visiting friends and relatives while the rain continued. The roads then improved enough for them to start the one-day journey to St. Louis. Mary's mother lived another three and a half years. During the next six years, however, Lane uncharacteristically drifted in his life in St. Louis and sought relief by traveling about the country. He also contracted a severe case of malaria.

It was a strange coincidence that General Stephen Watts Kearny's entry into Santa Fe had occurred within an hour of Ralph's death, but it is unlikely that the news of his arrival had yet reached St. Louis or that Lane at the time had an interest in the conquest of New Mexico. Even if he had, he could not have had any premonition that the events taking place in the Santa Fe Plaza would lead to his arrival in the same muddy place six years later.

But that was all in the future as he went down the Mississippi in early 1847 to get to a different environment and see old friends. His usual sense of purpose was gone, but the malaria was not. He first reported from New Orleans.

> I have had Fever, almost every night, since I left home, but the paroxysms have less and less force, & I feel more like getting well to-day, than I have yet done. In fact yesterday & today have been the only comfortable days, as regards temperature since I left home.[212]

However, he found the inhabitants still wearing winter coats and hovering over fires, because "The air was cold, damp & unpleasant."[213]

Three days later, he moved again – this time overnight on the little steamboat *Creole* to Mobile. Seasickness was now added to his other miseries: "Whilst we vomited, as if under the influence of double doses of Tartar & Ipecac." He understood his situation and continued describing it to Anne.

> Well here I am, some 1360 miles from Home, in the 58th year of my life, playing loafer, & that too for the first time, in my life; for, strange to tell, notwithstanding my disposition to wander, this is the first trip I have ever made, unconnected with business. But it is rather late now to commence traveling, for pleasure or improvement. – I once took much interest in everything around me & sympathized with everybody, in their good, or ill fortune – my curiosity was unbounded; now, I am no longer the same person; I look at persons and things with indifference, & would not walk a square, to witness what others would consider a fine spectacle.

His mind and understanding seemed as acute as ever, but the speed of his recovery did not reach his expectations. He had a fever almost every night as the rain continued, and he had a cold almost every day, which involved "more nose blowing and spitting, during the last 2 weeks, than in the previous 2 years." He did not turn to alcohol, but he was homesick and finally had enough. He was getting old.

He tripled his daily dose of four quinine pills and was determined to continue swallowing excessive amounts until the fever was gone. The strategy succeeded, for six days later he was back in New Orleans involving himself in a variety of matters and commenting on the behavior of others, despite what he had written Anne.

During the few days he had been in New Orleans prior to going to Mobile, he had visited friends, relatives, and dignitaries with little interest but though he thought he was slacking off, his energy and curiosity started to overcome the illness and depression. He was introduced to the governor, General Porter, and to John Slidell, a former ambassador to Mexico who had a "sinister look." He was pleased that the judges of the Supreme Court had departed when he was taken to meet them.

At the same time, he was intrigued by the complexity of a trial reported in a newspaper involving an inheritance that rested on two points of law – one, was the daughter of a second wife after the divorce of the first legitimate and, two, could a daughter who married without the consent of her father be disinherited, in this case of $80,000? Surprisingly, he withheld judgment.

Though his feelings of uselessness never disappeared entirely, they became more or less severe in relation to the continued bouts with colds and fever. He trudged through damp and unseasonably cold weather in a heavy coat and then issued detailed instructions to his family as he commented on people and current events.

Anne was told to be sure that the wages for a slave named Frederick be paid in full when the steamship *Louisiana* reached St. Louis and that he not be allowed to remain on board. Sarah was instructed to turn the cuttings of scupperwong grapes and chickasaw plums over to her husband, "Mr. Glasgow," for planting.

He simply could not suppress his wide range of interests. Sarah's uncle, Thomas Larkin, left him to see if his flatboats loaded with corn and pork had arrived—he expected to get $5,000—and if two others with corn were on the way.[214]

Though New Mexico was not of a primary interest, Lane did keep track of the war with Mexico, which he thought would be concluded after the battle of Vera Cruz. His opinion of General Zachary Taylor was not high, as he wrote to Mary. "You & I who have known Taylor personally for more than 30 years, never anticipated his present elevation. Pray, is it not a proof that man's destiny is fixed?"[215]

He also continued his commentary on religion, disagreeing with a minister who had moved from St. Louis to New Orleans and whom he considered foppish. He canceled a trip to see Old Masters, because the catalog said one painting was of the Almighty, and, thus, immoral.

These immediate distractions, however, could not overcome the overwhelming sense of grief. He had no long-range goals. "In health, I am back again, to the position I occupied about a week ago, - & my spirits are again good – when sick, my thoughts continually dwell upon the past, with painful intensity, - making life an almost insupportable burden.

As Wm. Glasgow in St. Louis struggled over naming a son Rafael, Lane speculated that it was intended to honor Ralph and also struggled.

> But if the name Rafael is intended, to commemorate my lost son, I beg you to change the name, before the Baptismal day. The name of *Ralph*, is altogether the most hallowed of names to me; & never crosses mind without producing strong emotions.[216]

Nevertheless, he was off again in the summer of 1848 to Chicago, Detroit, Windsor, and Toledo via rivers, the Great Lakes, and finally 226 miles on a canal boat to Lafayette—a "Purgatorial village."[217] Finally he took a stage to Terre Haute and then to Vincennes to see Mary's mother before returning to St. Louis. He still protested that his life of interest and activity was over. He wrote Mary, "My trip, so far, has done well enough, but my day for enjoying traveling or sight-seeing, - at least when alone, has gone by – never to return.[218]

He selected the mode of transportation as he went and, though beset with colds and seasickness on the Great Lakes, kept going.

The oppression of grief never left. "Believe me my dear wife – when I shall reach the end of my earthly race, I shall but repine. Time, thus far, does not reconcile me to our loss, & I fear it never will.

When he was in St. Louis, he maintained a medical practice, including staying with a Caroline Berkenlie until ten and returning at two in the morning when she died unexpectedly. Though his overall health had returned, he fretted that his faculties were diminishing and he might have to abandon his practice.

He and Mary went to balls and masquerades and a celebration put on by the "Germans" to honor Lajos Kossuth, leader of the 1848 Hungarian revolution. Not surprisingly, he had familiarized himself with the situation in that country and did not think the United States should get further involved. Despite his feelings and those of other leaders, Kossuth raised over $30,000.

He tended to Mary who, at the age of fifty-seven, suffered from frequent ailments. She, too, was getting old. He also worried about Ann, who was staying with the Breadings in Pittsburgh, repeatedly offering to send her money and imploring her, at the age of thirty-two, not to travel alone to Washington. He was not impressed that Benton had returned to St. Louis to live in a borrowed house so that he could run for the House of Representatives after his 1850 loss of his Senate seat.

He again headed east in May of 1852, this time by railroad, visiting Buffalo, Albany, New York, Boston, Newport, and finally Washington. Despite the sale of real estate, he had been dealing with serious debts since his powder mill blew up nineteen years earlier but now began to "breathe freely ... after toiling in want and sorry ... the wonder with me is, not that I am so shattered, but, that I am alive."[219]

The want and sorrow did not, however, keep him from living well, trading real estate, and investing while traveling. In New York, he made an offer for a warehouse on the St. Louis levee, $7,500 to be paid over two years, on behalf of his wife's trustee,

William Glasgow Jr. He planned to make the payments by selling other land.

He pursued information in both New York and Washington on a recently patented saw, which was reputed to cut 1,495 feet per hour, seeking the model on one of his many visits to the patent office. It is not clear to which Lane or Glasgow venture this was related.

He arrived in Washington on June 29, where he seemed to have regained his old energy. He visited landmarks, including Mount Vernon and the Smithsonian, made many trips to the patent office, and called on leaders, including Winfield Scott and President Fillmore. Whig leaders John Crittenden and Thomas Corwin were out of town, and Daniel Webster was sick. Thursday was fully occupied with the funeral of Henry Clay.

In the course of his eastern trip, he wrote frequently to his daughters in St. Louis, commenting on his surroundings and the advances of civilization. The return to activity started to bring back the health and energy that allowed him to pursue a frantic schedule in Washington.

Prior to reaching Washington, he had written Anne in Pittsburgh about the advances in transportation.

> I am looking back over 50 years, to the days of stage-coaches without springs, or backs to seats, - wild horses, - Drinking, or drunken drivers, - steep Hills, stumps, Rocks + gullies, with all their vicissitudes + hazards, - to say nothing of loss of sleep, etc. etc. The Turnpike, or McAdamized Road, - with spring-coaches, - made a mighty change, for the better, - to be, in its time, superceded, by the Railroad + commodius steam car! Pray what will be the next step, in the line of endless progress? Will it be the airship?

He wrote Mary from Boston on June 13 describing his trip from Buffalo to New York and then on to Boston. "On the morning of the 7th, at 8 a.m., I left Buffalo, in the Cars, + before night was in Albany, - 328 miles distant!! What you think of that rate of speed, in a cushioned seat, - upon a road so smooth, as to allow you to read, all day? The rate of speed was from 30 to 35 miles, an hour."

He stayed overnight and then went down the Hudson to New York City, which he described: "Everything is upon the high pressure principle in N.Y. All seem to be under high excitement; - all seem deeply absorbed, by their occupations; nobody walks; all run, - a foot, or in omnibus, the general mode of conveyance. The din, arising from the thousands of noises, on Broadway, from morn 'till night, resembles the roaring of a mighty storm."

He went to an Episcopal church on Sunday morning and described the sermon as a good one but could not refrain from expressing again his disdain for the Catholic church. "But I am perpetually worried, in our churches, by the slavish apings, of Roman Catholic usages, + the willingness manifested, to adopt the Doctrines of that Anti-Christian church, which, in Lord John Russell's language, 'enslaves the body + enchains the soul.'" He deplored the fact that the ministers stood sideways, not facing the congregation. "Amongst the primitive Christian churches, there was little, or no centralization, or tyranny in Church matters." "There was much diversity of opinion upon speculative points, - but all taught + believed, the same great and leading principles of Christianity. And, under this happy state of things, Christianity spread, 'like wild fire,' – and in all directions, - for 300 years. Then it was, that the first creed was proposed + enforced." He apologized for preaching without a license.

He went on to stay at Girard House in Philadelphia. "What a change is experienced, in coming from N. York to this city. Crowds, bustle, + bewildering noises, are exchanged for comparative quietude; + the change is more than acceptable to me." He had been to Newport but saw no reason to go to Cape May for sea air because "my health is too good to require it."

It is perhaps one of those odd coincidences that Lane arrived in Washington only a few weeks after the first governor of the New Mexico Territory had died someplace in Kansas while returning to Virginia for a much-needed rest. He had been inaugurated in March 1851 and was exhausted after thirteen months of establishing a civil government, dealing with Indians, and contending with Colonel Sumner, who had arrived in July 1851 as head of the military department. He and Calhoun received conflicting instructions from Washington. At the time of Calhoun's death, the only civil official in New Mexico was the Indian agent, John Greiner. There was good reason for the quick appointment of a new governor—and Lane was in Washington.

The Whig representative from St. Louis, John Darby, Edward Bates, and other friends proposed his name to President Fillmore. There was no opposition. In a matter of days, Lane was approved by Congress and admonished to get to New Mexico, which was almost in a state of anarchy.

TURMOIL IN ST. LOUIS AND WASHINGTON

Trade in St. Louis was booming in the spring of 1846 prior to Ralph's death and Lane's plunge into despair. In one week in April, fifty-nine steamboats landed at the levee. Six thousand passengers arrived, along with tons of freight, much of which was going west and already packed in wagons lashed to the deck and ready to travel over the Santa Fe Trail.[220] In 1850, the population was 78,000, including 4,000 Blacks of whom almost a third were free.[221] The need for slaves had been reduced because immigrants, largely German and Irish, flooded the city, ending a labor shortage.

Disasters, both natural and manmade, would, however, engulf the city in the next six years. The cholera epidemic in 1849 killed at least 13 percent of the population. In the same year, a fire that started in a stateroom on a steamboat swept through the city. Over one thousand men fought the blaze, but the water supply gave out, and so the fire was contained by blowing up buildings in its path. Three men died, and fifteen blocks of commercial and residential property were destroyed, along with twenty-three steamboats.[222]

Riots were common, usually involving the Irish. But in 1849, a particularly serious one occurred. Several months after the Great Fire, firemen were fighting a blaze that destroyed five steamboats. An altercation initiated by a dogfight led Irishmen to attack the firemen with stones and gunfire. The firemen then destroyed the saloon from which the Irishmen had come and three coffee houses. The firemen went home. The mob returned that evening with a six-inch howitzer but were turned back with the aid of a heavy rain.

Lane did not mention any of these events in the many letters written during this period, but confined himself to family matters and comments on religion, transportation, and other subjects that were of greater interest to him. The events in St. Louis seemed to have had little effect on him. However, the struggles in Washington and the Mexican war, which he mentioned briefly, would change his life dramatically.

It began in 1836 as Texas gained its independence from Mexico when Sam Houston defeated Santa Anna in the decisive battle on the San Jacinto River on April 21. The Texans had until then appeared headed for defeat after the slaughter of Americans at Goliad and the better-known Alamo. Most Texans hoped for annexation to the United States, but many later became determined to remain independent and expand to the West Coast.

Texas did remain independent, because neither the Whigs nor the Democrats were eager for annexation, fearing both a war with Mexico and the potential of another slave state. The issue, however, became a significant factor in the selection of candidates for the 1843 presidential election. The Whigs unanimously selected Clay, who some months earlier had expressed his opposition to annexation. The Democratic convention, however, was contentious, with Van Buren maneuvering in every possible way to regain the presidency. On the eighth ballot, James K. Polk was nominated. He had been a member of the House, serving two terms as speaker, was a strong supporter of Jackson, and was sometimes called "Young Hickory." Polk was a strong supporter of American expansion, including the annexation of Texas.

President Tyler, however, was not finished and was determined to consummate the annexation of Texas. After a series of fights in Congress, including overcoming the opposition of Benton, he succeeded by using his constitutional power to annex new states, which required a simple majority in the Senate, not the two-thirds required to negotiate a treaty with another country, which Texas was. Then much to everybody's surprise, he signed the bill three days before Polk's inauguration. The South had gained another slave state.[223]

Polk was determined to continue the expansion of the United States—characterized in the *Democratic Review* as the fulfillment of America's "manifest destiny."[224] The western United States was a vast area about which little was known other than the location of settlements, trails, and rivers. It was not even clear what the boundaries of the newly annexed Texas were. The Republic claimed the land as far west as the Rio Grande River to the west and the Arkansas to the north. The northwestern part of the United States, known as the Oregon Territory, included the present-day states of Oregon, Washington, Idaho, and parts of Wyoming and Montana. The area west of Texas and south of Oregon was Mexican territory, including present-day Nevada, California, Utah, Arizona, New Mexico, and portions of Wyoming and Colorado.[225]

At the beginning of 1846, Polk was faced with the possibility of two wars because of his expansionist goals. A war with England over Oregon would have been a disaster; war with Mexico, which was not a government in the modern sense, would be something else. In early January, he sent a resolution to Congress settling the boundary dispute with England at the forty-ninth parallel, not acceding to those raising a furor over "54-40 or fight."

He had earlier sent John Slidell, whom Wm. Carr Lane later thought had a sinister look, to Mexico to try to negotiate or bribe the Mexicans into handing over their provinces of California and New Mexico, which included Arizona and Utah, to the United States. As the English issues were settled, Polk received word that Slidell's overtures had been rejected. General Zachary Taylor was dispatched with two thousand US troops to the Nueces River and then on to the Rio Grande south of Corpus Christi. He was joined by undisciplined and largely Texan volunteers.

Taylor crossed the Rio Grande in April after, many claimed, he goaded the Mexicans to attack. Polk was frustrated that the war was not going well. Taylor did little to move forward but did plan to run for president. He was considered stupid by some, including Lane. Polk had to do something and finally, though he was a Whig, put General Winfield Scott in command. Scott, a brilliant and disciplined soldier, prepared his army and led a bloody five-month campaign from Vera Cruz to Mexico City, which he entered in September 1847, raising the American flag over the Halls of Montezuma.

The action in the war that had the greatest effect on Lane was the raising of the Army of the West under Stephen Watts Kearny, who organized an army at Fort Leavenworth, Kansas, while at the same time trying to train and discipline fifteen hundred Missouri volunteers. He first moved on to Bent's Fort in southern Colorado with the troops, volunteers, over fifteen hundred wagons, and almost twenty thousand animals—oxen, cattle, horses, and mules.[226] Traders' wagons, including Glasgow's, were part of the fifteen hundred. He left Bent's Fort on August 1, traveling for days over land with neither water nor vegetation; men and animals perished. They finally reached Raton Pass north of Las Vegas, New Mexico, and found water and feed.

Kearny entered Santa Fe on the afternoon of August 18. As he marched from Las Vegas to Santa Fe, he received conflicting reports of the intentions of Mexican Governor Manuel Armijo. At one point he was reported to have twelve thousand troops waiting in Apache Canyon east of Santa Fe. It is still not clear what combination of reality, cowardice, and bribery led him to abandon his city and flee south into Mexico with his entourage. New Mexico was conquered without a shot having been fired.

In accordance with the original plan, Kearny departed Santa Fe on August 24 with eight hundred men to go south and then west to conquer California. He reached San Diego in December. The Missouri volunteers had elected Alexander Doniphan as their leader. They were sent south with Colonel Price to join the American army in Chihuahua.

The signing of a treaty to end the war was complex, not only because of slow communications but because Polk's envoy to Mexico, Nicholas Trist, ignored instructions and negotiated a treaty in the town of Guadalupe Hidalgo near Mexico City on February 2, 1848. There was substantial debate in the Senate over ratification because of potential slavery issues and presidential politics. Those who opposed Polk because they thought he had instigated the war could hardly vote against ending it. Because modifications had been made in the original draft, it had to be returned to Mexico for ratification, which occurred on May 19, in large part to end American military occupation. The treaty would later play a major role in Lane's period as territorial governor.

The treaty did not signify the end, however. Oregon became a territory in August 1848, but New Mexico and California remained under military rule until the Compromise of 1850, through which

California became a state and New Mexico, which still included Arizona and Utah, became a territory.

SLAVERY—ALWAYS PRESENT

Lane in his 1846–1852 letters often referred to those working for him, but it was not always apparent whether they were slaves or paid servants. It was clear, however, that there were both. Frederick was a slave; Lane wrote from New Orleans to be sure he was taken off a steamboat when it arrived in St. Louis to avoid mistreatment. Frank, however, remains a mystery. He later accompanied Lane to New Mexico as his personal servant and constant companion.

The bitter fight between the North and South was always present in national politics but never simple. There were extremists on both sides, but many others had more complex reasons for taking their positions. One of these was David Wilmot, one of a group of young New York representatives who belonged to a new generation of Democrats opposed to slavery.

His name has become part of history because of the Wilmot Proviso, which he offered as an amendment to a two-million-dollar appropriation bill President Polk sent to Congress in August 1846. The intent of the bill was ostensibly to aid in negotiations to end the Mexican War. Many, particularly anti-slavery Whigs, saw it as a way to advance the president's plan for further territorial expansion. The amendment said, "neither slavery nor involuntary servitude shall ever exist in any territories acquired from Mexico as a result of the war."[227] The New York group of which Wilmot was a member was neither opposed to expansion nor particularly concerned about the plight of Blacks but wanted to ensure that White workers would not have to compete for jobs in new territories.

Polk increased the appropriation to three million dollars and succeeded in getting it passed without the amendment.

The defeated amendment, however, became the rallying point for northern anti-slavery Democrats along with similarly minded Whigs. One so-called Wilmot Democrat, Bradford Wood, spoke in the House. "It is a question whether, in the government of the country, she shall be borne down by the influence of your slaveholding aristocratic institutions, that have not in them the first element of Democracy."[228]

The amendment, and thus Wilmot's name, became the focus of the slavery issue that dominated the party conventions preceding the presidential election of 1848. Polk honored his commitment not to seek a second term. After a bitter fight, the Democrats nominated Lewis Cass. He had initially supported the amendment, but as his presidential ambitious grew, he not only withdrew his support but actively opposed it.

The Whigs met a few weeks later and, despite the continuing ambitions of Henry Clay and Daniel Webster, nominated the hero of the Mexican War, General Zachary Taylor. One of the general's appeals as a candidate was the vagueness of his political views. He hadn't been sure which party to join until shortly before the convention.

As a result, the hard-line anti-slavery Democrats bolted the convention immediately after the nomination and held their own convention. They were joined by members of the old Liberty Party and anti-slavery Whigs. The amalgamation became the Free Soil Party and nominated the aging Martin Van Buren.

Apparently seeking some form of moderation, the country elected Taylor with 163 electoral votes; Cass received 127 and Van Buren none.[229]

The struggles over the expansion of slavery continued until the middle of 1850. In January of that year, Taylor introduced a bill that would have admitted California as a free state immediately and New Mexico as soon as feasible. Southerners were enraged and met in Nashville; there was some talk of secession.

During the Mexican War, one critic of General Taylor described him as fat and sitting in his tent gaining weight. Perhaps he was correct. On July 4, 1850, Taylor spent much of an afternoon sitting in the sun at the unfinished Washington Monument eating raw vegetables and cherries and drinking iced milk. He continued in the evening, became seriously ill the next day, and died on the ninth of gastroenteritis. He was succeeded by Millard Fillmore.

Disputes had earlier reached a level of crisis. The Territory of New Mexico had ratified a free state constitution, which called for admission as a state in June. As a result, Texas started raising an army of volunteers to take all of New Mexico east of the Rio Grande, and Taylor had ordered the federal troops in Santa Fe to prepare for combat.

Fillmore as president, however, immediately put aside New Mexico's request for statehood and starting working with Henry Clay and others in Congress to resolve the problems. Finally, in September, a series of bills that became known as the Compromise of 1850 were passed. The effect was to admit California as a free state, abolish the slave trade in the District of Columbia, establish the New Mexico–Texas boundary at its existing location with a payment to Texas, and establish Utah and New Mexico, which still included Arizona, as territories with no reference to slavery. It was also made easier to recover fugitive slaves.

Thus, by the summer of 1852, when Wm. Carr Lane arrived in Washington, the general borders of the Western states had been established, Millard Fillmore was president, and the struggles over slavery continued. James S. Calhoun, who had been an Indian agent, was sworn in as the first territorial governor of New Mexico on March 3, 1851.

PART IV

New Mexico – The Culmination

1852–1854

THE LAND OF *POCO TIEMPO*

"Sun, silence, and adobe"—that is New Mexico in three words. If a fourth were to be added, it would be only to clinch the three. It is the Great American Mystery – the National Rip Van Winkle – the United States that is <u>not</u> the United States. Here is the land of *Poco Tiempo* – the home of "Pretty Soon," so wrote Charles Lummis in 1893.[230] Lummis, an Easterner, was one of the first promoters of New Mexico, The Land of Enchantment, but his characterization had a great deal of truth. People in the rest of the country knew little of the history or the different cultures of the territory.[AN-8]

Álavar Núñez Cabeza de Vaca, the first Spanish immigrant, appeared in New Mexico in 1636 with three companions after completing an eight-year journey from the Florida coast where their ship had been wrecked. The first planned expedition was led by Francisco Vásquez de Coronado, who set out from Mexico four years later in the hope of conquering "Cities of Gold" as Hernán Cortéz had in Mexico twenty years earlier. Coronado traveled as far east as Kansas but found no gold, only Indians living in mud pueblos.

Spain, nevertheless, was determined to colonize New Mexico and add to its empire. In 1598, Don Juan de Oñate set out to do so with four hundred men, 130 with wives and children, Indians to carry material, a large herd of animals, and oxen pulling eighty-three carts, including Oñate's fine velvet and satin clothes, his tent with a bed, and other refinements.[231]

They were accompanied by Franciscans who were to spread Catholicism and save the heathens. Colonies were established along the banks of the Rio Grande, which had been the site of Indian pueblos for generations. Santa Fe was established as the capital in 1607, though some claim that the founding was two years earlier. The Palace of the Governors in which Lane would live was constructed in 1610.

Many Pueblo Indians resisted Oñate's establishment of Spanish colonies, and the priests' attempts at conversion often resulted in violent clashes. The Pueblo of Acoma, located on a high and inaccessible mesa seventy miles west of the Rio Grande and the current city of Albuquerque, had first surrendered to Oñate but later lured another Spanish detachment to its slaughter. In February 1599, Oñate gained his revenge by overwhelming and destroying the pueblo. Only six hundred of the estimated two thousand inhabitants are thought to have survived. Some of those had their feet cut off. News of the fight at Acoma spread through the region, but killings and enslavement continued on both sides, as the Spanish colonized and assigned friars to pueblos to build churches while they confiscated the natives' food.

The growing Indian hostility came to fruition in 1680 with the Pueblo Revolt, inspired and led by Po'pay, who lived at Taos but was from the San Juan Pueblo. It was the only successful Indian revolt in American history. Thanks to a secret method of communication, the pueblos rose up simultaneously in August and murdered over four hundred friars and settlers while burning their churches and buildings. They then descended on Santa Fe and defeated the Spanish who had retreated to the Palace of the Governors where the women and children were barricaded. The Indians forced the survivors to surrender by burning most of the village and destroying the water supply. Spanish Governor Otermin led the garrison, women and children, and three friars, an estimated one thousand in all, to the southern pueblos, which already housed survivors, and then further to establish a camp near present-day El Paso.[232] The Indians occupied the Palace of the Governors.

Though several early attempts were made to recapture New Mexico, it was not until Don Diego de Vargas surrounded Santa Fe in September 1692 that Spain began to regain control. In the interim, the pueblos had tried to create a united force amongst themselves and attempted to make allies of the roaming Apaches, Utes, and Navajo. Not surprisingly, internal conflicts appeared, and Po'pay could not maintain a united front. More than a hundred years later, Tecumseh's similar efforts in the Midwest would also fail. It would be 1696 before the Spanish established reasonable control throughout the large area encompassing individual pueblos. De Vargas had executed seventy prisoners and sold four hundred women and children into slavery when he occupied Santa Fe.

Slavery was common. The Spanish held Indian captives; the various tribes and pueblos held Spanish and other Indian captives. It is not surprising that in this environment mixing of blood was common. A 1757 census listed Spanish and non-Indian 5,170, Pueblo Indians 8,694, Genizaro Indians 255.[233] The latter were non-Pueblo Indians living generally as Spanish. As late as 1868 hearings were held in Taos to free 363 Indians held in peonage or slavery, over 80 percent in the latter category. All were freed and the slaveholders charged.[234]

The period extending from 1598 to 1821 in New Mexico is

often described as the "Colonial Period." It would be inaccurate to describe the time as peaceful, but the pueblos had decided that they could not fight the Spanish rule. They submitted to abuse as they pretended to be converted to the Catholic faith. Some historians have said they were almost slaves. The Spanish still fought off raiding Apache, Comanche, and Navajo. This period of over a hundred years ended in 1821 when Mexico, which included New Mexico, obtained its independence from Spain. It is highly unlikely that this history of the Southwest was included in Wm. Carr Lane's education or that he was aware of the conquest and settlement that took place over a period of two centuries.

Nevertheless, rebellions and invasions continued. A major uprising that is a model of duplicity occurred in 1837, when eight northern pueblos rose up and were joined by Mexicans who objected to Spanish rule and taxes. One of the leaders of the Mexican plotters was General Manuel Armijo. The groups met at Santa Cruz de la Cañada, thirty-five miles north of Santa Fe, and proclaimed a plan of government on August 3, 1837.

Mexican Governor Albino Pérez assembled an unknown number of troops and, accompanied by friends, marched north on August 8 to put down the rebellion. However, when confronted by the rebels the next day, the troops deserted and forced Pérez and his friends to flee back toward Santa Fe to try to escape. They separated, most were captured, tortured, and killed. When Pérez was captured on the morning of the tenth, his head was cut off and paraded through Santa Fe on the end of a pole. The rebels entered Santa Fe the same day and elected as governor José Gonzales from the Taos Pueblo. The property of those killed was distributed among the rebels. A side effect of this action was the financial loss to American traders who had sold goods on credit to the Spanish.

A committee of three, including General Armijo, was designated during an assembly held on August 27 and 28 to prepare a set of grievances to be submitted to Mexico City. Armijo left for his home in Albuquerque, where he assembled troops and declared a counterrevolution supporting Mexico against the government he had just helped establish. His supporters marched north and occupied Santa Fe. He proclaimed himself governor.

While four hundred troops marched north from Mexico City to quell the rebellion, Armijo maintained peace with the rebels still in La Cañada until the Mexican troops reached Santa Fe early in 1838. He then took command and marched north. It has been reported that when they reached La Cañada, he decided to retreat but gave a junior officer approval to attack. The rebels were routed. Armijo then had his former comrades court-martialed and executed. José Gonzales was shot immediately.

Three years later, the president of Texas, General Mirabeau B. Lamar, presented Armijo with the opportunity to portray himself not only as a staunch supporter of Mexican rule but also as something of a hero. Lamar believed that it was finally time to establish all of New Mexico east of the Rio Grande as Texas territory, a claim Texas had made for years. He also believed that the New Mexicans would welcome the Texans as an alternative to Mexico. An expedition of six companies left Austin in June 1841 under the command of Brevet Brigadier General Hugh McLeod.

Armijo learned of the invasion, confined foreigners to their homes, and dispatched Captain Damasio Salazar to reconnoiter the eastern frontier. The Texans didn't know where they were going and were surprised to find the people of New Mexico did not regard them as saviors but as the foreign invaders they were.

An advance party reached the Pecos River roughly thirty miles south of Las Vegas. Salazar captured three men deemed to be spies on September 4 and sent them back to Santa Fe, where one was killed trying to escape and the other two executed on the orders of Armijo. On September 16, Salazar captured a party of six, lined them up, and had a firing squad in position but was dissuaded from saying "fire" by a prominent New Mexican.

In the meantime, Armijo had stationed himself in Las Vegas and on the seventeenth accepted the surrender of ninety-four Texans. The remainder of the Texans were found starving and lost further east on October 16. All of the invading force was marched to Mexico City. Armijo could now represent himself as the hero who had repelled a foreign invader.

That was not the case five years later when the US General Kearny arrived east of Santa Fe at Apache Pass. Armijo put up no resistance and fled south. It is possible that he had been bribed by St. Louis traders who traveled with Kearny and had preceded him to Santa Fe.

Armijo, however, always found a way to survive. He soon moved back to New Mexico and became a prominent and prosperous citizen at Limitar a few miles north of Socorro. Lane met with him there in 1852 and 1853.

NEW MEXICO IN TURMOIL

Lane did not remain in Washington after his Senate confirmation but returned immediately to St. Louis. He had sent word of his appointment ahead to Mary and Anne, but he reached St. Louis before the message. One can imagine the scene in the Lane household when he revealed what he was about to undertake after having said he was a shattered old man. Mary and Anne refused to go with him; Mary proclaimed in her usual gloomy way, "I'll never see you again." Despite her devotion to her father, Anne thought her mother ill-used.

Lane did not waste any time heading west to fill the vacant post. He left St. Louis on the steamboat *St. Ange* with his Black servant Frank on July 31.

By this time, Lane and his family must have known from a number of sources of the dangers in New Mexico. Though William Glasgow Jr. was not engaged in his uncles' trading enterprises, the

Lanes certainly had heard of the risks of going over the Santa
Fe Trail and of the difficulties in dealing with the Mexicans.
Prosperous Santa Feans sent their children to schools in St.
Louis—Anne and Sarah probably knew some of them. New
Mexicans began traveling east over the Trail in 1825 when the
governor commissioned Don Manuel Escudero to visit St. Louis
and Washington to encourage trade. He must have conferred with
Lane, who was then mayor. Lane was also a member of the Santa
Fe Trail Committee when he was a member of the legislature.
Frank Blair Jr. had been appointed US attorney in New Mexico
in 1846 by General Kearny.

The Santa Fe Trail was the link between New Mexico
and Missouri—and between Lane's life in St. Louis and the
governorship of the territory. The trail was opened in the fall of
1821 by William Bicknell, who traveled from Franklin, Missouri, to
Santa Fe and returned with a substantial profit from his trading. By
1846, the annual trade was estimated to have a value of $937,500
with a cost of $414,750 for outfits, insurance, wages, etc., leaving
a profit of $400,000, transported in 370 wagons pulled by 1,700
mules and 2,000 oxen driven by 500 men.[235]

The Trail had a single track from Independence, Missouri,
to the Arkansas River near current-day Dodge City, Kansas—
about 370 miles. It divided at that point, with the mountain route
following the river west and then turning south, over Raton Pass,
into New Mexico, and stretching almost five hundred miles to
Santa Fe. The Dry, or Cimarron, Route avoided the mountains
by going southwest toward New Mexico over the prairie. It was
about one hundred miles shorter, but there was no water available
during the first two-thirds of the route, and the exposure to
attack by Plains Indians was much greater. A well-documented
massacre took place in October 1849 when a Dr. White and his
party returning to Santa Fe were set upon at Point of Rocks, New
Mexico, by Apaches who killed White and four companions and

carried off his wife, their small daughter, and a Black nurse. The fate of the latter three remains a mystery, though it is fairly well established that the Apaches killed Mrs. White. The other two disappeared, though there were reports that a girl resembling the daughter was seen several years later in a Comanche camp. The assumption was that the Apache had sold her. The weather, with snowstorms or sandstorms, contributed to the hazards, taking the lives of dozens of men and hundreds of animals.

Because Manuel Armijo had fled south, General Kearny was welcomed by acting Governor Vigil y Alarid and the leading citizens of Santa Fe on August 18, 1846. The American flag was raised over the Palace of the Governors where they met.[AN-9] After the general addressed most of the population who had gathered in the Plaza, Vigil y Alarid responded in part, "Do not find it strange if there has been no manifestation of joy and enthusiasm in seeing this city occupied by your military forces. To us the power of the Mexican Republic is dead. No matter what her condition, she was our mother. What child will not shed abundant tears at the tomb of his parents ... In the name then, of the entire Department, I swear obedience to the Northern Republic and I render my respect to its laws and authority."[236]

Kearny acted quickly, naming officials, visiting pueblos, establishing the Kearny Code, which established a rule of law, and proclaiming that all persons living within New Mexico were now citizens of the United States. He added that those who remained peaceable would be considered good citizens, but that those resisting or inciting others to resist would be considered traitors. He named Charles Bent as Governor and sent detachments to remote villages and others to meet with the Navajo. On September 25, he left Santa Fe for California with three hundred American troops and four hundred Mormon volunteers. The latter were volunteers in name only. They had been recruited by Brigham Young with the aim of having them spread the Mormon word in California, where they would remain. Shortly after they had departed, he sent a representative to confiscate their advance pay. Colonel Alexander Doniphan left Santa Fe on October 26 with a regiment of regular troops and Missouri volunteers for his successful battles in Mexico. The army in Santa Fe was left under the command of Colonel Sterling Price to oversee the occupation.

The rumblings of dissent and some active resistance began to appear in the coming months, culminating in the murder of Governor Bent and five others in Taos on January 19, 1847. Bent was scalped. An insurgency had been organized by Mexicans and Indians with the aim of killing Price and Bent on Christmas Eve, but the plot was discovered, probably from information provided by Doña Tules Barceló, the proprietress of Santa Fe's leading gambling establishment.

Price moved quickly to destroy the insurgents. He left Santa Fe on January 23 with 350 men, including both regular troops and volunteers, and marched north, overcoming 1,500 rebels at Santa Cruz. He continued further north with his four howitzers and additional volunteers. They overwhelmed the Indians, who had barricaded themselves in the church at Taos. They agreed to peace on February 4. Close to two hundred rebels had been killed and up to fifty more executed. Many leaders were killed or executed, while the American death toll was less than 10 percent of that of the insurgents. Many prominent citizens in Northern New Mexico had sympathized with the revolt but remained silent.

Though the Americans had established control, there was still much unrest, particularly in the mountains east of Santa Fe and Taos. The Apaches, Comanches, and Navajos continued to raid villages and pueblos as the military launched retaliatory campaigns. The attempts to establish a government continued, with the underlying struggle between the military and civilian authorities always present.

The dispute was settled superficially with the swearing-in of James S. Calhoun as the first territorial governor on March 3, 1851, and the establishment of US territorial law. Calhoun, who had served under Zachary Taylor during the Mexican War, was forty-nine and had lived a comfortable life in Virginia prior to the war. Taylor had appointed him Indian Agent in July 1849, so he had been in the area for almost two years when he was sworn in as governor. He stated accurately in his inaugural address that "An era in the history of New Mexico commenced this day. The problem as to the capacity of the people for self-government is to be solved, preparatory to the assumption of a higher and more glorious position as one of the sovereign and independent states of the Union."[237]

Calhoun had accomplished a great deal prior to his death a little more than a year later. He had established a legislature, which passed an act called The Rights of the People, and had won the respect of New Mexicans and Pueblo Indians but not the Navajo, Comanche, and Apache, whom he thought would have to be contained on reservations. He had conducted a census for the purpose of legislative apportionment and found there to be 56,984 citizens, not including Indians.[238] About 95 percent had been born in the territory. He had, however, added to his stress by urging that the legislature pass a law preventing the entrance of free Blacks into New Mexico. He was denounced in the east for doing so. His requests for the means to protect people from Indian raids were largely ignored as disputes with the military continued. His speeches were similar in depth of understanding. He thought education, including that of women, was paramount. He left Santa Fe on May 6, 1852, with his wife, two daughters and their husbands, his secretary, five Pueblo Indians, a military escort of twenty, and his coffin, to visit Washington and to rest in Georgia.[239] His grave west of Kansas City has never been found.

ANOTHER INAUGURAL

Lane arrived in Santa Fe on Thursday, September 9, and was inaugurated as the second territorial governor of New Mexico on Monday, September 13, in front of a large crowd. The ceremonies included welcoming speeches, prayers, his acceptance, and a "thundering salute from Brooks' guns."[240] His remarks were limited to those appropriate for such an occasion. After he had traveled over much of the territory to observe the situation in New Mexico, he presented a comprehensive review of his conclusions. It was translated and read to the Legislative Assembly in Spanish on December 7.

During the forty-one days it had taken to travel from St. Louis to Santa Fe, he had not encountered any of the hazards that often confronted travelers, though he saw much evidence of their results. These included the graves of men who had perished because of weather or Indian attacks and the remains of three hundred army mules that had frozen to death.

His one serious medical problem, a sudden attack of renal calculus (kidney stones), laid him out thirty miles east of Point of Rocks, New Mexico, on August 25. On that day, he awoke on "his earth pallet" with a pain in his right side. On September 3, he wrote Mary from Fort Union, roughly a hundred miles east of Santa Fe, describing the episode. He had been moved from the ground to a bed in the carriage in which he was traveling. However, he was unable to keep anything in his stomach and obtained relief only from large doses of ether and chloroform. A doctor returning to St. Louis examined him and forbade him to take ether. Once he had gone on his way, Lane continued having it administered until the supply had been used up.

Major Carelton, in charge of the group, became so alarmed that he ordered a forced march to Fort Union with a detachment of six men, Frank, and the semiconscious Lane. They reached

Point of Rocks late in the afternoon and started again at midnight, reaching Fort Union at nine that night. He apparently passed the stones and was "relieved from pain of the most excruciating kind." He remained at Fort Union to regain his strength and was fully recovered by the time he left for Santa Fe on September 6.

He had written Anne earlier from Boonville, Missouri, three days after leaving St. Louis, reporting that he had gone ashore to vote the straight Whig ticket. He also felt some remorse. "Look to your mother – had I known that my departure, would have had such a crushing effect, upon her, that it has, I would have remained at home with her. As it is, I will surely return, next season, if it should please God to spare my life, + if she is in the same state of mind – I will never leave her again. My first duty on Earth is to do all I can to promote her happiness."[241] Though he often expressed similar sentiments, they never prevailed when a new challenge appeared.

He wrote in his journal that he had dispatched many letters back to St. Louis but was not sure they would be delivered. That may have been the case, for few survive. He also described the trip to Mary as "This dreary journey." The entries in his journal, however, are not consistent with that evaluation, nor was a letter to William Glasgow Jr. Throughout the trip he commented on the terrain, vegetation, food, water, stars, animals, content of the soil, and other travelers. His wide range of interests and curiosity had been aroused. He did not dwell on the misery he had left in St. Louis or the chaos awaiting him in Santa Fe.

He had embarked on the journey over the Santa Fe Trail at Independence, Missouri, where he and Frank boarded the mail stage, which had started monthly service to Santa Fe in 1850. The stage was drawn by six mules and the baggage wagon by four. The fare for Lane, Frank, and extra baggage to Fort Atkinson was $295. A herd of cattle was driven west with them. The Trail was simply a route followed by wagons, carriages, livestock, and riders.

As it crossed the prairie, they sometimes followed each other and sometimes traveled abreast. Deep ruts were cut in the soil—many can still be seen today. There were landmarks such as Pawnee Rock and many stream crossings that were commonly used.

The first day was through "eminently beautiful country." He "relished exceedingly" the dinner of fried ham, egg, pickles, crackers, and coffee. But they had brought no water with them, and he was very thirsty when they stopped at nine the next day. Fortunately, he discovered a pool of water that he mixed with brandy and drank "freely." He apparently was not concerned about consuming alcohol.

He noted on August 7 meeting seven groups of travelers going east; he counted the number of oxen in each team. There were also six lone travelers, "rough looking customers." The green horseflies were the most abundant of the many insects. Mill Creek was a "pretty stream lined with walnut, hickory, and elm trees with a luxuriant undergrowth of bushes." He made detailed entries in the journal about campsites and their daily progress.

They were up at four in the morning on August 8 and reached Council Grove, Kansas, at five in the afternoon. The grove, located on the banks of the Neosho River, was one of the most important stops on the Santa Fe Trail. In addition to the mail agent, Mr. Charles Whittington, the settlement included a Baptist mission, three trading firms, and a blacksmith shop. Lane stayed with Whittington and his wife at the cost of a dollar. He saw several survivors of Tecumseh's Shawnee who had been relocated to an adjacent reservation and were now wearing American clothes.

They made good progress after leaving Council Grove on the eleventh heading for Fort Atkinson, covering the roughly two hundred miles in six days. They had something of a feast on the first day, including cold ham, oysters, and pickles, for lunch "and had roasting ears brought from the Grove added to our repast." The corn undoubtedly came from the fertile soil along the Neosho River, but the origin of the oysters is a mystery. As they progressed, the grass gradually changed from tall prairie to buffalo and grama. There were days with no water, but "a good mule could go a day-and-a-half without any." One night the rain poured down while Lane was in the carriage and Frank slept under it. Wolves always followed them. The rabbits were much larger than those in Missouri.

At the Little Arkansas River, about ninety miles west of Council Grove, the driver told him they would now be at risk of an Indian attack. Mr. Whittington had told him that recently a war party of 375 Kaw, Osage, and Comanche had planned to attack the Pawnee in their own territory but withdrew when they discovered the encampment included two thousand Pawnee, Omaha, Missouri, Fox, and Iowa. The Kaw leader thought it such a dishonor to retreat that he rode alone into the encampment and killed a woman before he was killed. Mr. Whittington thought they were preparing for another attack.

Dr. Lane described the remains of a murdered Delaware. "His clothes and some of his remains were found as follows: the lower jaw, the backbone, thigh bones, 1 scapula; the humerus, radius, bones of both hands and some other portions of his bones; also a lock of his hair, plaited. His clothes were still clotted with blood." Presumably, because he was an Indian, he had not been buried.

"By the way, we passed three graves by the wayside: 1st, the grave of a foot passenger who froze to death last winter; 2nd, the grave of the deserter who was murdered by his fellow deserters for his money; 3rd, the grave of somebody unknown to our party; with the frozen man was buried about 70 dollars in gold. The grave has not yet been violated to recover this treasure."

At Fort Atkinson Lane changed to an army ambulance, a kind of carriage with springs, accompanied by "a Company of Dragoons, 1 brass canon, 2 Baggage Wagons and 1 ambulance" all under the commander of Fort Union, Major Carleton. The company took the shorter and more hazardous Dry Route.

They started out on August 16 for Fort Union, a little over three hundred miles away; it took them eleven days climaxed by a forced march. They were accompanied for the first ten miles by a Major Buckner and Miss Marie Chouteau on horseback. There is no explanation for the purpose of Miss Chateau's visit to the fort. Again, the days alternated between a lack of water and rain. They soon passed "four Kayoway Indians going to the Fort, with perhaps 2,000 or 2,500 horses."

Saturday August 21 was "A splendid morning, Venus being some degrees south of the sun's place of rising and about thirty above the horizon and shining brightly." On Sunday they camped at Upper Cold Spring where there was an abundance of water and vegetation. "At dinner we had perch five inches long and a dessert of perfumed grapes which I ate with unusual pleasure."

He recorded the changes in terrain and the increase in elevation. "This tableland is broken and washed away, in many places much resembling architectural ruins." He climbed a hill of lava. On Tuesday when they were opposite Round Mound, he estimated that they were now at six thousand feet. Even though he was accustomed to an elevation of five hundred feet, his health and breathing were excellent. He did note that his vision was much sharper in the thinner air and objects appeared much closer than they were. He proved it by estimating that Round Mound was three hundred yards away and then pacing off a longer distance.

He arrived at Fort Union twenty-seven days after leaving St. Louis and thrived until the attack of renal calculus. He seemed to have particularly enjoyed riding alone with Major Carleton several miles ahead of the rest of the party. Hs curiosity did not lessen during his nine-day recuperation. He showed particular interest in the Post garden irrigated by buckets fastened to an endless chain and powered by six mules: "fine Pumpkins, Corn in the roasting ear, various Berries, Turnips, Peas, Parsnips, Cabbage, poor cucumbers, Radish, fine Okra, Beets, and indigenous Potatoes."

The methods of travel and environment were a dramatic contrast to those of his journeys south and east after Ralph's death, but his curiosity and enthusiasm were unchanged. In the East and South he expressed his opinions about education, religion, progress, people, politics, and on and on. Traveling to Santa Fe, he described every aspect of the environment and human activity. He never mentioned the problems he would find in New Mexico. While in Washington, Lane had mentioned the first signs of recovery from the despair that had plagued him since Ralph's death; a recovery was complete by the time he reached Santa Fe.

He had been invigorated by his new experiences in what might almost be called a vacation, but that would change gradually during the four days required to cover the one hundred miles from Fort Union to Santa Fe. He left on Monday morning in an ambulance with Captain Shoemaker, his little son, and a Dr. Byrne. Major Carleton was in another carriage with another officer. "Baggage wagons and an escort of 6 dragoons completed the party."

On Tuesday they entered the pass through the Sangre de Cristo mountains. "The scenery yesterday and to-day has been most delightful ... Stopped at Las Vegas – 2,600 inhabitants." His identity became known. A rancher, "upon being informed that I was the *Gobernador*, a sort of divan with half a dozen cushions was spread for me alone." The county sheriff asked Major Carleton to escort two prisoners back to a jail in Santa Fe from which they had escaped. The major agreed after Lane ordered that they be shot if they tried to escape again. "Thus it happened that my first official or rather semi-official act in execution of the law has been one of terrible harshness ... The poor wretches of prisoners both of them on one little mule." They passed the ruins of the old church at the abandoned Pecos Pueblo—"ruins are somewhat imposing. In length it is some 125 feet by about 50, some of the woodwork rudely carved is quite sound." North of the church there "were immense structures and many stories high in some places."

His new role commenced unofficially just before noon on Thursday, when he was met about ten miles east of Santa Fe by John Greiner, secretary of the territory and acting governor, accompanied by many Mexican citizens. As they continued, many others in carriages and on horseback "joined the escort with great spirit." He continued to the Plaza filled with people and arrived "amidst a thundering salute from Col. Brooks ... Passed the rest of the day receiving visitors and resting myself."

On Friday, Lane wrote, "Col Sumner left the city for Albuquerque, his new headquarters; was introduced to many citizens." He spent the evening with a Baptist missionary and missionary families. On Sunday he went to the mission church and wrote his inaugural address, which was translated into Spanish by Don Manuel Álvarez the day after he read it. His address was similar in tone and understanding to those he had delivered years earlier in St. Louis.

> Gentlemen, I have come amongst you with two objects in view; namely, to employ my time honorably to myself, and usefully to the people of this Territory ... The task before us, public and private, now is to build on that which has been torn down by revolutions, to harmonize conflicting laws, and to reconcile conventionalities in social life, so as to produce civility of action and goodwill through the land.[242]

The oath of office was then administered by Judge Baker.

As the ceremonies were nearing their end, the platform on which the dignitaries were seated fell two feet to the ground "without oversetting a single chair or making it necessary for any body to leave." He remarked to the aged Vicario, "who was sitting near me 'that a <u>bad beginning</u> would, I hoped, make a good ending.' … I was conducted, by the Vicario to his church, - where a Te deum was performed, - the feeble choir being assisted, by the music of two violins, a Bass drum + some other instrument that I don't recollect. This part of the ceremony was not acceptable to some part of the American population, who are protestants."[243] His sense of observation and commentary had not been dulled by the long trip or new environment.

"Another thundering salute from Brooks' guns closed the ceremony … Dined with Col Brooks and visited Mr. Ortiz, his clever little wife, Col Brooks, and Major Carleton. She played on the Spanish guitar and sang for us; we took leave at nine."

On September 14 he wrote, "Am now fairly inducted into office." He would be sixty-three in December and about to undertake the most complex job of his life in an almost foreign and often hostile environment.

Run Over with Red and White Thieves and Robbers

Lane had to know that he was taking on a major responsibility in an environment entirely different than any he had ever experienced. He would be not only governing people of very different cultures and languages but also dealing with Mexicans, many of whom still deeply resented the Americans they considered intruders. Added to that was the contrast between peaceful pueblos and the Navajo and Apache who raided Mexicans, Americans, and Pueblos. Perhaps of the greatest importance was the basic difference in cultures: the Americans were individualist, the Spanish and Pueblo Indians were essentially communal.[AN-10] Violence was far more prevalent than in St. Louis during its roughest periods, when dueling had at least a veneer of fairness.

He had, however, not been prepared for the lack of governmental organization and finances or the hostility of the army and its refusal to support the civil government. The defiance of the army commander, Colonel Edwin Vose "Bull Head" Sumner, was particularly obstructive in dealing with raiding Indians. Lane was also Superintendent of Indian Affairs.

The actions of the Catholic church complicated the environment further. New Mexico had originally been a missionary enterprise for the Spanish. Its priests were Franciscans. Earlier, there had been a few secular clergy, but these came from Mexico until early in the nineteenth century, when five New Mexicans attended the seminary in Durango.[244]

A major upheaval occurred in 1850 and 1851 when the church replaced Durango as the seat of the Catholic church with the Vicariate Apostolic of Santa Fe and assigned Bishop Jean Baptiste Lamy with his boyhood friend Vicar Joseph Projectus Machebeuf to lead it. They had grown up together in the French province of l'Auvergne.

Many decrees were imposed by the bishop and his associate that were in accordance with the doctrines of the Catholic church, which Lane had decried in his writings for years. Two American authors, Willa Cather in her 1927 novel *Death Comes to the Archbishop* and Paul Horgan in his 1975 biography *Lamy of Santa Fe*, have painted a widely accepted heroic picture of Lamy.

Not only was Lamy's view of Catholicism doctrinaire, but he gravitated toward those who spoke English and whom he considered cultured. While the claim was ridiculous, he was charged by the 1856 New Mexico legislature with favoring Protestantism. No action was taken. Nevertheless, he did not approve of the native religious statues, *bultos*, or paintings, *retablos*, which he often replaced with formal European representations. He did not approve of the use of musical instruments in church because they were also used at lively dances known as *fandangos*. He determined how masses should be conducted and imposed tithing on local, destitute parishes.

Prior to Lamy's arrival, New Mexican secular priests had

received little guidance from Durango and often met community social needs in addition to their pastoral duties. Not surprisingly, the imposition of rigid rules by foreigners resulted in widespread resistance.

Governor Calhoun had arranged the welcome for Lamy, which Horgan described as a "triumphal entry with festive thousands, including all the leading citizens riding in the finest carriages gathered from the city and the country for miles around."[245] In contrast, Lane never refers to a meeting with Lamy or mentions his name. Horgan cites Lane briefly on three pages of his 440-page biography. The "aged Vicario," possibly Juan Felipe Ortiz, who invited Lane into the church on the day of his inauguration could not have been Lamy, who was then thirty-seven. Thus, the two most important and powerful men in the territory seemingly had no contact, though their offices could not have been more than three blocks apart.

Lane remained in Santa Fe for only a month before setting out on a fourteen-day, three-hundred-mile trip to gain a better understanding of the Territory. He had not relaxed during his time in Santa Fe, but had confronted the turmoil in the government and the customs of the Indians and Spanish.

Colonel Sumner had already taken the only emblem of the American government, the flag that had flown over the Palace of the Governors since 1846, to Albuquerque. His denial of Lane's request for its return because he "was not authorized by the government to furnish him with government stores" almost led to a duel. [246] He had left only enough troops in Santa Fe to guard the military stores and reprimanded Colonel Brooks for firing the salute recognizing Lane's inauguration, saying that he "wished it understood that civil government in New Mexico was not to depend in any way upon military authority." Colonel Sumner had reported to the War Department that a civil government in New Mexico was not feasible and, during the lapse between

Calhoun's death and Lane's arrival, seemed to have assumed all responsibilities, except for those of Indian Agent Grenier, with whom he had ongoing disputes.

Lane held Sumner responsible for the chaos. He had to intervene with personal funds to prevent prisoners from starving when Sumner stopped the practice of feeding them from government supplies. Lane later wrote Sumner:

> Never was an executive officer in a more pitiable plight than I was at this time. I was an utter stranger to my official duties, without having a competent legal advisor, and with scarcely an official document on file to direct or assist my official actions; the secretary of the Territory was likewise lacking in experience in civil affairs; two of the Territorial judges and the attorney-general absent in the States, and one Indian agent and one acting only in the Territory; not a cent of money on hand, or known, or known to be subject to the draft of the governor, Superintendent of Indian affairs, or the Secretary of the Territory; not a cent in the city, county or Territorial treasuries, and no credit for the country ... nor was there a single company of militia organized in the whole Territory, nor a single musket within the reach of a volunteer ... and you, Colonel Sumner, must have been, from your official position, duly informed of these things.[247] [emphasis added]

He wrote to Mary on September 25 and William Glasgow Jr. on the 26th describing some of the daily frustrations. "Under the Spanish + Mexican rule, the Senor Gubernado, was supreme ruler in every department of the Provincial Government; and since the conquest of the country, by the U.S., the Governors have, to a great extent, exercised, arbitrary powers; This is a source of great trouble to me, - for applications of every kind, from all quarters of the Ter. – are daily presented and after a tedious examination of the nature + merits of the case, have to be referred, to the proper offices for adjudication. Thus, you see, I have probably ten-fold more duty to perform, than appropriately belongs to my office." He was working from eight in the morning to eleven at night.

To Glasgow he described a custom that he had to adopt reluctantly, "you hear or read – 'Governor,' or 'Gobernador,' every 5 minutes besides getting at least 50 embraces from Indians + sometimes from Mexiques, daily. These people embrace, with much grace + dignity; but the custom does not fit the taste of one of us." He had set up a mess with the Secretary and several others with Frank as Major Domo. His health was excellent. To Mary, he wrote, "I eat heartily at every meal, + (will you credit it) eat mutton, real sheep meat, with pleasure, at almost every meal!!!" To Glasgow, he said, "As for the palace here, of which you speak, it is nothing else but a mud-house white washed, inside + outside, one story high, with a plaza in front, + a flat roof, of earth, - with apartments oddly arranged, - rudely furnished + badly ventilated. – Fortunately the air is so very pure, that all this bad management, cannot produce sickness, - to any extent." The legislature met in crammed rooms on each side of his quarters. He also wrote both Mary and Glasgow that he had immediately dispatched Colonel Brooks to meet Señora Ortiz, a young, beautiful, accomplished + pious lady and wife of a wealthy Mexican, when he learned she wanted to meet the governor. He was surprised that "perhaps 7 out of every 10 Americans, in this city, as it is called, - go constantly armed, and I do not know anybody, that does not sleep with pistols, under, or near their pillows. I conform to this custom, but under a conviction, that there is no kind of necessity, for any such precaution."

He had not severed his St. Louis financial interests and so forwarded instructions to Glasgow. "As to old Grey, if not already sold, let him go for what he will bring – never keep an <u>old</u> Horse unless there is something to attach you to him." He would have kept old Grey had he been in St. Louis to ride him. It is not clear what the dispute was about, but advised, "under the favorable disposition that <u>I know</u> the Judge to be in, upon the subject, - will be able to get the suit of the city dismissed; but if he can not, I think it will be unsafe, to go to trial, in my absence."

"As for my Land-warrant, let the matter rest, until I have time to attend to it. But certainly there never was as stupid a set of men, in any public office, as can be found in the Bounty-Land offic. … Never mind I will have the whole of the 160 acres, if I have to expend double the value of the Little patch, in getting it. But I find I must attend to it in person." He praised Glasgow for building on the "pond property," thought he had built on the ground "near the Powder magazine, very advantageously," and that his plan "to run a Diagonal street to the Railroad" to be "the best."

If not entirely acclimated, Lane had settled into his new job in Santa Fe before he set off on October 5 to tour the territory. He was accompanied by the territorial librarian, Samuel Ellison, the carriage driver, a peon and Frank in a four-wheeled carriage, and a horse. No troops had been assigned as an escort.

He visited with army officers, judges, legislators, *alcaldes*, ranchers, businessmen, and *vicarios*. One was Henry Connelly, who had been a partner with the Glasgow brothers in their Mexican trading enterprises and would become the sixth territorial governor in 1861. Another was the ever-surviving Manuel Armijo, who had returned to New Mexico and established himself comfortably at Limitar, approximately forty miles south of Albuquerque. He led a "cavalcade of citizens" to accompany Lane to town. He also had dinner with Lamy's right-hand man, Vicario Joseph Machebeuf, but no mention was made of the bishop.

The contacts with powerful and important men offset his experiences in Santa Fe. He did not let first impressions control his actions. He had traveled south of Albuquerque, visiting the haciendas and ranches of thirty-one prominent Spaniards and Americans. When he returned to Santa Fe he wrote in his journal that "of the nine counties which comprise the whole Territory, I have visited 7 – Doña Ana and Rio Riba being the counties which remain to be visited. This visit has dispelled much error of opinion as to the condition of the inhabitants and strengthens my hopes of being useful in my official capacity."

The exact dates of the forty-day session of the Legislative Assembly are not clear, but he recorded in his journal that it met on November 6 and "I gave my third and last dinner to the members to-day. I'm glad the dinnering is at an end and that the session is near its close."

His first and only message to the Legislative Assembly, read in Spanish and English, was comprehensive in outlining not only the existing problems in the Territory but also the potential for growth. He had in a short period of time come to understand the situation in New Mexico. Brief excerpts show the range and insight of his observations and conclusions.[248] He started with the existing state of affairs.

> It cannot be denied that the first aspect of things in this Territory is discouraging.
>
> We are very distant from the States, difficult of access and surrounded by barbarians of doubtful faith.
>
> The population, which does not exceed 60,000 souls, is widely scattered through distant valleys, over an area so immense that 20 companies of United States troops are insufficient for its protection against the Indians, and your own

People are so badly armed that they cannot protect their own property from depredations.

Your highways are in a bad condition and the schoolmaster (an indispensable functionary in popular government) is rarely seen amongst you.

The country is run over with red and white thieves and robbers.

Your revenue laws are so defective that sufficient funds are not provided for the ordinary purpose of government.

Business amongst you languishes and much discontent prevails.

He then moved to the potential.

These discouragements would be appalling were it not evident to every reflective mind that all these difficulties are either temporary or removable by proper exertions.

Your country is one of the very healthiest on the globe.

Your agricultural products are various, your soil rewards your labor abundantly, and your tillable lands may be increased, perhaps more than a thousand fold, by improved *acequias* and *tangues.*

Your facilities for stock-raising are unequalled; and a well-organized militia force will protect your stock from red thieves, and a penitentiary will rid you of white thieves.

Your rich mines of gold, silver, copper, lead and iron, and your abundant supply of common salt, coal, gypsum, marble, nitre, and soda only require time, capital and industry, with good roads, to

make them available, as great sources of public
and private wealth.

He recommended changes in laws but cautioned of the dangers
of moving in haste in a short forty-day session.

> The whole body of laws of this Territory needs
> revision and amendment, besides extensions into
> objects now unprovided for.
> The criminal laws need your attention.
> I recommend the repeal of the law which
> authorizes the licensing of gambling houses and
> that the property of the poor shall be exempt from
> taxation.

He ended by saying that he had reported to the War
Department that there had not been a shot fired between Kearny
and New Mexicans, that the Territory should not be treated as
conquered but annexed, and that the laws introduced from the
States were often not appropriate. He believed all citizens should
learn English, but "nor do I advise them to change any of their
beneficial or praiseworthy customs, nor do I advise them to forget
their parent stock and the proud recollections that cluster around
Castilian history. I do not advise them to disuse their beautiful
language."

He was occupied during the next two months in getting
better organized and carrying out his official duties. He engaged
a secretary, Miguel Antonio Otero, who attended St. Louis
University, was admitted to the Missouri Bar, and was a member
of the Legislative Assembly when Lane arrived in New Mexico.

As Superintendent of Indian Affairs, he instituted a policy of
making peace with the Apache and Navajo by providing rations
and promising support. The first of these agreements was entered

into with Apaches north of Santa Fe in the early months of his term. He spent about $20,000 of his own funds in providing supplies, but when his treaties were not approved by Congress, the Apache raids increased in number and brutality.

He also found time as usual to write long letters to his family describing New Mexico and commenting on the health of friends and relatives in St. Louis, particularly after the monthly mail stage arrived—one brought seven family letters. He wrote John Darby, a member of Congress, requesting that mail be delivered twice a month.

On October 24, he wrote Anne and Sarah: "For a time, after my arrival here, I had the horrors terribly, but now I do much better." The mountain scenery took him back to his boyhood, "spent amidst, Hills, Vallies + Rocks." "The first aspect of New Mexican civilization, is absolutely forbidding – Their Houses + their fields, are of a piece + have a most forlorn, - I may even say – revolting aspect." "The Dwelling Homes, churches, + other buildings, are sad specimens of architecture. They are uniformly built of sun-dried Bricks, coarsely made + very large. A dwelling House resembles a Brick-kiln, more than anything else that I ever saw." "In building them, the plumb-line + the level, are not used." "Inside the Houses, you find much more neatnesses + comfort than might be expected, from such an unpromising exterior."

He described the furnishing in great detail. It required only a short time to become accustomed to the enormous change from St. Louis, with its brick buildings and eastern furnishings, though he thought, "it takes sometime to wear away these first impressions."

He always liked the people. "The people are extremely polite + hospitable. They embrace you at meeting, +, for the most part, offer you their Houses. Much error has gained currency about the depravity of their morals." "The people of this country, are far from being lazy. – But as they have few conveniences, or labour-saving contrivances, a great deal of toil, makes but little show." He used cornbread as an example. In St. Louis the cook started with meal; in New Mexico she started with corn that had to be shelled, steeped in lye, washed, ground between stones, and then kneaded. He wrote that the Chavez, Perreas, Oteros, Bacas, Ortiz, Pinos, Vigils, Gutierrez, and Armijos families and others owned the land in areas he had visited on his southern trip and intended to keep it. Marrying close relatives was one way of doing so.

"My acquaintance with Females is very limited in this town, or City. I know but two Mexican Ladies … A notable senorita called the wild-cat, promises me a Fandango."

He closed with "I never have enjoyed better Health + Frank is getting Fat." He was still their father and admonished them not to do likewise.

He was getting the affairs of his office in order with his secretary, taking on many routine chores and Frank managing his personal affairs. He had even gotten some fresh pork, always had "Fine Beets + Beans + excellent onions, and Fresh Eggs. Then we have some starved chickens: they are so miserably poor, that I wonder how they can muster up spirits, to crow as much as they do."

Lane could not, however, avoid involvement with Black slavery, even in New Mexico. On November 18, 1852 he assumed the debts of a Major James Henry Carleton and gained title to two slaves, twenty-one-year-old Benjamin and twenty-eight-year-old Hannah, both of whom the major had purchased in Missouri as "slaves for life." Carleton had also incurred debts totaling $619 starting in 1848 and owing in Maine, Missouri, New Mexico, and the Cherokee Territory and to the US Treasury. The transaction, which established a trust, was recorded on the November 19 and is thought to be the first sale of Black slaves in the Territory. Lane could hire them out or sell them with the proceeds placed in a trust. Any funds in excess of the debts were to be paid to Carleton's wife. Lane did not mention this transaction in his journal or letters, nor is it known what happened to Benjamin and Hannah.

Whether Lane became involved in this to settle a military problem or for humanitarian reason is not known, yet he clearly did not do it for profit.

Lane remained in Santa Fe, taking care of his myriad duties and possibly sending Benjamin and Hannah east, though they could have stayed in New Mexico and possibly been freed. He also, rather surprisingly, made no mention in his journal or letters of Christmas, although on January 8, he wrote, "Have never passed so pleasant a winter in my life as to climatic influences. Health excellent."

He set out on November 20 to take care of official business in Taos and to visit one of the two counties he had not been to, Rio Arriba, accompanied by a Dr. Massie, his private secretary Señor Otero, Frank, and the driver, Joe Collins. He was alone in the carriage, so Frank led his horse. They stopped twice for the night before Lane rode his horse on to Taos because the road was impassable to carriages. While in Taos he visited the pueblo, met with the circuit judge and others, attended a fandango, saw the end of an Indian dance, went to mass, and saw some cockfighting. He then returned to Santa Fe after dark on November 26, traveling the same route on horseback and by carriage.

Seven days later, he set out for New Placer (Golden) thirty miles south of Santa Fe with Judge Baker also in the carriage and Frank and James Webb on horseback. He stayed with Don Serafin Ramirez, a member of the assembly, while he visited the gold mines. In addition, "my business mission to the Placer was to recover stolen horses for Baca, to take to their owners – the Comanche Indians."

He was back in Santa Fe on February 7, 1853 and remained there until February 28, when he embarked on a long, more significant, and potentially hazardous journey to go as far south as El Paso, and then to an Apache stronghold near present-day Silver City, and to visit the ninth county, Doña Ana. The constant activity of his earlier years had returned.

ON HIS OWN

Now therefore, as the United States has been wrongfully deprived of the portion of the territory, even should the Mexican Republic have a rightful claim to it, which is denied; and as by the law of nations, the United States is justly entitled to exercise jurisdiction over the same and protect the inhabitants thereof in all their rights until the claim of the Mexican republic shall be fully recognized by the United States, and, as the probable time of settlement of the boundary question is indefinitely postponed, and the interest of the United States and the rights of the inhabitants of the territory are inadequately protected, I, William Carr Lane, governor of the Territory of New Mexico (upon my own official responsibility and without orders from the cabinet at Washington) do hereby, in behalf of the United States, retake possession of the said disputed territory to be held provisionally by the United States until the question of boundary shall be determined by the United States and the Mexican Republic.[249]

The proclamation was preceded by six paragraphs that established both its legal basis and practical need. It was followed by the designation of the boundaries and issuance of orders to civil and military authorities to enforce the laws of the United States and the Territory in the disputed area. Because the area was annexed to Doña Ana County, the proclamation was signed in the town of Doña Ana on March 13, 1853.

The question of Mexican or American sovereignty over the area of almost thirty thousand square miles was rooted in significant errors in Disturnell's *Map of Mexico*, which had been relied on in the Treaty of Guadalupe Hidalgo to establish the Mexico–New Mexico boundary. It showed El Paso roughly thirty miles too far north and the Rio Grande River 120 miles too far east. The map itself was a reprint of an 1828 plagiarism of a January 1826 reproduction of a map published in Philadelphia in 1822.[250] The area was important because of the rich Mesilla Valley along the Rio Grande and the copper mines southeast of current-day Silver City, New Mexico. In addition, Southern interests wanted it as a southern route for a railroad to California. Commissioners from both countries had met in San Diego to survey and establish the California border. They had completed the job successfully in a year and moved on to El Paso to establish the New Mexico line. It was then that the errors in cartography were discovered.

The Mexicans wanted a line that would have given them possession of the valley and mines. The Americans believed the area was part of the United States. The commissioners reached an accord, the Bartlett-Garcia Conde Compromise, which did not satisfy anybody, certainly not the Americans. President Pierce and Congress refused to accept the agreement or to fund a further survey unless it confirmed the American position.

Lane reported in January 1854, in a letter presumably to Congress, "When I went to New Mexico in the summer of '52, I was urged by the delegate from that Territory to claim jurisdiction over the Mesilla district and take possession of it by force. For reasons that will be apparent to you, I refused to adopt this course, but as soon as I was informed that the government of the United States had repudiated Bartlett's line (which was in February) and after consulting the attorney-general of the Territory, I issued a proclamation and claimed jurisdiction of the country until the boundary line should be established by the two governments."[251]

His action roused the Mexican military, got national attention, forced President Pierce to take action, and, some believe, almost started a second Mexican War. Secretary of State Marcy approved of the claim but did not want the military used to enforce it. The US ambassador to Mexico did not approve. The New Orleans *Picayune Report* expressed what seemed to be eastern public opinion. "It certainly is not for the Governor of a territory of the United States to anticipate the decision of the federal government of a question of so delicate a nature as the drawing of a boundary between that territory and a foreign state.[252]

Feelings ran high in the Mesilla Valley. Many Americans had moved in, forcing Mexicans off what they considered to be their land. Lane believed American rights were not protected. President Antonio López de Santa Anna ordered the governor of Chihuahua to dispatch troops into the valley to resist an American occupation. After Colonel Sumner rejected Lane's request for US troops, Lane raised a body of Texas and New Mexico volunteers to enforce the occupation. At the same time that he had issued the proclamation at Doña Ana, he had sent it in a dispatch to President Pierce.

The president had previously shown little interest in the boundary dispute, but the mobilization of Mexican troops and the gathering of a militia that would not be under the army's control got his attention. In the fall, he ordered James Gadsden to Mexico City as envoy extraordinary and minister for the United States to settle the growing problem. Santa Anna, who was always short of funds, agreed on December 30 to sell the almost thirty thousand square miles for ten million dollars, or about thirty-five cents an acre. The final treaty was not ratified until June of the next year. The US military took possession in 1856 but could not prevent Indian raids that forced the abandonment of a stage route from Texas to California in 1860. The population near the copper mines, however, continued to grow.

Lane had two goals when he left Santa Fe on February 28, 1853, for the southern part of the Territory – a trip that would cover 1,123 miles by his calculation. He did not return to Santa Fe until April 28. The troubles in the Mesilla Valley, which made up a sliver of the Gadsden Purchase, had started before he reached New Mexico. He had wanted to protect American citizens but waited until there was a legal basis for taking action. His other objective was to eliminate, or at least reduce, the raids being carried out by bands of Apache in the Territory and in Mexico.

The Apache roamed through the mountains and across the deserts with no desire to settle down. They lived in bands, each local group with its own leader. The bands had no tribal government or annual ceremonial gathering and often fought each other. Revenge was paramount. If a Mexican or American killed an Apache, he or a substitute was sought out and turned over to female relatives of the slain Apache for disposition.[253]

The Spanish and then the Mexicans had fought with the Apache for centuries before the Americans arrived. Raids into northern Mexico were so devastating that the states of Sonora and Chihuahua were almost abandoned more than once. An Apache leader later said they wanted some Mexicans to remain and raise livestock that could be stolen.

The Spanish worked the mines as early as 1804 but could not make peace. The Mexicans, however, later had some success. The Americans arrived in 1846. General Kearny stopped at the mines to meet with several leaders, including Mangas Coloradas, who could not understand why, with the Mexicans as a common enemy, the Americans were trying to prevent the raids, particularly as Americans purchased stolen livestock. One old Apache leader said, "You have taken Santa Fe, let us go on and take Chihuahua and Sonora; we will go with you. You fight for the soil, we fight for plunder; so we will agree perfectly." The raids could not be stopped, even though the Treaty of Guadalupe Hidalgo required the Americans to do so.

The composition of Lane's party changed as the territory

through which he traveled after he left Santa Fe changed dramatically. The journal he maintained throughout the trip again included not only distances, overnight stops, and people but also observations about the environment.[254] When they left Santa Fe on February 28, "Jo Collins drove my 4 mule, + carriage, + Mr. Sam I. Ellison Translator of the Ter. rode with me in the carriage. My colored servants Frank + Dr. Massie's Jack, and Jose Maria, a well bred Indian from the Pueblo of Tesuque, rode on Horse or Mule back."

They would travel twelve days, covering roughly 170 miles before stopping at Doña Ana and then continuing to El Paso before returning to Doña Ana to undertake the second and more hazardous part of the trip.

As Lane traveled south, he met with political and business leaders of the Territory as well as Baptist missionaries, Catholic priests, and military officers. He spent one night with the governor of the Sandia Pueblo and left two dollars, though no payment was expected, in contrast to the Americans and Mexicans, who expected compensation. He kept account of all his expenses. The Captain Pope with whom he met would become the well-known Union general. On March 4 he arranged payment of $1,509.82 to the Navajo and $1,659.82 to the Apache and ordered Indian Agent Baird to attend a Comanche council to settle a grievance.

Daily entries covered a wide range. "A Sandia Indian, who reports the sick mule left on the road dead + Jose's Mule sick." "The Carriage Mules yesterday were so exhausted, after getting them out of the mudhole (with the assistance of some Mexns.) that they could scarcely draw the carriage – walked." "Have no confidence in Jo Collins. He is both Drunkard + Gambler, + g-d knows what else." "Made Ft. Fillmore and was obliged, unwillingly, to quarter with Col. Miles, a walking sponge, martinet + a ___."

However, he was encouraged by much of what he experienced. "Saw abundance of mistleto, on the dwarf cotton trees, near Dr.

Connelly's. Drank excellent Wine, at Dr. Connelly's at Oteros."
"The people are sowing, by estimation, 50 per cent more wheat
than last year, + are preparing for planting an increased amount
of corn land. The American plow is coming into General usage
in the Rio Abajo, + plowing how much deeper, + I presume less
irrigation will therefore be required." "The sun was so hot, on
the 6th + 7th that my face was dreadfully burned." "We had Hail,
of about the size of small cherries, so as to cover the ground
completely."

He continued to learn about the Territory and be surprised.
He was particularly intrigued by the report of Dr. Connelly that
he had dug a hole in the dry bed of the Arkansas which filled with
water, with fish three inches long swimming in it. Though Lane
was skeptical, he wondered if eggs could spawn in sand. He was
surprised by the wheat yield. The same Dr. Connelly told him that
Don Perea, his father-in-law, in Bernalillo, reaped 40 fahegus (63.2
bushels) of wheat for one sown upon manured land. "This yield
was supported by" a gentn. whom I saw at Genl. Armijo's, told
me, that 100 had been produced from 1. This seems incredible."

The party had spent four nights at Fort Conrad on the trip
south to rest the animals and await the arrival of a military guard
before crossing the *Jornado del Muerto* – the Journey of the Dead.
The *Jornado* had earned its name both because there was virtually
no water and because travelers were frequently attacked by Apache
and Comanche.

On March 10 they sent the wagons ahead and a rider back
to Peralta and Socorro to thank Dr. Connelly and to instruct
Prefect Baca how to treat Comanche prisoners. "March 11, Friday,
left the Hospitable Ft. Conrad, under an escort of 30 Dragoons,
commanded by Lt. Albey, expecting to overhaul our 2 freight +
1 Baggage Waggons, before we reach Fra Christoval where there
is water, + to encamp some 10 or 12 miles in the *Jornado*." They
watered the livestock and filled the casks.

"Sat. 12 March. Rose at 3 A.M. + after a cup of coffee set out ... made the Lagunas, 1 ½ miles apart, by ½ past 8 A.M. 15 miles or thereabouts. Mr. Allison says we are 30 miles from the 'point of rock,' a place of great danger, + 57 miles from the end of the *Jornado*." Lane described the *Jornado*, "thus far, is a valley from 30 to 50 miles wide, (when there is an occasional expansion), between parallel ranges of mountains running N. + S. some 1900 or 2000 feet above the level of the valley. Not a tree is in the Vale or on the Mountains + the Mountains appeared to my vision to be bare even of bushes ... The valley was covd. with grasses of various kinds, some of which was not dead ... the soap plant + different species of Cactus abound."

After a long rest at Lagunas, they set out at three in the afternoon and traveled forty miles, stopping at eleven. The livestock had no water or feed, and Lane slept in the carriage, where he "suffered from the cold." They again made an early start and reached the Rio Grande, where they had breakfast before traveling another eight miles to Doña Ana. On Sunday, March 13, he issued the proclamation. While there, he was "Entertained kindly by Don Pablo Melendez + his 3 daughters, Trinidad, Josephita + Jesusita. Invited to a Ball. It is Lent, but as the Priest goes, we may venture to go also." The next day, "went to the Ball last night but the Padre was not there. The music consisted of a violin, Harp + Guitar, + (a part of the time) by 2 extemporaneous Singers, (one of them singing second), who sang sentimental verses, that would have done credit to people of more external refinement ... The Ball was got up, in honor of my visit, + did not continue long, after I retired, which was before 11."

The next day they traveled on to Fort Fillmore a short distance south of Las Cruces. After one night there with the detested Colonel Miles, he went on to spend four nights enjoying the hospitality of Hugh Stephenson at his 900-acre estate on the current site of El Paso, Texas. On Saturday, March 19, he returned to Fort Fillmore and the next day continued back to Doña Ana. It is not clear who was assembling the volunteers to protect the Mesilla Valley, but Lane now concentrated entirely on the second part of his journey.

Both the purpose and the environment would change dramatically. He would travel on roads and trails that were used much less than the road from Santa Fe south and camp in the open for eighteen of the next twenty-five nights. There would always be the threat of an attack by an Apache band, particularly those under the leadership of Mangas Coloradas, who could be brutally cruel. The gold discovered by the Boundary Commission in 1851 near the copper mines had attracted prospectors. Though Mangas Coloradas had assisted a group of prospectors, they repaid him by tying him to a post and administering a whipping. As a result, many a miner died in the future with his head over a fire or buried in an anthill. On the other hand, a doctor who treated Apache was given all the gold he could carry.

Again Lane, though on a hazardous mission, made detailed entries in his journal describing the country, particularly the mountains and forests, as they moved westward. He had never seen anything like it.

When Lane had set out from Doña Ana on Tuesday, March 29, he was accompanied by "Mr Otero in the carriage with me, Anselmo + Frank on Mules, + my Saddle-Horse led by Frank." He had sent a Mr. Ward ahead the day before with the freight wagons and some number of cattle. It would require five days to travel the approximately eighty miles to Fort Webster where he would meet with the Apache.

He had "Left of the Indian goods (100 sheets + 50 Mex. Blankets + a lot of Tobacco), for the Mescalero + other White Mountain Apache Indns. To be distributed, by Don Pablo Melendres according to his discretion." When they encamped on the second night, he was alarmed by gunshots, but they came from a party cutting timber. He was enthralled by the country, especially the "Canon, as it is called, that calls to mind Stephens description of Petra, in Ancient Edom. The sides of the Canon are perpendicular cliffs of Black Volcanic conglomerate, such as I have never seen before, with a metallic luster, where it is exposed to the weather." "There is a fall of 6 or 8 feet, in the Canon, with two escapes for water, separated by a mass of Rock. One of these cascades empties into what is not inaptly termed a *tenaha*, a Mexican water vessel." "A few yards, below the *tenaha* there are 2 depressions in the Solid Rock, resembling mortars (for pounding hard substances), of the size of a large Apothecaries Mortar. No man can look at these excavations, + not feel they have not been made by man, for Mortars. But when + by whom?" On the fourth day they "exchanged our 4 ½ yoke of broken down oxen for 5 yoke, in better condition, + exchanged Train conductors, for the better, I hope."

The first Fort Webster was located at the copper mines near Santa Rita and was established in January 1852 as the first army outpost in the area roamed by Mangas Coloradas's bands. In September, the troops were moved approximately fifteen miles northwest to a location on the Mimbres River in the mountains of the same name. It was at the second location of Fort Webster that Lane met with the Apache. He had arrived on Saturday. After several days of meetings with a large number of Apache, he wrote the treaty on Wednesday and signed it on Thursday. The agreement again reflected his belief that it was far better for both sides to live in peace than to be constantly fighting. He promised to provide food and supplies as immediate relief and also promised support for three years in return for the cessation of raiding. He advanced funds from the territorial treasury to initiate the process, particularly to plant crops.

Lane found time to write Mary while he was negotiating the treaty. He described the first thirty-six days of the trip and the effect on his health. "You are, I dare say, anxious about my health. I wish you could see me; you would begin to think, that my application for an extension on my lease on life, had been granted. I have neither ache, nor pain; + have never felt better in my life. On my journey, I sometimes ride, in the carriage, + sometimes on Horseback, + sometimes I walk for recreation. A tramp of a league, does not fatigue me, + sometimes I walk 2 leagues, with little inconvenience."[255] (While there is not a standard definition of a league, it was probably close to three miles.) This report of robust health came from a sixty-three-year-old man who a year earlier had thought his life was over.

He also described the distances between towns with no houses—30 to 120 miles. "And to pass over those solitudes, with from 10 to 25 miles without water, you must go, in strong companies, well armed, - to meet real, or supposed danger, - from Indians or Robbers."

After signing the treaty, he started west for the Gila River, a distance of approximately sixty miles, to determine if the river valley were suitable for farming and, thus, a location in which the Apache could settle. He would return to Fort Webster eight days later and then go on to Santa Fe. The party traveling to and from the Gila included an Apache chief, Ponce, who would continue to deal with the Americans for over twenty-five years. He was afraid of "Lawless Indians, but Lane assured him his party could protect itself. "Major Steen has 16 men, + he makes the 17th. My party consists Mr. Otero, Sec. Mr. Ward, Intr. The 2 drivers, the 2 coloured men, 3 Mexs. + 3 Indns. (1 of which is detached to find other Indns.) in all, myself included, 13, making a total of 30 men, all well armed, except the 3 Apaches who have Bows + arrows. I fancy we could successfully resist 300 Apaches, armed as they generally are, with Bows only."

They reached the Gila River on the fifth day, first heading south by the copper mines and then west and northwest over the

Continental Divide in the Burro Mountains. [256] As usual, Lane recorded his observations and their progress. "Set out at 7 oclk, course nearby south, upon an Old Trail, over which Waggons had once tis said passed." "Our trail thus far, is the old Mexn. trail from Sonora to the Copper Mines." They crossed the rejected line of the Boundary Commission.

"At the 1st water, Ponce discovered a track, + fearing it was a vidette, of the Sonorians, with our consent, sent his peon, to a watering place, to spy. In the evening he returned, with a mule which he had found, but he brot. no tidings, of Sonorians or Indians, to Ponce's great relief."

"After attempting to pass down the Canon, on which we lay, we found it to be impassable, some 3 or 4 miles down, + the waggons + carriages were forced to return, to camp + take another canon." "Took our line of march about 7 A.M. passed westward down an arroyo, then N. some 45° W. across a mesa. Thence down an arroyo, a little S. of W. until we reached the object of our march, the Rio Gila, at noon."

His observations along the way were wide-ranging. He didn't say who was drinking too much but recorded that "We have done well in all our traveling arrangements, but if there had not been a Brandy bottle, nearer than 500 miles, we would have done much better."

"Night uncomfortably cold (we slept in the open air)." "Many Wolves prowled + howled around our camp last night, + many herds of antelopes have been in sight, but our 2 Indian Hunters have not brot. in any fresh meat." "Saw yesterday, 3 varieties of the mescal (*maguey*), out of which the Indns., prepare an excellent article, for food, in great quantities." "The flax is in bloom, + grows upon the Hills, as well as on the low parts of the vallies." "The cañon in which we are encamped, is not on an average 50 yds. wide, with perpendicular, or nearly perdendr., walls (of a singular conglomerate), which appears to me to be about a 1000 foot high, but wh. my companions say are more than 3 times that height." "This day, is Gov. Lane's (as the party are pleased to call it, because I am the first Gov., that is supposed to have entered it), has been exceedingly uncomfortable from the excessively high wind. Collected some specimens of curious stones, + picked up a Grape Vine for Mr. G. St. Louis. It is late, but perhaps it may live. The night was very cold, + everybody suffered somewhat. Ice was twice as thick as a dollar in the Water Bucket." A partridge had been killed with a stone. "It was exquisite eating. A prarie dog + a rattlesnack were also shot, + an antelope shot at. A Huge Wild He goat of the common species brot. up the rear of the herd of Antelopes. He was, no doubt, a Stray from the Indians, or Mexns. When I saw him I thot. of Moses 'Scapegoates in the Wilderness.'"

The treaty Lane had signed with the Apache was based on the assumption that they would be able to raise crops in the Gila Valley. He wanted to assure himself of the validity of that assumption. He had ridden ten miles north to observe the land, and others in the party had traveled further. "The soil of River bottoms, where they are subject to be overflowed, are Sandy + unfit for Cultivation; above this level they are fertile + easy of irrigation, as the flow of the fall in the river, here, must be twice as great, as it is, in the Rio Grande." They went further south to camp on the river and had "a view of the Valley of the Gila, (in all), for about 25 or 30 ms." They then returned to the campsite they had occupied two nights earlier. "My visit to the Gila, was for the purpose of ascertaining its fitness for a future location for the Apaches. It will do, well for that purpose."

The party, on its return to Fort Webster, retraced the route it had taken to reach the Gila. They made good time, covering almost fifty miles in one day. "We went right across the immense plain, regardless of ravines +hills, down + up, with our 8 Mule Waggons + 4 Mule Waggons + ambulance, to the amazement of our Inds." Lane and three companions attempted to take a shortcut over the mountains on horseback but had to turn back. The next day they succeeded on another shortcut, "but it only made the ride more tiresome." "The furthest way round would have been the nearest way home."

He completed his business with the Apache leaders at the fort and rode down the Mimbres River to join the rest of the party for the first night of the eleven-day return trip to Santa Fe. "Heard Turkeys Gobbling, saw Bear tracks + killed an immense Rattlesnake with 13 rattles. Night pleasant."

They continued to retrace the route they had followed going west from the Rio Grande and reached the river on the third night. He had been intrigued earlier by the even water level in the Tenaha, because there was no apparent source of supply. "It has probably not recd. any supply of water, from above ground, since last Sept; and in all probability, not less than 500 men, + the same number of animals, have encamped + watered here, since that time. Allowing each man to have used 1 quart + each Horse Mule + Ox, to have drank 4 galls. upwards of 2000 galls. must have been drawn out, in the meantime; possibly even double that quantity, as the water is wasted in being used for cattle, by being pounded into an excavation in the sand. The place is a puzzle to me."

They started north on the twentieth heading toward Fort Conrad at the northern end of the Jornado del Muerto without a military escort. None of them were familiar with the road. Lane had miscalculated, thinking they would reach the fort that night, but they did not do so until the twenty-second. He had sent wagons ahead, One turned over and was badly damaged. On the twenty-first, "Traveled until 10 o'clk before we could find a suitable place to encamp. This has been the most fatiguing day of our whole journey, say 42 miles to-day." It may have been impossible to gather the level of support they had on the trip south, or Lane may have decided to plunge ahead.

Lane continued to comment on multiple things on the

three-day trip to Albuquerque. "Saw 3 Flocks of Sheep + Goats this morning, the first was in charge of 2 men + 1 dog, + numbered 600 + upwards. The 2nd division was in charge of 2 men + 1 dog, + numbered 600 + upward. The 2nd division were in charge of a merry little Boy, who sang as he followed his herd of Ewes + goats, with their Lambs + kids; + such Bleating of young ones + their dams, I have never heard before, the flock numbering 700 + upwards. The 3rd herd was very limited in numbers + was composed of large sheep, with the heaviest fleeces I have ever seen in the Terr. They were attended by 1 man, who was engaged in spinning coarse yarns, by means of a stick." "Capt. Ewell says, stone coal (Bituminous) abounds West of Las Lunas, of a good quality. He believes the strata to be 3 or 4 feet thick." "In trimming grapes, in N. Mex. the vine stalks are never more than from 1 to 2 feet high." "Made Albuquerque, + stopped at Dr. Abodies. Crossed the River, in a Govt. Ferry Boat, manned by unskillful Mxns. with the worst oars I ever saw."

After a late start on the twenty-sixth, they stopped at Algodones, started early the next day, and reached Santa Fe in the evening.

"Was met by a calvacade of citizens."

A Contested Election

The results of the presidential election in the fall of 1852 caused Lane to resign as governor. He declared his candidacy for the position of territorial representative to the US Congress on August 9, 1853, the day after his replacement, David Meriwether, arrived in Santa Fe. Lane had not waited to be fired because of his party affiliation but had the lead. He continued to carry out his duties until Meriwether was inaugurated.

The national party conventions prior to the presidential

election in the fall of 1852 were riven with fights over slavery and sectionalism, both of which led to many candidates in both parties. The Democrats settled on Franklin Pierce of New Hampshire on the forty-ninth ballot. The Whigs required fifty-three to nominate General Winfield Scott. The Free Soil Party met the next month, quickly nominated John P. Hale, and changed their name to the Free Democratic Party. General Scott won only four states and the Free Democrats none. The country was bitterly divided by slavery—Pierce received only 50.9 percent of the popular vote.[257]

Lane concluded early in December that his term as territorial governor would not continue under a Democratic president and wrote his friend Representative John Darby on December 31, "I have written to [Senator] Geyer, by this mail, + have told him, that if President Pierce wishes to make an appointment, for this Island, all he has to do, is signify his pleasure, to Geyer, + that my resignation, will be in his hands, as soon as the mail can go from Washington, to St. Louis, + back again." He concluded, "I have 1000 + 1 things to say, but time is not allowed me to write, or for you to legislate, upon my suggestions. We need every thing here – I have had a rough time of it, but I am getting things 'shipshape,' + into harmonious action."[258]

He knew he was in a tenuous position when he started his trip south in late February, but that did not deter him in any way from taking aggressive action to resolve the boundary dispute with Mexico and deal with Apache raids. After returning from his southern trip on April 27, he remained in Santa Fe carrying out the duties of his office until August 9, when he started his election campaign. He had written Darby that, initially, he had intended to serve the full four-year term but would not do so even if asked because of his family's unhappiness with his absence.

He had achieved both the objectives of his southern trip by forcing President Pierce to acquire the disputed territory and making peace with the Apache. The latter, however, would be only a short-term success because Congress refused to ratify the treaty. His acknowledgement of the various cultures of the various tribes and pueblos was consistent with the views he had expressed to the Missouri legislature thirty years earlier.

This differentiation was apparent in May when he became the center of a dispute involving residents of the pueblos of Nambe and Pojoaque. He had written on May 6 that "The Pueblo Indians of N. Mex. are civilized communities; each being governed by its own Laws, administered by its own officers; + all being subject to the authority of the Govr. of the Ter. of N. Mex. as supt Indn Affairs. There has been no interference with their Laws, which are merely their Ancient Customs, except when appeals were taken, from the decisions of the Pueblo Tribunals to the Tata, Gov. of the Ter."

The immediate situation involved both Catholic and Pueblo traditions. After two years of courtship, a twenty-four-year-old young man from Pojoaque was married to a fifteen-year-old girl from Nambe in a Catholic ceremony during which the young man promised to live with his widowed mother-in-law. His father, however, soon demanded that he and his wife return to his home. In accordance with Pueblo law, he was physically restrained and returned home while his wife remained with her mother. After several attempts at a resolution failed, the families, Pueblo elders, and others appeared in Lane's office. He often commented in his journal about the appearance of women and this time noted that the mother-in-law "was a rather pretty woman, of some 35 years of age, tall, slender + graceful with a remarkably pensive countenance. She was moreover eloquent, + spoke with her own language, + the Spanish, with remarkable fluency."

He referred to himself in the third person in his description of the proceedings.[259] "Much argumentation ensued, + the Tata or Father, of all the Pueblos was not a little perplexed, in making a judgment in the case. Whereupon the Judge took up the Bible and gave a decision ... Genesis Chapter 2, versus 24. 'Therefore shall a man leave his Father and his Mother, + shall cleave to his wife and they shall be one flesh.' Deuteronomy chap 24 verse 5 'When a man hath taken a new wife, he shall not go out to war, neither shall he be charged with any business, but he shall be free at Home, for One Year, and shall cheer up his wife, which he has taken.'" Lane decided that the couple should live with the mother-in-law for one year and that a final decision be postponed until that date.

There was much commotion, "Whereupon the Father stamped his foot, + commanded that all should submit to his decision, in silence, which was done without another word. The Mother, the young wife, the Husband, + the Men of Nambe, followed the Govr. from the Indian office to his quarters, to embrace + thank him for making so righteous a decision; and then went on their way to Nambe, rejoicing." Six weeks later, "All parties interested in the judgment above mentioned perfectly contented."

Several weeks later he was not in such a judicious mood when he exploded in fury during a meeting with Colonel Sumner and a group of Navajo. The Indians refused to turn over the murderer of a Mexican, and Lane thought his policy of peaceful dealings was at risk. Sumner refused to carry out the reprisals Lane demanded.

Lane's Apache treaty was probably doomed the day it was signed, though there were reports that Apache leaders, including Mangas Coloradas, were favorably impressed when they visited the Gila Valley. The failure of Congress to ratify the treaty would have been enough to assure failure, but there were ever-changing local policies. The new Governor Meriwether, at least initially, favored use of force and was not disappointed when Congress rejected both the treaty Lane had negotiated with the Mimbres and the one he had signed with Jicarillas in northwestern New Mexico. The army had fed the latter while awaiting ratification but stopped as soon as the treaty was rejected. Open warfare soon started when a detachment of dragoons killed a number of

Apache, including women and children. The Apache retaliated with their bows and arrows, killing twenty-four.[260] In the south, the Mimbres concentrated on the Anglos while continuing the raids into Sonora, killing 170 in July.

The changing situation was compounded by sometimes dishonest Indian agents, miners, and land-seekers who often confiscated supplies intended for the Indians while plying them with alcohol. Clashes with the Apache in the south continued well into the 1880s.

Lane remained in Santa Fe for the next three months, "contending every day with 'the world, the flesh + the Devil,' + am by no means happy. I am not quite satisfied with myself. I am perpetually under the influence of impulses, which cause me to say + do rash things, and I begin to learn that selfishness is so intense + overwhelming in this region, that I receive no disinterested counsel from Friends, + as for my Enemies they would exterminate me if they had the power. The task of a Reformer is a hard one."

He attempted to stop the prefect of Santa Ana County from building a road across an *acequia* at the Jemez Pueblo and made social calls. One was "to Señora Maria Guertrudes, said to be from 105 to 110 years old. Her hearing is bad, her sight better, her appetite good + health good." He concluded, after looking at her daughter, and calculating the possible date of birth, that the mother was probably 90 – certainly no more than ninety-five.

He wrote to Anne on June 8 to describe at great length the ceremony of taking down the cross on the last Sunday in June as part of the Fête of Corpus Christi. Crosses that had been raised in private homes were taken down until only one remained in a lavishly decorated chamber with a similarly elaborate altar. "There was no Padre present, + the religious services were devoutly performed by the Females. The ceremony commenced by all kneeling, + an audible prayer – recitations, responses + chants followed, + then the cross was lowered one step. The same ceremonies were thrice repeated, with corresponding lowering, each time; + then the cross was devoutly held, by the person who had erected it, – she being richly dressed, with her head covered, with a Black Lace veil, - kneeling, + it was then kissed, by each Female present, on her knees. It was then presented to a Lady, who was also kneeling, who was richly dressed, + had a Black Lace veil, over her head; and she bore it away. And it will be this Lady's task, to erect an Altar next year, at her own house."

He was the only man present. The women then adjourned to the next room for "indifferent pastries and liquors" and then went on "to the Dancing Room, where Quadrilles + Waltz were danced, to the Music of the Harp, until a late hour. I did not enjoy myself much + left early." Some men were already in the "Dancing room," others had gone to the placita where "pistols were fired during the whole ceremony. Thus ended the ceremony of the taking down of the crosses (<u>Descuelgo de la Santa Cruz</u>), which I never Witnessed before, + which I have no desire to Witness again."[261]

He settled his personal finances, forwarded accounts to Washington, and assured Mary he would soon be home. "Again, my health has been, + continues to be, robust (after my nephritis attack), on the plains, - cold, cough or other ailment; + have only lacked the society of my Family, to make life quite pleasant … Traveling relieves me + hence it is that traveling is so agreeable to me."[262]

Lane during his ten months as governor had come to understand the Territory and received much praise, as he had earlier in Missouri. "He was a man of superior ability"[263] "Though his administration was short, Lane had accomplished much in New Mexico. He had been instrumental in saving the Mesilla Valley for New Mexico and the United States. By his affection for the people and by his travel among them, he added stature to the governorship. His kindness, mature understanding and appreciation for things New Mexican won friendship and respect for the governor's office."[264] "During his term in office, a statement appeared in the *Baltimore American*; 'There is a bold and brave public servant in the administration of national interests at present in New Mexico.'"[265] He also attended to more mundane matters raising revenues for the state and counties, auditing accounts of public officials and removing them from office, limiting gambling, and prohibiting providing liquor to Indians in any manner.

Lane must have considered running for territorial representative during the eight months that elapsed between the submission of his resignation and the arrival of his successor, but perhaps not, for he was by his own admission prone to impulsive actions. Despite his frequent comments about the condition of New Mexico, he had clearly become attached to it. His trips and experiences, as varied as the pueblo judgment and taking down of the crosses, had to have been fascinating. He reveled in travel despite hardships: the trip to the Mimbres seemed to be almost an outing. And then another challenge was there, and he accepted it, despite his frequent statements about returning home and staying there.

He left Santa Fe on August 16 on a campaign trip that would take him south of Albuquerque to Limitar, back to Santa Fe, on to Las Vegas, and finally northwest to Mora and through the mountains to Taos, where he arrived two days prior to the election. He had spoken with every element of the population, except the Pueblo Indians—he apparently knew that would not be necessary.

He visited with many important merchants, ranchers, political officeholders, and military officers with whom he had met on his trip the previous September and continued to document events and comment on personalities.

Dinner at Custillos
1st course   Boiled mutton + green chile Tortillas
2nd "   Boiled Fowl + Rice
3rd "   Frijoles
4th "   Curds + Mexican Sugar

On August 23, "Roads inundated, reached Juan Perea's between 8 + 9 p.m.; but could not be heard by any of his family inside his gate. Went on to the residence of Jose Leander Perea, whose reply to my Mex Servant, who applied for Lodging for us was: 'It is not a proper time of night to take in Traveler!' He shall hear from me." There were no other incidences of a lack of hospitality and the electioneering was successful.

"Rain all day. Made Santa Fe about 9 p.m. The night was so dark that Mr Ellison was obliged to walk in the Rain, + we had to light paper occasionally to see the road." He stayed only two days and then headed east with three companions, including Frank, for Pecos and San Miguel, where they stayed with Señor Diego Romero. They stopped with Mr. Moore in Tecolote and met with Dr. Connelly, who had seen Lane's family in St. Louis. On August 30, "made Las Vegas before 11 a.m. roads very muddy. Met that mass of Folly, egotism + dishonesty, Facundo Pino"—he was suspected of involvement in the 1846 Taos rebellion.

On August 31, "Mr. N. N. Smith returned in the carriage to Santa Fe, + I set out accompanied by Mr Geo. W. Meritt + Frank for Taos, on Horse and Mule back." They stopped at one o'clock because of rain but started for Mora in the sunshine after breakfast the next morning. There he "met Capt Valdez + many enthusiastic political friends amongst others Gen Simpson." They rode up the Mora Valley, which he thought to be beautiful, to the foot of the mountains which they crossed, traveled down a valley, climbed over the mountains, and then rode down another valley to Taos. They had ridden over forty miles in two days. "Being unused to riding on Horse back, this days ride over, the excessive bad roads, + Steep Mountains + Hills, have been painfully fatiguing to me, + worrying to Kitty Houghton My Mule." His discomfort did not prevent him from observing that "The natural features of the country + the productions of the soil were exceedingly interesting." He noted in some detail the many kinds of trees.

While in Taos he stayed with Judge Beaubien, who in 1846 had been appointed judge by General Kearny. but more importantly Beaubien owned the Maxwell land grant, which included well over a million acres in northern New Mexico and southern Colorado.

Lane's opponent was Padre Jose Manuel Gallegos, who had been the very popular pastor of the church in Albuquerque until Bishop Lamy withdrew all his privileges and faculties and sent Father Machebeauf to replace him. This event was one of a number that occurred during the bitter struggle between Lamy and the native priests. The bitterness is apparent in Machebeauf's statement after he had replaced Gallegos, "There was no doubt about his talents, and he used them to good effect in his new field, for through them he worked every kind of scheme until he succeeded in getting himself elected to the Congress of the United States as Delegate from the Territory of New Mexico."[266]

The view from the side of the native priests was stated with similar vehemence by the respected scholar Fray Angélico Chavez in his 1985 biography of Padre Gallegos entitled *Tres Macho—He Said*. The title itself reveals admiration for the padre. The reference to Lane as James Carr Lane is surprising but perhaps indicates a one-sided view. Chavez described the Gallegos of 1840, "It also looks as though, already at this time, his spirited nature had begun expressing itself in various ways, and verging on the political. At the same time signs of cockiness and indiscretion are beginning to show."[267] Gallegos had been a member of the assembly in Santa Fe prior to the American conquest and continued in the legislature afterwards. Because he spoke only Spanish and knew nothing of the Democratic Party and differences with the Whigs, he sought out Meriwether, the new Democratic territorial governor, to learn about political parties. Meriwether also introduced him to the US Constitution.

On August 5, 1853, Gallegos organized a convention of the Democratic Party and was nominated. Chavez described the situation. "This caused an immediate uproar in the Capital among those politicians calling themselves 'the American party,' and mostly English speaking." They nominated Lane. "And now there began a campaign which became the model for every successive political fight in New Mexico to this day. It was characterized as what in our times has been called a "Hispano-Anglo" contest, although influential and well-heeled natives were backing Lane, not to mention native Democrats like Donaciano Vigil who were against Gallegos. Even Padre Martinez of Taos was later accused of being against him."[268] It was to be a complex—and disputed—election.

Lane had been optimistic about the success of his campaign, writing Mary from Santa Fe after his southern trip. "The prospects are decidedly in favor of my being elected; but nothing is certain, and especially in N. Mex."[269] He wrote again four days later from Las Vegas and was less hopeful. "In point of fact, the opposition, to every thing American, is so uncompromising, that if this county should turn against me, you must not be surprised. But 'all is not lost that is in danger.' They say, they have no personal objection to me, but that they are determined to elect one of their own race; but that I am the most acceptable of all the Americans; but that they must try a Mexican. God bless them. If you knew how little the very best informed know, you would be amazed at their conceitedness."[270]

He hoped a victory would provide an endorsement of his administration and avoid the expense of contesting the results. As usual, there is no record of Mary's reaction.

Lane remained in Taos until September 8 to learn the results in Taos County. He won by 104 votes of 1,078 cast. He went to a, "crowded + too warm, retired early, women not petty + men homely." At sixty-three, he must have been one of the older participants. He wrote William Glasgow Jr., "will set out, for Sta. Fe, tomorrow morning. The Road to Sta Fe., is very bad, + we must cross a very high Mountain; this will make the ride a fatiguing one. Frank will ride a Horse, + I will ride a Mule; + the Guide will be mounted I know not how." Parts of the area through which they traveled were still subject to Navajo and Apache raids.

They stayed at Santa Cruz de la Cañada on the ninth to get the results from Rio Arriba County: a margin of 442 for Gallegos out of 840. "But the estimate is by no means reliable, particularly as it regards El Embudo precinct." He received a report of victory. "Mr. Gorman came up from Santa Fe in the middle of last night, with the news that I am elected. His Mission is to the Prefect Court, at the counting of the Votes, to prevent the altering of the Poll Books in favor of my opponent." He then received the governor's report of Rio Arriba County, which gave Gallegos a margin of 698 but again omitted El Embudo, which, if included, would have reduced the margin to 129.

"My Electioneering Tour is now terminated, in which I have traveled 375 miles in a carriage, + 150, over the worst possible roads, on Mule-back, making the entire excursion of 525 miles." He remained in Santa Fe until October 1. In addition to monitoring the vote counts, he settled his many accounts, wrote letters, attended various social events, and commented on the quality of the food. "The apples of Sta Fe, as tested by me, are uniformly sweet, The Grapes + Peaches which are brot there, from a distance, are uniformly sour. The Raspberries are intensely sour. The Apricots grown here, are not very good. Melons are very poor." On October 29, he "Stole a moment from business to join my Brethren of the Masonic Fraternity, + the 'Odd Fellows'" to dedicate a cemetery. "I became a Mason in 1814 + was advanced, to the degree of Master Mason. Since the year 1815, I have not been a member of any Lodge, merely joining the Brethren, upon public occasions."

He had many business and related affairs with which to deal. He settled his accounts with local merchants, closed his bank account, and paid several whom he had employed. He counted the gold and silver in his possession and recorded the balance almost every day. He also had the county issue a bond in the amount of $500 at 6 percent interest to be paid over five years to reimburse him for the money he spent to pay for food for prisoners when Colonel Sumner would have let them starve. He was pleased to receive private correspondence concerning John Bartlett, under whose direction as boundary commissioner the Mesilla Valley dispute had occurred. The Gadsden Treaty had not yet been settled. "I am to use this correspondence, according to my discretion, to check-mate Bartlett. No doubt now remains, on my mind, that this quondam Boundary Commissioner, is both Foul + Knave; + this private correspondence, furnishes proofs, of both these characteristics." Lane had moved out of the Palace of the Governors weeks before Meriwether arrived.

His major efforts during the ensuing three weeks, however, were directed at the ever-changing election results and suspicions about manipulation. On the eleventh, good news arrived from Doña Ana, Socorro, Valencia, Bernalillo and Santa Anna, "which makes my election certain if the illegal votes in Rio Ariba + San Miguel can be set aside. A report on the thirteenth of the vote in San Miguel County gave Gallegos a margin of 1,152 of 1,666 votes cast. On the twentieth, "Much excitement against the Gov for granting a Cert of Elections to Gallegos, + no little agst the Secreterio, for his doings in the premises." The certification is not surprising, for Meriwether had tutored Gallegos on the Democratic Party and the Constitution. Two days later, he reported, "went into an investigation of Roll Books of late election. Reports an error in the count of the Gov + Sec. + that I am entitled to a Certificate of Election." Gallegos arrived in Santa Fe the next day, and Lane initiated the steps required to contest the counts.[271]

Five days later the Secretary of the Territory issued the final and official results.

Under 1st Abstract of Votes
Lane 4,530   Gallegos 4,322
        under 2nd abstract
Lane 2,378   Gallegos 2,866
        under 3rd abstract
Lane 4,206   Gallegos 2,962
        under 4th abstract
Lane 4,732   Gallegos 5,243

It is not clear when the various abstracts were computed or why the total in the second is so low, but Lane's total in the other three remained fairly consistent, while Gallegos surged at the end.

The final count supported by the Thirty-Third Congress in February 1854 accepted the fourth abstract count for Gallegos but reduced Lane's by 197. The results Lane submitted to Congress gave him 4,233 votes and Gallegos 3,717. Except for minor differences, the discrepancies were concentrated in three counties: San Miguel and Rio Arriba, which he always thought to be subject to fraud, and Doña Ana, which was a surprise.

Though he had considered returning to St. Louis via Texas and New Orleans, he finally decided to ride in the Independence mail stage, retracing the route over the Santa Fe Trail he had taken a little more than a year before.[272] The citizens of Santa Fe gave a dinner and a ball for him on the 28th. He toasted them, "The Moral + Social reform which has been so happily commenced in N. Mex. + in which so many of the native citizens have cordially cooperated upon a late occasion. Truth is Mighty + will finally prevail over error + vice."

He met with his Masonic brethren the next day and on the 30th made final preparations, including accepting $500 in gold to be delivered to Glasgow & Bros. in St. Louis and carried at Mr. Aubrey's risk.

The mail party included two passengers in addition to Lane

and Frank, the driver, a mounted conductor, a mounted outrider, and the driver of the baggage wagon. "I was accompanied, to Arroyo Hondo, by a number of citizens in carriages and on Horse back. At the Arroyo speeches were made + complimentary Toasts were drunk, songs were sung (one written for the occasion), and I was overwhelmed with compliments + kind offices."

> Governor Lane[273]
> In sunshine and storm, in censure and praise,
> Long Live Governor Lane.
> He speaks what he thinks and he means what he says,
> Viva Governor Lane!
> No tricks, nor no bribes, nor no silly blunder
> Shall steal our worthy governor's thunder,
> We'll stand at his back till the day we go under,
> Long live Governor Lane!

Lane had to be disappointed by the election results, even though the apparent fraud must also have made him confident that he would prevail in Washington. The send-off at Arroyo Hondo would certainly have lifted his spirits.

The mail stage required twenty-one days to reach Independence, nineteen days less than Lane's trip west the year before, nine of which had been spent recuperating at Fort Union. During the three-week eastward journey, he continued to record lengthy observations about the food, the weather, buffalo, other objects of interest, and, as always, the behavior of individuals.

On October 3, at a home in La Vegas, he wrote, "The Breakfast was purely American, a treat, coffee with good cream, Fresh Butter, + Hot Flannel Cakes. God Bless the women of the States, + their cookery, + their general habits." Two days later, "Breakfasted at noon, fried Ham, crackers, coffee, molasses, + some Sweet Butter, that was put up for my own use." A week later, "Dined on

Duck-soup, a new dish, which was palatable, but perhaps it was my appetite, that made it so good. It cannot be denied that Frank is a good cook, after his invention of Duck Soup." Two weeks later near the dry Little Coon Creek, he reported, "The water which was procured, was too badly tasted, to encourage me to take any more of the coffee, than about half a cup. Besides, there is nothing in any part of the Breakfast that is not so disgusting, the Ham excepted, so I eat little." "Encamped at Walnut Creek, to feed the Mules with corn (which had been brought from Council Grove); + made a long halt, every body cramming themselves to the throat with Buffalo meat, the Hump Ribs of a Cow. But the cooking did not please me."

On October 18, they reached Council Grove and again the home of mail agent Whittington and his wife. There the days of often miserable food ended. "Mrs. Whittington spread an excellent table for us, but none of the Party partook but myself. God bless the women of the states."

Throughout the journey he recorded detailed descriptions of the land, vegetation, birds, and animals. He frequently mentioned the wolves that hovered about their camp, sometimes entering it, and admired "the extraordinary courage" of the dog, Caw, who drove off three wolves that were feasting on the guts of an antelope the conductor had shot. They saw herds of antelope – nobody seemed to be able to shoot precisely, for Caw had to chase down the wounded animals. He was particularly interested in the buffalo. "We have passed a succession of Herds, for at least 10 miles + if I were to estimate their numbers, at many hundred thousands I presume I would not err." He was also prescient. "The Buffalo is rapidly disappearing, +, in a very few more years, will entirely disappear from the plains. Our Ind policy must therefore be changed, to enable the Inds to subsist." He was curious about a centipede he found and was fascinated by a large grasshopper he had never seen before. "If edible, its great size, might make it available, as an article of food." He mistook a large skunk for a fox but "suffered little from his odors."

The hardships of travel were always present. On the fourth, he walked ahead of the carriage five miles, but a wheel broke before it overtook him, and he had to retrace the five miles. The damaged wheel was carried back to Fort Union to be repaired. It was returned at three in the morning, and they started again at sunrise. "We had no tent + went to bed without supper. The Dew fell heavily, + the night was cold. I slept uncomfortably, but rose fresh + wet." "About 10 oclk, it commenced raining, + continued to rain all night. The Passengers + Frank got into the Stage Coach + Baggage Waggon; + the men got under the Waggon. I did not move my bed, relying on my India Rubber Cape, to save me from the wet; but by Sun-rise I was well-bathed in Cold Water." There were many days during which there was not only no rain but no water for the animals.

They met parties traveling west; Lane knew a few from St. Louis. They spent a day with the mail coach headed for Santa Fe. Two German dukes with their retainers were camped west of Council Grove to hunt buffalo.

He had no official duties to take care of and seemed to be on an excursion, though on the eighteenth day he did note, "I am tired of the Journey + am not anxious to make it again." None of the hardships or pleasures prevented him from making his usual observations about life and men's behavior. "To be good is better than to be rich." "He who will not change his opinions, will never correct his errors." "Intellectual cultivation, without moral culture, may be of little benefit."

The final day was not easy. "The rain + wind has steadily increased + is now noon, somewhat violent + this however did not prevent our onward march, amidst the Rain which continued until the middle of the afternoon, when the rain ceased + the wind + cold increased to an uncomfortable extent. Our Dinner-hall at

'Lone Elm' was full of discomfort, from the wether wet ground on which we were obliged to spread our meal + set, the wind, smoke + cold: And last of our poor fare, fat bacon fried, the last of the crackers + a scanty supply, a bit of pickle apiece + Tea without sugar, water boiled in the coffee pot. But being our last meal on 'The plains' no-body grumbled."

"Arrived at 'Independence' 1 ¼ p.m. + took lodging at 'Noland House.' Thus ends a Journey across 'The Plains,' in the stage, of 800 miles ... which has been performed, without suffering, + without any accident."

He embarked on the *UB Honduras* on Monday, October 24, and reached St. Louis in the evening on Friday. They were stranded on sand bars three times; once it took a full day to get afloat because the Missouri River had been very low and full of snags. Mary was expecting him, for he had telegraphed from both Independence and Jefferson City. He reached home after eight, and they went immediately to the Glasgows' for dinner. He had been gone three days shy of fifteen months.

He left again in four weeks with Anne for Washington via New York and Philadelphia to pursue his challenge and settle his government accounts. He would not return to St. Louis until late April.

PART V

Washington to St. Louis: The Final Years
1855–1863

DEFEAT IN WASHINGTON

Lane took care of his family and business affairs in St. Louis while continuing to deal with unfinished business in New Mexico. He and his daughter Anne embarked on the Alton Railroad for Washington on November 24. The primary purpose of the trip was to challenge the election of Padre Gallegos as soon as he was sworn in as a member of the House of Representatives. In addition, Lane petitioned to be reimbursed for his personal expenditures in New Mexico and hoped he would also be reimbursed for the expenses incurred in connection with the journey to Washington.

Determination was always evident in his actions, but his pursuit of the New Mexico seat in the House of Representatives was relentless; Lane behaved like a hedgehog rather than his usual fox. He had become attached to the territory and its inhabitants and believed he could represent them effectively. He was also deeply offended by the slanderous remarks aimed at him and what he considered to be a fraudulent election that had denied him victory.

Before leaving St. Louis, he spent several days at his farm, Bienvenue, north of the city, arranging with a T. G. Adams to farm it in partnership. He paid particular attention to the Glasgow family. "Willie is better, Victor is somewhat ill, from Chills, + my Daughter Sarah is Much out of health."[274] He did not elaborate on Sarah's illness. He was also working with his son-in-law to obtain patent reports from the Smithsonian Institute.

The first stop on the journey east was the Sherman Hotel in Chicago. After a night there, they continued by train to Albany by way of Buffalo, staying at the Delavan House, and then departed at five in the afternoon on the overnight journey to New York City. They remained in New York for four days at the Metropolitan Hotel, "the most magnificent Hotel + the best in all its various appointments I ever saw."[275] The hotel had recently been sold for $800,000. He purchased a silver tea set for Mary for $260, paying $175 in cash and $85 in silver bullion.[276] While in New Mexico he had a solid silver coffee mug made for her, probably in Mexico. He did not comment on the frenetic nature of the city as he had during a prior visit.

They then departed for Philadelphia, staying again at Girard's House. He left Anne there and went on to Washington to establish himself at Brown's Hotel on Pennsylvania Avenue, where he would remain until April. Anne traveled frequently during this time and exchanged letters with her father.

Lane's manner of travel and purchases indicated that his dire financial circumstances were in the past. Nevertheless, he kept a detailed expense report, including of spending ten cents for three apples. Expenses at the Delavan House, including a twelve-cent haircut, were $6.12; at the Metropolitan in New York, $15.75. He made no comparisons between this trip and the arduous journey over the Santa Fe Trail two months earlier.

His evaluation of Washington, DC, on December 2 was the culmination of years of multiple contacts. "Looked about, in this great Fermenting-Tub of party politics, intrigue + Vice, but could ascertain little of what is going on under the Surface."

Lane had to wait over two weeks for Padre Gallegos to appear. Finally, the new representative was seated with a translator fourteen days after Congress had convened. Lane had taken a seat as a contestant on the second day of the session but could not file his official documents until Gallegos had been seated. There is no explanation for the padre's dilatory approach to claiming the most important position he would ever hold.

Lane was busy as ever during the thirteen-day wait, writing letters, meeting people, keeping track of Gallegos's anticipated arrival, and commenting as usual on a myriad of subjects. He deposited $442 in gold at Brown's Hotel. His correspondence involved business and family affairs in St. Louis and lingering matters in New Mexico. He called on judges, politicians, and businessmen in Washington while he attempted to settle his accounts and waited. He met with the cartographer John Disturnell, who had prepared the map that had almost precipitated a second Mexican War. There is no report of their conversation.

He met with President Pierce on December 15 but was not impressed. It reminded him of "Ovids account of Phoetin's [sic] attempt to drive the chariot of the Sun, + its disastrous result, which I read as a school boy, + which I have not read since."[277] He did not say what actions of President Pierce had led him to this conclusion, but it is consistent with the general historic evaluation of Pierce. He had another encounter with the president on January 1, 1854. The occasion was a grand reception for the general population. He took Anne, who reported in a letter to Sarah that, as they approached the White House, she saw "Mrs. Pierce at an upper window ... and never saw a sadder face." "The interior of the house offered some strong contrasts – the diplomatic corps in their court dresses, officers of the Army and Navy in their uniforms, side by side with an Irishman who did not seem to have seen water for some time. I am glad I went once, but don't catch me ever doing it again."

Earlier, Lane had been introduced to a US Navy Lieutenant, J. C. Strain, who had been designated by the secretary of the navy, "with fear + trembling, to run a line of levels from Caledonia Bay, to Panama bay, (I believe), the distance is about 40 ms + has a River at each end with a single hill of 150 feet in height, near mid-way, the harbours at each end being good. It is proposed to cut a Canal from ocean to ocean, without a lock to be 150 feet wide at the bottom, so as to allow the largest Ships of War to pass each other in the Canal."[278] He goes on to describe the tides on each end and expenditures allocated for the survey— $1,380. Construction of the Panama Canal would start in fifty years.

The memorial contesting the election was finally filed on December 19 and immediately referred to the Committee on Elections, which could not take it up until after the holidays. Lane did not slow down, meeting with the head of the post office about service to New Mexico and having breakfast with a Judge McLain, who believed that "the scale of morality in the country was descending so rapidly that despotism would ensue." Lane did not disagree. "I have had my own misgivings, for some time. Ever since the Presidency of Gen'l Jackson, for whom I voted the first time, (but not the second), from which may God preserve me."[279] He said he was not very well, a significant change from the reports of his health while in New Mexico. He visited the Smithsonian.

Anne was in Washington for Christmas, which Lane deemed the quietest he had ever experienced. She went to the Episcopal Church and "I afterwards to the Unitarian Church + heard a Transcendental Pantheistic Sermon, from Dr. Channing, which I could not comprehend."[280]

The stay in Washington would not end soon, for the Committee on Elections did not issue its final report until February 27; an effort in the House on the twenty-ninth to reconsider the rejection of Lane's memorial was voted down.

Thomas Hart Benton, now a Representative, had risen in the House on December 19 to present the credentials of "Senor Jose Gallegos, a delegate from the Territory of New Mexico; and that he be sworn in and take his seat."[281] Two identical sets of results were presented, one certified by Governor Merriwether and the other by the territorial secretary of New Mexico, William S. Messervy. Each showed an identical tally of the official count on September 20.

Count of the entire vote

Jose Manuel Gallegos received	4,971
William Carr Lane received	4,526
Majority for Jose Manual Gallegos	445

After throwing out such returns as were not made in strict accordance with the law, the results stand as follows:

Jose Manuel Gallegos received	2,806
William Carr Lane received	2,267
Majority for Jose Manual Gallegos	539

The certified figures do not match even approximately those recorded as the first, second, third, and fourth abstracts and reported by Lane following his investigation in Santa Fe. The results are even murkier, because the final Committee report contained entirely different results and did not refer to the tally after questionable ballots were "thrown out."

Lane presented his results:

Lane	4,233
Gallegos	3,717
Majority for Lane	516

The Committee established the final results:

Gallegos	5,243
Lane	4,535
Majority for Gallegos	708

It is impossible to determine the real cause of the discrepancies. Lane had believed both during the election and immediately after it that there was chicanery in some counties and in the secretary's office, which was likely supported by the governor given his party affiliation and his tutoring of Gallegos. During the long wait for the committee results, Lane reported frequently on forces working against him in Washington and Santa Fe. It is impossible to know what combination of fraud and primitive procedures created this morass. The committee thought it to be the latter.

After examining all the poll books provided by the territorial secretary and interviewing unidentified witnesses, the committee officially denied Lane's claim. Its report is long and verbose, but several conclusions stand out. "That there was very great irregularity in the returns is fully admitted; but not more so than might reasonably be expected under all the circumstances. The government of the Territory of New Mexico has been but recently organized; the people are not accustomed to the precision and accuracy of our election forms; they do not understand our language or our system of laws." They rejected the existence of any evidence of fraud or "that the returns were not made in the most perfect good faith." They did acknowledge that in several precincts in San Miguel County the judge had submitted only the abstract of the results, not the poll books as required by law. They found a loophole in New Mexico law that allowed fifteen days for late returns to be collected by a special messenger but again acknowledged that there was no proof that had been done. It obviously would have been easy to make the poll books consistent with abstract after the fact. The committee gave Gallegos 1,397 votes from San Miguel County; Lane claimed the padre had received only 476. Rio Arriba and Santa Ana had smaller differences, but the three alone account for Lane's loss, with San Miguel accounting for the majority.

The committee also rejected the votes for Lane cast by the Taos Pueblo Indians and 202 by the Laguna Pueblo, though it is likely that the Treaty of Guadalupe Hidalgo had guaranteed them that right. The committee, thus, supported the territorial law that denied them the vote. "They retain their tribal characteristics; form a distinct community from the whites, make their own local and separate laws, are governed by their own chiefs (there are no chiefs in pueblos), and do not differ essentially from other savage tribes." Until 1948, the New Mexico Constitution prohibited Indians living on reservations, which included pueblos, from voting in either federal or state elections. In that year, returning World War II veterans challenged the provision in court and won. Another lawsuit in Arizona removed a similar ban.

In all likelihood, the basic reason for the committee reaching the convoluted conclusion was the almost two-thirds Democratic majority in the House. Lane was a Whig, and his successor, the Democrat Merriwether, had trained Gallegos to be a Democrat. Lane had suspected during his long wait that there was political maneuvering taking place. The House refused to pay for a translator for Gallegos.

In a bit of historic irony, Gallegos was reelected two years later, but this time the challenge by his opponent and former secretary to Lane, Miguel Otero, was upheld by the Committee of Elections. Gallegos returned to New Mexico. The official tally gave Gallegos a margin of 99, but the committee gave Otero a margin of 290.[282] He had undoubtedly learned from the failure of the earlier challenge and was better able to document fraud, such as voting by Mexicans who had not established United States citizenship.

Fray Angélico Chavez in *Trés Macho—He Said* comes to a very different conclusion, describing the contested election essentially as a heated dispute between the Catholic supporters of Bishop Lamy and the Hispanic priests who campaigned for Gallegos, one of their former members. Chavez said Otero was really not a New Mexican, though he had been born in the territory, and cited as evidence his claim that he could address Congress in English. He also entitled his description of the reversal, "The Shame of Congress."

Prior to the committee's decision, Lane had not only commented on the "jockeying that was resorted to against me" but pursued the settling of his accounts, written letters, and visited sites that interested him. On January 22 he and a Mr. Law took the train to Annapolis to see a midshipman at the Naval Academy. He described the grounds of the Academy as "surpassingly beautiful; + the school itself, has a high character. The present numbers of Cadets, at School, amounts to 120 – some as young as 13."[283] "This is my first visit, to this antient, + antiquated looking, Town, - which has not a single sign of 'progress' about it." "The Town, or rather city (it was the state capital), has the quietude of mid-day of other places, at midnight."

His veneration of George Washington continued as he described a picture of the general resigning at the end of the Revolutionary War as "the most moral spectacle which the world ever witnessed."

"I spent the evening, at the House of Commodore Morris, last week. He is now 72 years old, + altho 'shot thro' the body from side to side, in the engagement between the *Constitution* + the *Guerriere*, he is still stout." Lane then recorded the details of the battle as reported by the commodore, which concluded, "The Constitution then bore down, on the opposite, + gave another tremendous broad side, - which completed the destruction of enemy. Never was such utter destruction effected, in so short a time."

His letter to Sarah in St. Louis on February 19 covered a variety of subjects, particularly relating to her children. "As far as revaccinating (smallpox), I advise that it should be done. The doing of it can do no harm, to the patient, + causes little expense; + it may perchance, do much good." He explained that confusion in letter writing was the result of Anne and he having far-separated rooms in a large hotel and rarely seeing each other—he often did not know where she was. "I do not expect to engage in the practice of my profession again, - at least I indulge the hope, to be able to make my living, in some other way."

He commented on the health and character of many friends and acquaintances. He took pity on "Poor Die Kearny. She has not deserved so sad a fate." Her husband had apparently abandoned her. "Bid her to wait patiently, for a turn in the Scale of Fortune. 'It is a long lane, that has no turn,' and whichever way the turn may be, must better her condition." He had a different view of others. "As for the Edwards, no terms of contempt, are too strong, for their deserts."

He wrote William Glasgow Jr. on February 19 covering very different subjects. He had Glasgow take care of some personal business and assured him that he would be home "before the April Court. It is my opinion that I had better compromise that suit if the current City Atty. remains." "Old Merriwether, has been writing, secretly and openly gross libels against a Ex Inc Agent, + indirectly attempting to implicate me. He has however failed, + is perfectly well understood, at the Department. – I may notice these slanders thro' the newspapers, when all my business is done here. My Family may rest easy, in the perfect assurance, that every act of my life, public + private, in N. Mex. will bear the Severest scrutiny." He was uncertain about the timing of getting his accounts settled. "I am charged with money expended, - out of the Navajo + Utah appropriations, (not needed, for those Indians), for the Apaches; + cannot get a credit for these expenditures, until the Deficiency

Bill, so called, passes." "The Gadsden Treaty, is before the Senate, with some prospect of being confirmed, - notwithstanding the high price we pay for what we get." He seemed to think the United States should simply have seized the area, as he had.

Surprisingly, he writes almost as an afterthought that "The Nebraska Bill, it seems to me, is losing favor; but, at this time, has friends enough to pass it, in both Houses." He did say, "Congress is getting into a snarl, + things will be worse before they are better" but indicated no position on the Nebraska Bill that ultimately split the country, divided the political parties, and affected him for the remainder of his life. The bill was passed by Congress as the Kansas-Nebraska Act in May 1854.

The genesis of the act lay in the push to continue expanding westward, this time by railroad through Nebraska. That construction would require establishing Nebraska as a territory and taking control of Indian lands. Stephen A. Douglas of Illinois was the act's sponsor in the Senate, at least in part because he owned substantial real estate in Chicago that would grow in value with a western railroad. He had already had similar success with a southern route. The House passed the bill in March 1853, but the Senate tabled it. The bill essentially encompassed all of the land north of 36°30', which the Missouri Compromise of 1820 had established as non-slave territory. Southerners rose up in fury.

The railroad objective was lost in the bitter fight over an amendment that expanded slave territory. Every member of President Pierce's cabinet was opposed, except for Jefferson Davis and one other. However, Douglas, Davis, and other supporters of the bill, which repealed the 36°30' slavery boundary included in the Missouri Compromise, forced their way into the White House on a Sunday and told the president he would lose the South if he did not provide support. He capitulated. The Senate also killed a provision that would have established 160-acre homestead grants, because it would have encouraged free farms. The votes in both the Senate and the House were split by region, not party. The vote for passage in the Senate was 41 to 17 and in the House 115 to 104.[284]

The regional split was further exacerbated by the inclusion of the Fugitive Slave Act that allowed federal agents to assist in the recapture of free slaves who had traveled as far north as Maine. In a more dramatic attempt to expand slavery, Narciso Lopez in 1851 led a privately funded expedition from New Orleans to annex Cuba as a slave state. The expedition failed in a disastrous fashion.

The efforts to annex Cuba, however, did not end. President Pierce, always anxious to add territory, appointed Pierre Soulé Ambassador to Spain with quiet instructions to offer to buy Cuba. Southerners were eager to add a slave state and blunt a possible uprising similar to the one that had occurred in Haiti. Soulé proceeded to gather the US ambassadors to England, James Buchanan, and France, John Mason, at Ostend, Belgium. There they issued a manifesto that effectively said Spain had to sell Cuba or the United States would take it. The subsequent uproar among anti-slavery Northerners forced Pierce to abandon the idea. He was still reeling from the effect of the Kansas-Nebraska Act.

The exact date of Lane's return to St. Louis was not recorded, but it was probably in early April. He had written two of Sarah's children late in March describing the ability of a blind man who lived at Brown's Hotel to move about Washington and of a Mexican in Taos who had been blinded in childhood by smallpox and who, at the age of twenty-seven, supported his family by cutting firewood eight or ten miles from town and bringing it back on a donkey to sell. He also cut grass three or four miles away to bring in and sell. He also herded cattle. Lane advised, "My dear children, the example of these two poor people, ought not only to make us thankful, for the great blessings, which we enjoy, but ought to convince us to accomplish, almost anything that we undertake to perform. Therefore, be not disheartened, when you do not easily learn your tasks – try and try again, + you will accomplish your object, in the end."[285]

A year later, T. G. Hunt reported that the efforts in Congress to reimburse Lane for the trip to Washington and finally settle his accounts had not yet succeeded. He thought he would have to wait for the next Congress.

Lane returned to St. Louis for the last nine years of his life at the age of sixty-four, presumably accompanied by Anne. He died in January 1863 at the age of seventy-three.

RETURN TO ST. LOUIS

Lane may have known when he left St. Louis in May 1852 that the trip would end in Washington, but he could not have known that he would be appointed governor of New Mexico while there. He had barely paused in St. Louis as he headed west for Santa Fe. He would not live at his home again for almost two years, except for the four weeks in November 1853 when he once more paused before leaving for Washington.

It would be an exaggeration to conclude that he returned a beaten man, but he held no official position, and his medical practice, which he did not want to reestablish, had essentially disappeared. His real estate holdings appear to have been in good order, though there never was a clear accounting of what they were at any given time.

He was in any case able to live well and remain in generally good health until his final illness. However, the increasingly bitter and unyielding disputes over slavery that resulted in the outbreak of the Civil War almost two years before his death generated both fury and serious distress. The situation was aggravated because Missouri was a divided border state and St. Louis the center of Union restrictions imposed on Southern sympathizers, of which Lane was one of the most prominent.

As the nation remained seemingly inevitably split over slavery, Lane took care of his family and personal affairs, seldom mentioning the dispute, though he wrote many letters. Strains within the family grew, particularly in relation to Sarah's husband William Glasgow Jr., whom the Lanes cared for and respected. However, he was a Union supporter, and they were not hesitant to tell him that they simply could not understand his position. Lane suffered another blow four years after his return when Sarah was crippled, apparently by rheumatoid arthritis. Despite trips to various hot springs in the United States, she continued to suffer almost constant pain. Finally, in the fall of 1861 after the start of the Civil War, her father and husband persuaded her to travel to Wiesbaden, Germany, for the baths. She departed with her husband and five oldest children.[AN-11] She would remain in Germany for three years while Glasgow traveled back and forth at least twice a year. This travel had to be difficult with the war raging. It is likely that he took the train to Chicago and then east to Albany and down to New York City to board a ship, but no mention of the route was recorded. It was, however, obviously costly. Lane and Glasgow each provided $8,000 per year and Anne $2,000, for a total of $18,000.

The Whig party of which Lane was a member had always been split on the issue of slavery. There were Northern Whigs and Southern Whigs; he presumably would have been identified with the latter. The passage of the Kansas-Nebraska Act, which he had only briefly mentioned, destroyed the party. The Democrats in the North were similarly torn apart, though they remained dominant in the South, where they largely absorbed that branch of the Whig party. At the same time, attempts grew in the North to establish a militant anti-slavery party. The name "Republican" apparently was first used in Ripon, Wisconsin, and then adopted in May 1854 by thirty Congressmen.[286]

It is likely that Lane had no party affiliation after this time, for he could not embrace the generally anti-slavery Republicans and, after his denunciation of Jackson, could hardly be a Democrat. Thomas Hart Benton had opposed the Kansas-Nebraska Act because it extended slavery, not because he was an abolitionist. Stephen Douglas returned to Illinois to defend the act and his position that local governments should be entitled to make their own choices.

Abraham Lincoln had disagreed in a debate with Douglas that preceded by four years the six famous Lincoln-Douglas debates. Lincoln said in the 1854 debate:

> When the white man governs himself that is self-government; but when he governs himself, and also governs another man ... that is despotism ... The Negro is a man ... There can be no moral right in connection with one man's making a slave of another." "Let no one be deceived the spirit of seventy-six and the spirit of Nebraska, are antagonisms ... Little by little ... we have been giving up the old for the new faith. Near eighty years ago we began by declaring that all men are created equal; but now from that beginning we have run down to the other declarative, that for some men to enslave others is a 'sacred right of self government.' These principles cannot stand together ... Our republican robe is soiled and trailed in the dust. Let us repurify it ... Let us re-adopt the Declaration of Independence, and with it, the practices, and policy, which harmonize with it ... If we do this, we shall not only have saved the Union, but we shall have so saved it, as to make, and to keep it forever worthy of the saving.[287]

If Lane followed the speeches in the 1850s, he did not record his reaction. His position, however, was clear, and he would never waiver from the statement he made about the White, Black, and Indian races in the Missouri legislature twenty years earlier: Each required a different form of government.

Similarly, he did not indicate any interest in the presidential election of 1856, which put the ineffective James Buchanan in the White House. The political parties were still sorting themselves out when they convened. The first to meet was the American party, which hoped to salvage the Whigs. However, when the convention failed to call for repeal of the Kansas-Nebraska Act, seventy northern delegates walked out to form the North American party. The remaining delegates nominated Millard Fillmore.

The North American convention chose John C. Fremont on the first ballot because he still retained a popular image as "The Pathfinder" and had no public record to defend, despite his checkered career. The ambitions and connections of his wife, Jessie Benton, would be a plus, though her father, Thomas Hart Benton, maintained his position as a Jacksonian Democrat and voted against his son-in-law. The Democrats nominated Buchanan on the seventeenth ballot after Franklin Pierce and Stephen Douglas withdrew. Buchanan had held so many public positions – ten years each as a congressman and senator, a five-year stint as an ambassador, and four as secretary of state – that he was known as "Old Public Functionary," not quite "Old Hickory." The campaign almost devolved into two—Buchanan battled against Fillmore in the South and against Fremont in the North. Fremont won 114 electoral votes in the North, but Buchanan gained a total of 174, including all of the South, to win easily. He won only 45 percent of the popular vote.[288]

St. Louis had suffered twin disasters in 1849 with the cholera epidemic and the Great Fire. By 1850, however, the epidemic had abated and larger buildings were rising from the burned-out areas. The city was about to enter a decade of prosperity and growth.

Lane, the Ewings, and the Glasgows always seemed to own substantial amounts of real estate. Even when Lane had been forced to sell all his property at a sheriff's sale, a Ewing bought it at bargain prices. There is no record of what they lost in the Great Fire. Though Lane was not one of the new class of wealth that developed in the 1850s, he seems to have prospered.

St. Louis was still a river city, with up to 120 steamships tied up along the levee on a single day, but it also began to become a land transportation hub with the start of construction of a railroad to the Pacific Ocean in 1851.[289] Businessmen moved in to start manufacturing enterprises, open retail establishments, and build hotels. The Excelsior Manufacturing Company, for example, built over one million stoves by 1893. Thirty-six breweries produced more than 216,000 barrels of beer in 1854. The luxurious Planters' Hotel could not meet the demand for its rooms—Planter's Punch was invented in its bar. Financial institutions grew along with the demand for their services. Construction of mansions, some with indoor plumbing, accompanied the increasing wealth, as did the growth of cultural institutions and social events.

As always, there was the darker side: dozens of children living on the streets, prostitution, violence, and always slavery. In 1854, a major riot broke out during the election when some foreign-born citizens were disqualified from voting. A mob of five thousand was confronted by the Irish opposition. The police force of sixty-three was clearly outmatched. By the time the rioting had ended, ten were dead and many more injured. "Hawk-Eye Bill" set fire to the Pacific Hotel the next year killing sixty. What is thought to have been the last duel was fought in 1856, but random murder continued on the streets.

The composition of the population changed drastically as Germans moved in. A similar migration in 1830 had consisted largely of well-educated immigrants, but the new surge was made up largely of peasants and artisans. Germans constituted one-third of the population by 1860. This influx greatly affected slavery in St. Louis and Missouri.

The St. Louis population of 77,860 in 1850 included 2,656 slaves and 1,398 free Blacks.[290] The number of slaves had been declining in both the city and state and continued to do so as the German immigrants filled the demand for labor. As a result, St. Louis became a center for selling slaves and sending them south. By 1859, one of the most active traders occupied a two-and-a-half-story building complete with barred windows. A woman bought slave babies to raise and sell. The traders were shunned by the general population, but nevertheless, the brutal practice continued, even though the traders had to sneak their captives to the river for the trip south to avoid being mobbed. Their practices were brutal. Older slaves had their gray hair pulled out, backs were inspected for lash scars, which would indicate disobedience, and many were forced to strip.

Individual and often remarkable stories reflected this abuse. One woman who had been the mistress of a Southerner escaped to St. Louis, though pregnant. After the baby was born, she was discovered and sold. The baby died on the trip south. When the body was thrown in the river, the mother tried to follow but was restrained and given fifty lashes for her misbehavior. She again escaped in New Orleans, made her way back to St. Louis, married a Frenchman, and moved to France, where it was reported they lived long, happy, and affluent lives. It seems unlikely that Lane sold his slaves south, for he did not report any such transactions— nor did he comment on the trade.

Lane's life during the period of almost nine years between his return to St. Louis and his death was dominated by Sarah's illness and the Civil War. Mary apparently was in St. Louis for this period, probably because her father had died in 1846 and her mother four years later. Lane's few letters to her were written when she was in Hot Springs, Arkansas, with Sarah. From the time of Sarah's departure from St. Louis to the time of Lane's final illness, however, there was a steady stream of letters to Sarah and her husband, first to Arkansas and then to Germany.

Anne curtailed her travels to help take care of her sister's younger children and stopped altogether after the start of the war. She then also wrote frequently to Sarah.

Lane's letters between March 1858 and July 1861 were devoted almost entirely to the health and activities of his grandchildren and friends, except for those to Glasgow, which dealt frequently with business matters. He opened a letter to Sarah on February 10, 1859, with the startling and perhaps revealing statements, "I am at a loss to determine whether to write to you, or Mr. G.; but have concluded, as I have so very little to say, - that it shall be to you." "We move on, in the same daily routine, ... enjoying, Health, peace – plenty – undisturbed sleep + a reasonable share of happiness. The children desire the return of their Parents, - who are so dear to them; but, one + all, have ceased to fret, at the separation."

He wrote Glasgow in January 1859 about one of his real estate ventures, which appeared to be substantial. "I went out to your Buildings today. The stone-work of the cellars, of 7 of the Buildings, (except the Range-work) are completed; and the Excavation, for perhaps as many more, is done, some masons + casters were upon the ground; and a mass of Joist-lumber, was on hand. – All this, in mid-winter, looks like an early completion of the Block. The Houses look small, to me –" He went on to describe the status of the street construction.

He corresponded with his old friend John Darby, who was his attorney in a lawsuit and was scathing in his description of the defense. The case finally went to the Missouri Supreme Court in March 1859, where Lane, who was approaching seventy, had to explain who he was. Darby gave a dinner party on June 1, 1858, for twenty-one leading citizens who had been in business when he had been admitted to the bar in May 1827. Dr. William Carr Lane was number two on the guest list, following Colonel John O'Fallon.

Sarah's children were under the care of her sister and mother. Lane, in another surprising comment in a letter to Anne, who was in Cape May, New Jersey, in August 1860, reported on Mary, "Your Mother is quite well, + and astonishes me by her cheerful discharge of her present duties, + her successful management of the children – she pets one – coaxes another + bribes a third one."

CIVIL WAR IN ST. LOUIS

The opening shots at Fort Sumter, located on an island in the harbor of Charleston, South Carolina, were fired by General Beauregard following the orders of Confederate President Jefferson Davis. The small and starving American garrison under the command of Major Robert Anderson responded as best it could, but was forced to surrender two days later. The American flag was replaced by the Confederate.

The attempts during the preceding months to avoid war had included a Southern demand for the surrender of Fort Sumter. The dithering James Buchanan was overwhelmed. Some threatened to hang him if he gave in. He finally decided to neither reinforce Sumter nor hand it over, as it was easier to let Abraham Lincoln deal with the crisis. The new president also hoped to avoid war but knew he could not surrender. His attempt to resupply the fort forced Jefferson Davis to choose war or peace, and he chose the former.

During the years preceding Lincoln's election in 1860, violence, speeches, and publications had stoked the anti-slavery sentiment in the North. The most influential of the latter was Harriet Beecher Stowe's *Uncle Tom's Cabin, or Life Among the*

Lowly. Three hundred thousand copies were sold in the United States in the first year after it was published as a book in 1852—the equivalent of three million today. It had appeared earlier as a magazine serial.[291]

Enforcement of the Fugitive Slave Law seemed to prove her point. Anthony Burns escaped from slavery in Virginia in March 1854 but was arrested by US marshals in Boston in May when his owner came to reclaim him. Abolitionists stormed the jail but were repulsed. President Pierce responded by sending marines, cavalry, and artillery to Boston as well as a naval ship to carry Burns back to Virginia, saying, "Incur any expense to insure the execution of the law."[292] The judge ordered him returned and refused offers to buy him, which his owner had agreed to. This episode cost the country $100,000, over $2 million today.

Violence on a wider scale broke out in Kansas in May 1856 as a result of the Kansas-Nebraska Act. David Atchison, senator from Missouri, president pro-tem, and always described as "foul-mouthed," fomented attacks. Free-Soil New Englanders sent emigrants to Kansas to assure it would be a free territory, while pro-slavery Missourians illegally crossed the border to vote. Atchison organized a mob of border rowdies in 1855, saying, "There are eleven hundred men coming over from Platte County to vote and if that ain't enough we can send five thousand – enough to kill every God-damned abolitionist in the Territory.[293] Pierce listened to Atchison and not only refused to stop this violent charade but replaced the Free-Soil territorial governor with an adamant supporter of slavery. The Free-Soilers stood their ground and elected their own legislators. There were now two governments.

A perhaps even more dramatic event occurred in the US Senate on May 22 when a congressman beat Senator Charles Sumner over the head with a gold-capped cane, reportedly more than thirty times. Opposing bills proposing the entrance of Kansas as a free state and slave state had been introduced; neither could pass, because Republicans controlled the House and Democrats the Senate. Sumner spoke eloquently and stridently for two days, including an attack on his colleague from South Carolina, Andrew Butler. "Don Quixote who had chosen a mistress to whom he has made his vows, and who ... though polluted in the sight of the world, is chaste in his sight – I mean the harlot, slavery."

The violence of these events was emblematic of the bitterness infecting the country. They set the stage for the election of Abraham Lincoln in 1860 and, thus, to the establishment of the Confederacy early in 1861. Seven Southern states, including Texas, Arkansas, Tennessee, North Carolina, and Virginia, joined after the fall of Fort Sumter.

The Democrats had met in January 1860 in Charleston. The Northern delegates intended to nominate Stephen Douglas, but the Southerners refused to yield their slaves. William Lowndes Yancey of Alabama presented their position. "Ours are the institutions which are at stake; ours is the property that is to be destroyed; ours is the honor at stake."[294] After fifty-seven ballots, there was no agreement, so the convention adjourned to meet again in Baltimore in June. Little had changed. The Southerners left the convention to nominate Pierce's vice president, John Breckenridge. The Northerners remained to nominate Douglas.

The Republicans met in May in Chicago without the same rancor but with many competing candidates. Seward hoped to win on the first ballot. There were the first of what came to be known as dark horse candidates, including Lincoln of Illinois and Bates of Missouri. Seward did not achieve his first ballot goal and gradually lost delegates as Lincoln added them. Delegates from a number of states began switching to Lincoln during the third ballot. The final four from Ohio put him over the number needed. The estimated crowd of 40,000 inside and outside the convention center, largely Lincoln supporters, erupted with enthusiasm. The Constitutional Union party composed of generally elderly former

Whigs had nominated John Bell of Tennessee just before the Republican convention, hoping to keep the country together by not taking a position on slavery.

The campaign was again in two sections—Lincoln against Douglas in the North and against Breckenridge in the South. Lincoln did not campaign in the South and was not even on the ballot in some states. Douglas did venture into the South to warn of disunion but got little response.

President Buchanan had not only been weak but also presided over what many consider the most corrupt administration in American history. Continued revelations of misdealings further aided the Republicans. Lincoln won only 40 percent of the popular vote nationally but 54 percent in the North. Breckenridge won 45 percent of the Southern popular vote and Bell 39. Lincoln easily won the electoral vote with 180 while needing only 152. Adding to the Southerners' anguish was the Republican triumph in Congress—three quarters of the Republicans would be anti-slavery. Stephen Douglas threw his support behind Lincoln after the election, hoping to avoid disunion. After the loss of Fort Sumter, he said, "There are only two sides to the question. Every man must be for the United States or against it. There can be no neutrals in this war, only patriots – or traitors." He died a month later.

Lane did not leave an extensive record of his concerns during 1860, but he did predict the coming of the Civil War. He wanted Missouri to stay in the Union as a slave state. His wish came to pass, but not in the way he had hoped. He was particularly critical of Lincoln and his cabinet members whom he considered abolitionists. Two of them were from Missouri, Attorney General Edward Bates and Postmaster General Montgomery Blair, brother of the powerful pro-Union Frank Blair. Lane had to be acquainted with the two Missourians. Bates was a distinguished attorney who had sought the Republican presidential nomination in 1860. Blair, also an attorney, had defended Dred Scott before the Supreme Court.

Missouri was split into three factions: abolitionists, slaveholders who wanted to secede, and those who wanted to stay in the Union. Governor Jackson was a Southern sympathizer who had stated in his inaugural address, "Missouri should make a timely decision to stand by her sister slave-holding states."[295]

Francis Blair Jr. was a strong pro-Union Republican member of the US House who had the strong support of the more than 50,000 Germans in St. Louis. The old Southern and Creole elites had their social positions and real estate but not the political strength of the new businessmen, who generally thought in terms of the east-west trade by railroad rather than north-south transport by the river. A state convention, which was to decide the question of secession, met on March 4, 1861, in St. Louis after an inconclusive meeting six days earlier in Jefferson City. Five days later, the convention reported that there was no adequate cause to secede and that the state should work for peace and the equality of all states.

Lane had been adamantly opposed to the country splitting before the assault on Fort Sumter. After the war started, he wrote letters to congressmen, generals, and others to urge a peaceful solution. He did not believe the North could win. He was also concerned about the St. Louis trade down the river. He thought Lincoln and "his slaves" would hang themselves in the end. In July 1861, he wrote to abolitionist leaders in the Kansas-Missouri boundary struggle suggesting a truce. In September he wrote an open letter to General Winfield Scott urging an armistice between the Union and the Confederacy. He thought Congress should stop Lincoln in his tracks. Lane was now seventy-one. and, while his views were deeply held, his proposals were unrealistic and did not seem to recognize the changes in the population of St. Louis.

The center of attention in St. Louis now shifted to the federal arsenal, in which a substantial store of munitions was located—60,000 muskets, 90,000 pounds of powder, 1.5 million bar cartridges, 40 field pieces, siege guns, and machinery to manufacture arms.[296] Governor Jackson had not given up his goal of secession and plotted to capture the stores for his Southern-supported Missouri militia, with the probable aim of transferring it to the Confederacy. Blair, however, moved more aggressively to assure that such a takeover was thwarted. He recruited, armed, and trained a militia while at the same time maneuvering to have the arsenal commander, whom he suspected of Southern sympathies, called back to Washington.

Jackson remained determined to lead Missouri into the Confederacy. He seized a much smaller arsenal at Liberty near Kansas City, took control of the St. Louis police, and requested arms from Jefferson Davis with which he could capture St. Louis. In early May, four cannons with ammunition arrived in St. Louis from Baton Rouge in crates labeled "marble". Nathaniel Lyon, now in command of the arsenal, mustered his German volunteers into the Union army and started sending muskets to Illinois. The shipments had their own drama. On one night a crowd of Southerners who had been tipped off gathered at the river to stop the shipment. Lyon, however, was also tipped off. The mob seized a few boxes of ancient flintlocks at a decoy steamship while 21,000 modern guns were taken safely across the river.

The cannon from Baton Rouge were moved to Camp Jackson, which the governor had established with Missouri militia on the edge of St. Louis. Lyon, disguised as Frank Blair's mother-in-law, rode through the camp in a carriage on a personal reconnaissance foray. The next day, he surrounded Camp Jackson with German-Americans and regular troops and captured it without a shot being fired. However, as the prisoners were marched through the city, mobs hurled insults at the "Damned Dutch." When one of Lyon's officers was shot, soldiers fired back. Twenty-eight civilians and two soldiers were killed and scores wounded. That night several lone Germans were murdered on the streets. It is unlikely that the mob entered the area in which Lane lived, but St. Louis was in a state of panic. At one point before the violence started, a group of prominent citizens had met to try to arrange a truce. Lane was not listed as one of them.

Jackson, with the Mexican War General Sterling Price who had gone over to the Confederacy, retreated to Jefferson City. A conference between the two and Blair and Lyon failed to reach any agreement. Lyon then drove them from the capital, then Boonville and then all the way to the southwest corner of Missouri. He had organized, trained, and equipped an army and won the first important Union victory. He was a hero. He had kept Missouri in the Union, but it remained torn by dissension and was beset by brutal raiders on both sides.

The next series of events that shook St. Louis came on July 25, 1861, with the arrival of the always ambitious and cocky John C. Fremont as commander of the Western Department, which in large part meant Missouri. He was as usual accompanied by his even more ambitious wife Jessie. They had delayed their departure for St. Louis for three weeks while remaining ensconced in the Astor Hotel in New York while the general ordered arms and invited old friends to join him in the West. Both Lincoln and Frank Blair, who at the time was a Fremont supporter, were impatient because securing Missouri was a major part of the president's strategy—he did not want the state or Kentucky to slip into the Confederacy.

The Fremonts finally moved into a St. Louis mansion with enough room to house not only the Fremonts but also his large staff, which soon grew even bigger and required the requisition of neighboring houses. The staff was made up largely of old friends, including Hungarian and Italian officers with strange names, fancy uniforms, and unclear designations, such as military registrar and expeditor. Whatever their military prowess in Europe had been, they did not understand Missouri and were derided by the citizens of St. Louis. Fremont set up a series of security barriers to prevent both St. Louis leaders and Missouri farmers from seeing him. During the first evening in St. Louis, Jessie sent a letter to Postmaster General Montgomery Blair demanding funds, troops, and arms. She added, "It is also my own to say that I don't like this neglect," to which Fremont added, "Money + Arms without delay + by the quickest Conveyance."[297]

Lyon, now under the command of Fremont, had earlier occupied Springfield in the southwestern part of the state with his 5,500 troops, but General Price was determined to reclaim his reputation.[298] His 8,000 ill-equipped Missourians had been reinforced with 5,000 Confederate troops under the command of the experienced General Ben McCulloch. Fremont refused to reinforce Lyons; the ninety-day enlistment of half his troops was about to expire. However, rather than retreating, he decided to attack Price and his allies. He probably would have succeeded by using his unorthodox tactics had it not been for his death in the battle and the mistaken identity of Southern troops by one of Lyon's commanders, who thought because of their gray uniforms they were Iowans and let them approach. They then wiped out a significant portion of Lyon's forces. What could have been another Northern victory became a Southern triumph shortly after the success at Manassas (Bull Run). Both sides suffered over 1,300 casualties at what is known as the Battle of Wilson Creek. Price continued north to occupy Lexington east of Kansas City.

Fremont in a period of two months lost half of the state. Confederate guerrillas increased their activities, unrest in St. Louis grew, and former supporters, including the Blairs, turned against him. They initiated the steps necessary for his removal. Throughout this period, Fremont had worked on elaborate plans to raise a large army and navy and sweep down the Mississippi. He also requested the resources to ring St. Louis with fortifications.

Finally, on August 13 with no authority, he issued a remarkable proclamation through which he took over all "the administrative powers of the state," specifically:

- Declared martial law;
- Ordered the execution of guerillas caught behind Union lines; and
- Confiscated all of the property and freed the slaves of all Confederate activists in the state.

Lincoln immediately ordered Fremont to withdraw the proclamation, understanding that Union soldiers would be shot in retaliation and that Kentucky could well be lost because of the abolition of slavery. Fremont refused to do so unless it were done in a way to create a public confrontation with the president. He sent Jessie to Washington to meet with Lincoln and expound on her husband's superior wisdom and prestige. The next day, Lincoln publicly demanded the withdrawal of Fremont's decrees. Fremont, in a final effort to restore his reputation, gathered an army of 38,000 to drive Price from Lexington. Price, however, by that time had lost half his troops and had already retreated to the southwest. Fremont was not with the Union troops that reoccupied the state with no opposition.

Two investigations of Fremont, one by Montgomery Blair and the other by the secretary of war, confirmed both his incompetence and his arrogance. They also discovered rampant corruption, including $4.5 million of unpaid bills. The fortification of St. Louis was stopped. Lincoln formally removed Fremont, who was trying to proclaim a victory over Southern troops who did not exist. He had been in command of the West for one hundred days. He would not give up. He organized a splinter party in 1864 to oppose Lincoln but then withdrew—another failure.

In November, Lincoln appointed General Harry W. Halleck to replace Fremont. The general found an army administration in shambles and surrounded by defiant citizens in St. Louis.

Missouri Governor Gamble and other leading citizens attempted to work toward a mutually satisfactory solution to the growing north-south rift, but Halleck, who was drinking heavily, would have none of it. In December, he issued orders that led to the confiscation of the homes and property of suspected Southern sympathizers in St. Louis, the censorship of their mail, and levying of random assessments.

Wm. Carr Lane reached the age of seventy-two in the same month that Halleck issued the decrees, which would plague Lane during the remaining months of his life. A month later, the conflict that had engulfed Missouri would for a short period overwhelm the New Mexico Territory. Lane was not affected by that conflict, but he had developed strong feelings about the territory and was not pleased with the Union victory.

Confederate General Sibley set out in January 1862 at the head of 2,300 Texans with the goal of moving up the Rio Grande to capture Santa Fe and Albuquerque, move on to Fort Union northeast of Santa Fe, and ultimately go to Colorado to cut off the supply of gold to the Union. He moved rapidly with considerable success, defeating New Mexico volunteers at Fort Craig about one hundred miles south of Albuquerque in late February and then occupying Albuquerque and Santa Fe in March. The Confederate flag flew over the Palace of the Governors that had been occupied previously by Spanish, Indians, Mexicans, Americans, and now Confederates.

Colorado Governor William Gilpin had learned of the defeat at Fort Craig and immediately dispatched Colorado volunteers under Major Chivington to Fort Union with the intent of recapturing Santa Fe. The volunteers included 210 cavalry and 180 infantry. They first encountered the Texans on March 27 at Apache Canyon twenty miles east of Santa Fe, the same easily defended location from which Mexican Governor Armijo had fled sixteen years earlier. The battle continued over a period of three days. The Texans were finally forced to flee south after Chivington with 400 men climbed out of the canyon, bypassed the Southern troops, and destroyed their supplies in the rear, killing 1,100 mules, burning 64 wagons, and leaving nothing to support the Texans. Casualties were high: up to 250 were killed, about two-thirds of them Texans. Sibley retreated all the way to El Paso, and the American flag again flew over the Palace of the Governors.

SEVENTEEN MONTHS

General Halleck issued orders twelve months before Lane's death that shook the city and put Lane under enormous pressure. One of the most severe orders was the levy on suspected Southern sympathizers. Another simply said that women displaying the Confederate flag or expressing sympathy for the South could be arrested. No proof was required.

A direct personal blow had occurred five months earlier as Lane contemplated the departure of Sarah, her husband, and their five older children for Wiesbaden, Germany. He had then written the first entry of what he termed a diary. He must have suspected that he would never again see his younger daughter and five oldest grandchildren. Sarah did not return until after his death. She was still crippled.

He wrote on July 21, 1861, "I now commence a Diary of Family affairs, which will be so exceedingly minute, that it will prove a bane, if not a nuisance, to all, save only the <u>Mother</u> of the little ones, - of whom I will speak. To <u>her</u>, no incident will be uninteresting, - no narration tedious, for a Mother's love is as strong as Iron, + as enduring as life." He did not entitle anything in the future as a "diary" but did write many letters with details of family life to Sarah and Wm. Glasgow. Anne also wrote to her sister.

A few months later, the party of seven departed for Germany. The seven-year-old twins, Allan and Frank, and Sarah,[AN-12] then three, along with their nursemaid, moved from the Glasgow home on the edge of the city to the Lane's house, which was not large and already housed Lane, Mary, Anne, and assorted servants.

Sarah must have been similarly distraught at the separation, for she had already lost two children, one at the age of two and the other at six. In 1866 after the family had returned to St. Louis, Victor Carr died at the age of sixteen, a year older than Victor Carr Lane (Ralph) had been when he died in 1846. William Glasgow Jr. was as devastated by his loss as his father-in-law had been twenty years earlier.

Despite what Lane had written in the July 21 "Diary," his letters were not confined to the activities of his three grandchildren. He was focused on the war and the reports of battles and arrival of wounded in St. Louis. In April he wrote, "This Civil War is a painful theme, which thrusts itself before us, at every turn; but I adhere to the opinion which I heretofore expressed that it will end by the 1st June. This conviction is however by no means universal, for the Northern people insist upon an unconditional surrender, or the overthrow of the south, neither of which is within the range of probability or even possibility. The Daily cost of the War to Lincoln's admin. is quoted at 5 millions of Dolls, + yet there are more defeats than victories. Another army of 100,000 men is needed to keep down secession in this State - + an army required to retake New Mexico."

He thought the North would be unable to fill the "deficiencies in the ranks of the army." "I hope and pray for peace + if the details of the peace should not be perfectly satisfactory, then details may be afterwards amended satisfactorily."

At the end of September as the war continued past his predicted June 1 ending, he wrote, "The Confederate states cannot be subdued by a long continuance of the war – most completely they are slave states + I can see no hope of terminating the war but in European interference in some measure. In point of fact, this is necessary to save the North from utter ruin, as well as the south. Christendom ought to make immediate interference or close their churches and admit that Christianity is a myth + all preaching is hollow hypocrisy. If Christendom would with one voice – command peace, the war would end without any other interference … I therefore say – let the good offices of Foreign interference come + come quickly."

He was tormented and had to be aware of prisoners and wounded soldiers pouring into St. Louis. St. Louis women organized to care for the wounded, gathering supplies, enlisting nurses, and opening fifteen hospitals. By May of 1862, over nineteen thousand patients had been treated. The first Confederate prisoners arrived in St. Louis in December 1861. The prison population grew to over 600 housed in miserable conditions. Local citizens were forbidden to bring prisoners food or clothing because of a justifiable fear that they would assist in escapes.[299]

Lane's hopes and recommendations were clearly unrealistic and grew out of some combination of horror of the toll the war was taking and his unwavering belief in the rectitude of the South's position. While he had been active during the seven years since his return to St. Louis, he had held no elected or appointed offices and thus had no direct means of affecting policy locally or nationally— and he was seventy-two. By the time he wrote his plan for the intervention of Christianity in September, his health had started to fail. The plea, however, did reflect his beliefs about Christianity, which he had expressed decades earlier. The overarching effect on his life, however, was the constant and severe punishment of Southern sympathizers in St. Louis.

He wrote the Reverend William Greenleaf Eliot in February criticizing his actions as an influential opponent of slavery. Eliot had founded the Unitarian Church of the Messiah and Washington University. More importantly, he was a close and influential friend of William Glasgow Jr., and Lane believed him responsible for Glasgow's support of the North.

"Rev'd Mr Eliot, D. Sir.: I claim for myself Pure + patriotic motives in all my political acts + will not presume to deny to others + equally to yourself like good motives, but we all must be judged by our acts, + I am not aware that any Christian can offer a sufficient excuse for advising a Civil War of ten years duration. Again you are supposed to have had the favors if not to be intimate with each of the commanding generals of this dept. Now have you availed yourself of your position to save individuals from imprisonment + Banishment + from Robbery. Have you counseled the making of Peace. Every days continuance of the war will make matters Worse + worse until finally the tables will be turned upon the North with terrible retribution."

Lane's predictions of the length of the war varied, but he was steadfast in his appeal to a Christianity that would support slavery. Despite his scorn of Glasgow's position on the war, he continued to hold him in high regard and depend on him to manage his business affairs, particularly his real estate. Anne, however, did not forgive Glasgow until she saw his devastation at the death of Victor Carr.

The punishment of Southern sympathizers based on Halleck's edicts was administered in many ways. One was the censorship of mail. Anne in one of her letters to Sarah said, "Make of that what you will, Mr Censor." Far more serious was the assessment of penalties and seizure of property if the fines were not paid. The most drastic was banishment from the city, which sometimes included imprisonment. The forced housing of refugees posed an additional threat.

Lane immediately began his tirades against the military rulers. He wrote on January 15, "The Civil War is our only trouble. A nomadic population gypsy-like in habits – have come amongst us since the commencement of cold weather. These creatures pretend to have been torn from their Homes + Substance + come here to be taken care of – At first our humane + law abiding Mil. Rulers proposed to billet these miserables on our citizens, but have now determined to quarter them in St. Louis + support them out of a contribution, which has been + will continue to be levied on such of our citizens male + female who may be spotted by the secret police + new night court of inquiry, as persons who have sympathies with secession – Assessments of sums varying from 1 to 500$ have been levied by Genl. Haleck, by means of his provost Marshallship + Provost – Marshall Genl. Farrar, assisted tis said by a council of B.R. Knaves – God forgive me, but the truth will out in spite of prudence."

"Assessments have been levied upon Messrs. Benoist - $4000. H. L. Patterson – Alex. Keyser – Col. Grimsley Dorsheimen – Funkhouser – McLaran – January each $3000 – Mrs. Site I believe $100. Mrs. Schaumburg + Mrs. Wills each $500. Dr Engleman told me yesterday that Arch. Bp. Kenrick had been assessed $1000, but Mr. North denied the truth of the allegation to-day."

"I am + always have been a legal citizen – but over my sympathies I never pretend to exercise control, + as I am Southern by lineage my leaning is to the Southern side in spite of myself." The last sentence might indicate some level of doubt, but no similar expression appeared elsewhere, and not too much can be read into this single statement.

A month later he reported, "Last week Mr. Sam'l Engler – a peaceable and law abiding citizen of St. L who is a manufacturer of Star Candles – was ordered to pay a large sum of money, by the Secret Tribunal of which that unscrupulous shallow Pate Barney Farrar is the executive officer. Mr. E declined to pay the 'assessment,' as it is called – his property was seized by Farrar + upon his serving out a write of Replevin from Judge Rebar's Court, he was imprisoned for contempt of the Abolition Court + banished from the State – some say to Cin'ti – but nobody knows, certainly to what point – so we go + I hope Mr. G. suffers no disquietude, as I am sure his everlasting busy + medling friend Mr. Eliot does not."

He apparently could not resist making stabs at the Reverend Eliot nor at the entire US government. "And so the <u>law</u> as declared by Lincoln's Cabinet, in which a crude notion of military 'necessity' + 'expediency' of some upstart Jackass, with a sword at his side + a file of mercenary soldiers at his heels; all our rights of persons and property have vanished + we are subjected to the hard necessity of seeking the protection of some better Govt. is a signal failure - + the question will be, where can we go for greater security – But go somewhere is positive duty – and absolute necessity."

He continued expressing his anger until September. "The Higher law doctrines have prostrated every safeguard and left us at the mercy of a Briefless Brat of a yankee lawyer, a stupid, ignorant Missourian + their unscrupulous German hirelings." Anne also wrote to her sister during this period, citing similar horrors and views. There is no way of knowing if any of the targeted citizens were in fact engaged in subversive activities.

Lane apparently was assessed, but there is no record of the date or amount. He was listed on page 95 of *A List of Disloyal and Disenfranchised Persons in St. Louis County* (compiled from Official Documents, St. Louis, 1866) as "No. 4516, Lane, William Carr, assessed. Secessionist, city."[300]

It is rather surprising that Lane did not suffer more severe penalties because of his strident views and personal attacks. He almost asked for such action by using his exact address in letters to the family and highlighting it, presumably for the benefit of the censor. He did spend some time at Bienvenue, the family farm north of the city, in the summer, probably at the urging of his family. It seems quite possible that the prominence of the Glasgow family and their close friend the Reverend Eliot shielded him.

Lane, as he had promised in his July 1861 "Diary," did write to Sarah in great detail about the well-being, activities, education, and deportment of the three younger children. He also offered advice concerning the five older ones in Germany. His opinions on the subject of education were as strong as ever, but he did not venture into religion.

The first sign of health problems appeared in January 1862. He wrote Sarah on January 15 that he had suffered an attack of an ill-defined illness with the advent of cold weather. It came late this year, but "Engleman and Hodgin took me in hand without any delay – my ankles were ornamented with mustard – my chest with a Blister, + my Temples with scarification + cups – the everlasting cathartic was also admin'd - + here I am now, sitting by the Stove, eating everything before me + more too." The treatments don't provide much evidence of the nature of the illness, but he survived it and the cures. Early in February he reported further progress. "My own Health is reestablished, with a good appetite, but my strength is not completely restored."

By mid-April he wrote to Glasgow that, "My own health is entirely restored – my wt being 220# - 10½# more than I have ever reached before. In fact, Mrs. L. has forbidden me any drink but a simple glass of wine + cup of Tea - + has restricted my diet, to prevent further increase in flesh."

The combination of the war and overwhelming threat of assessment finally wore him down. While it is not known how much was levied, he fretted that it might be as much as $500,000. In July they took him to Bienvenue to be somewhat removed, but he kept writing. The country must have provided some distraction, for he wrote, "A Mocking Bird + a cat-bird have each a nest in the Garden, + perhaps have hatched their eggs by this time." "The Whip-poor-will is also there + repeats his melancholy note nearly the entire night, from his perch near our sleeping rooms. During the day the Partridge is constantly calling out 'Bob White.' Years ago the great owl used to Hoot around the house + occasionally carry off a poor chicken. Now Mr. Owl has retired into the depths of the Forest, where he prefers all his time, to the great relief of the Poultry."

He was back in the city by mid-September, and he wrote Glasgow a long letter discussing thousands of dollars of real estate dealings. He continued to visit a few old patients. The family had hoped that he could travel to Wiesbaden in January with Glasgow, to get relief from the daily torment. In August he had been required to present himself in person to obtain an exemption from the draft. It became apparent, however, that he did not have the strength to travel.

It is not clear when his final illness set in or if it were anything more specific than the effects of old age -- he was seventy-two. The final decline seems to have started in December. After his death, Anne wrote Sarah saying she had for several weeks given him sips of brandy. He had the strength to proclaim when told that various doctors were consulting about his condition, "that a consultation always make a mess." His condition continued to worsen after New Year's, and he died on January 6. He was able on the same day to understand the birthday greetings that had been sent from Germany.

Anne wrote, "Well he is at rest now – the brain that was always thinking for the benefit of someone, the heart that asked for the distresses of all is still and we must bear our loss as we can. His life was as he always wished not prolonged after his usefulness was diminished." "How often he said he would rather wear out than rust out."

EPILOGUE

Wm. Carr Lane led a long, adventurous, and productive life that encompassed a tumultuous period in American history. He was born in the eighteenth century. His beliefs of governance and the structure of society reflected those of that century and of the founding fathers. He revered George Washington. Lane did not describe at any length any other president who held office after George Washington, except for Andrew Jackson, whom he came to detest. That feeling had less to do with what he must have considered Jackson's undignified behavior than with the change from a well-ordered society governed by educated, intelligent, White men to one of populism and political parties. He criticized Jackson's successors for incompetence and finally railed against Abraham Lincoln for destroying the country.

He was a man of unquestioned curiosity, restlessness, intelligence, courage, integrity, fortitude, and independence, but could be both stubborn and impetuous. His broad formal education and basic character traits often combined to place him in a position of leadership, whether as a militiaman in the War of 1812 or as a US Territorial Governor forty years later. He was not without personal ambition, but it was rarely directed at a single goal. The fox-hedgehog comparison is apt.

His basic characteristics kept him on the American frontier as it moved west, first to the Midwest and then to the Southwest. It put him in situations that required personal courage, whether on lone travels from Fort Belle Fontaine, Missouri, to distant outposts or to meetings with the Apache in the Mimbres Mountains of New Mexico. Of greater importance, his character and intelligence led him to positions of responsibility in Missouri and New Mexico that had a major influence on the organization of governments in a new state and a new territory.

His extensive writings revealed the strength of his positions related to religion, politics, governance, and education. They also showed him to be a keen observer of the environment of the areas through which he traveled and of the people who inhabited them. He was always fascinated by new experiences and respected as a physician, though the extent of his business enterprises is not clear. He reported much about his real estate transactions but certainly not everything. His large powder mill enterprise ended in disaster and there were references to a business in Ohio and even a hacienda in Cuba, but much remains a mystery.

He was reportedly a large, gregarious, and kind man, but one with a violent temper. One can only speculate on the clothes he wore, but he probably was attired in a coat and tie even as he crossed the Santa Fe Trail and traveled in New Mexico. He often commented on attractive women, but certainly no kind of dalliance was ever reported—it wouldn't have been.

His marriage to Mary was the most inexplicable aspect of his life but led to the revelations of his thoughts and character in his hundreds of letters to her. There can be little question that her personal traits were almost the opposite of his and that she could be extremely unpleasant and difficult to live with. Her lack of education and interest in his many activities were almost certainly the result of a woman's role in the nineteenth century, not of individual deprivation. However, her months-long stays in the Ewing home outside Vincennes could not have been typical. They could perhaps be explained by that house's greater comfort than her husband's various homes in St. Louis, but that would not account for her failure to return for her daughter's wedding. Yet, the continued written professions of devotion were certainly sincere, even though he regularly broke his repeated promises to stay home.

There can be no doubt that he was devoted to his children—the death of Ralph almost destroyed him. He sparred at times with the unmarried Anne, who was like him in many ways. He obviously cared enormously about Sarah and her children, his relationship with William Glasgow Jr. was more complex. Lane was repulsed by Glasgow's Union sympathies but at the same time held him in high regard and relied on him for business advice.

The views he formed early in his life never changed. One can consider that as steadfastness, inflexibility, or inability to acknowledge cultural and political change, particularly with regard to his failure to deal with the fundamental cruelty of slavery. He also on at least two occasions proposed policies which, while visionary in a sense, could not possibly have been put into practice. The first was expressed to the Missouri legislature with the description of separate White, Black, and Indian societies and the second during the Civil War with his belief that Christian European churches, presumably Protestant, should intervene to end the conflict.

Slavery was a central factor throughout his life, first simply as an accepted part of society and in the end as the cause of him being labeled an untrustworthy person after he had devoted his lifetime to loyal public service. That designation was crushing. The devastation was compounded by Sarah's crippling disease, which resulted in her departure for Germany with his five oldest grandchildren. He would never see them again. His life ended in tragedy, though he "never rusted out."

Author's Notes

#1

The St. Louis in which I grew up in the 1930s and early 1940s still reflected the attitudes relating to Blacks that existed prior to the Civil War. Everything was segregated, except for public transportation. Black servants were common. My father was a professor at Washington University, but we had a cook who prepared all meals, except Thursday and Sunday evening dinners; a laundress three days a week boiling and ironing clothes in the basement; a cleaning woman one day a week; and a yardman who came every morning, except Sunday. We actually lived in University City beyond the city limits. Most Blacks lived in a depressed area known as Mill Creek Valley, west of downtown St. Louis.

My grandmother, Wm. Carr Lane's granddaughter, lived with my family, but she died before I was born and her husband four years later. The old attitudes, however, continued, combining personal consideration and kindness with natural separation. I remember my father expressing disdain because Charles, the yardman, lived in a condemned house. For some reason, I was offended at the time. My parents, who always had season tickets to the St. Louis Symphony, debated a long time whether they could continue to go when Blacks were admitted in the 1960s. To their credit, they did. Also, my father accepted being taken care of by Black men for the last ten years of his life when he was confined to a wheelchair. I'm not sure what triggered my early unease with many of the racial remarks I heard growing up in a White society. But soon after my wife and I moved to Chicago in 1960, I became a member of the board of the Community Renewal Society, which fought the racism prevalent in Chicago, and continued for seventeen years.

Note:

Mill Creek Valley became the focus of major redevelopment projects in the 1950s – 454 acres were cleared; 1,772 families and 610 individuals were displaced.

#2

Anne Ewing Lane was eighty-five when she died in 1904. My father, William G. B. Carson, was then thirteen and had often visited "Auntie Lane." He remembered that during her final years "she was enthroned … on a prosaic chair by a second-story bay window … from which point of vantage she could survey the coming-ins and going-outs of her various relatives and friends who then inhabited the neighborhood The house had an elevator to take her to the ground floor for meals.

Wm. Carr Lane attempted without success in the mid-1830s to drop the "e" from "Anne" because he thought having two of them adjacent in the name was confusing. There was also some thought of changing "Sarah" to "Louise" or "Sidney."

Note:

Carson, William Glasgow Bruce, *Anne Ewing Lane*, *The Bulletin of the Missouri Historical Society*, St. Louis, January 1965, p. 87.

#3

The property, somewhat reduced by condemnation proceedings to build waterworks, roads, and parks, remained in the Glasgow family until after World War II, when it was sold to a California developer and named Glasgow Village. The Lane name was lost as the streets were given Scottish names. It had a population of 5,500 in 2010. My father fondly remembered going to the farm, Bienvenue, as a boy. There was a scattering of houses but nothing very elaborate. There were, of course, hayrides and other ventures. I remember in the 1930s being driven up there and thinking it all pretty dull. Whatever accommodations had existed had by that time either collapsed or burned.

It is perhaps ironic that no Lane or Glasgow descendent had any interest in retaining the farm. In stark contrast, the Ewing farm north of Vincennes has remained in the family and is currently occupied by sixth-generation direct descendants, who have donated a conservation easement on the acres to assure the land remains agricultural. The property now includes the much-enlarged main house, Mont Clair, and historic farm buildings. The Ewings manage the soil, water, orchards, and woodlands in accordance with the highest level of conservation practices. In 2010 they were honored with the John Arnold Award for Rural Preservation presented by the Indiana Landmarks and Indiana Farm Bureau.

#4

As I was growing up, it was a wry family grievance that William Glasgow Jr. had sold the winery. The purchaser had started selling Cooks Imperial Champagne, which was still popular one hundred years later. I don't know how many owners it has gone through since Cook bought it from Glasgow, but it is now produced in California and promoted on the Internet with the same name.

#5

These institutions remain in various forms today. The Mission Free School continued as an orphanage with approximately thirty children until 1959, when it became the Division of Child Psychiatry of the Washington University Medical School. It continues as a division in the school. My mother, Elisabeth Chapin Carson, was a member of the board for many years.

My father, William G. B. Carson, attended Smith Academy, graduating a few years ahead of the poet T. S. Eliot. It later changed to St. Louis Country Day School, from which I graduated in 1946. My wife, Georgia Sims Carson, was teaching at Mary Institute when we were married in 1956. The two schools have merged to become MICDS.

#6

One of Sarah's children and Wm. Carr Lane's granddaughters, Susan Glasgow, was born in 1851 and married a prominent St. Louis physician, Norman Bruce Carson, in 1888. Three years later, their only child and my father, William Glasgow Bruce Carson, was born. Dr. Carson had come to St. Louis as a child, graduated from St. Louis Medical College in 1868, and then studied in Vienna for two years. He died in 1931 at the age of eighty-seven. Though he and his wife lived with my parents, I was in my third year when he died. She had died in June 1928, six months before I was born. My only memory of him is seeing him in bed tended by a nurse. My late older brother was also named Norman Bruce Carson, but not Junior or the Second—I never knew why.

#7

It is unlikely that the farm north of St. Louis was included in this sale, for it remained intact. It would probably be impossible to trace the ultimate disposition of all the property that was sold because of the many families involved. William and Sarah built a large house, Glasgow Place, in the city and later enlarged it and developed the surrounding property. It was sold in the 1890s to Barnes Hospital. However, the hospital decided to build further west on Kings Highway. Various family members then rented it from time to time until it was torn down in 1915 and the Wm. Glasgow Jr. school built on the site. It was renamed "Dunbar" when it was designated a Black school within the segregated St. Louis school system. There is some irony in this because Glasgow was the one member of the family to support the Union during the Civil War.

#8

Although the New Mexico of the twenty-first century has atomic labs, millionaires with second and third homes, and all the trappings of modern life, it still is the only state that includes "USA" on most of its automotive license plates. Natives delight in stories such as the Atlanta Olympics official demanding to see the visa of a New Mexico official. In 2010 a little over 2 million people, roughly 790,000 in three metropolitan areas, were spread over 121,000 square miles. Almost half the population was Hispanic and 10 percent Native American. Seventeen pueblos continue to function as active communities, while the Apache and Navajo occupy large reservations. Though the violence ceased long ago, the Pueblo and other Indians are still taking steps to shed the Spanish influence. The modern names of pueblos were bestowed by the Spanish. However, in recent years many pueblos have taken the original names; for instance, "San Juan" is now "Okay Owingeh."

#9

A most uninspiring portrait of General Kearny now hangs in the New Mexico History Museum, which includes the Palace of the Governors. There is little wonder that it is inauspicious, for it is a bad copy painted by a picture framer of the original inferior portrait. The original was the property of Mrs. Western Bascum, Nellie, a daughter of the general. She was a good friend of my father's family in St. Louis. In 1903, former New Mexico Governor Bradford Prince requested that she give her portrait to the Historical Society of New Mexico. She was not about to give it up but then remembered the terrible copy that the frame maker had made on his own while cleaning the original. She quickly retrieved it and, along with my grandmother, Wm. Carr Lane's granddaughter, and my father, took the train to Santa Fe for the grand presentation on August 13, 1903. y father was twelve. The former governor made an eloquent speech, proclaiming it was the only existing portrait of the general. The original is now owned by the Missouri History Museum. Nellie Kearny reportedly had a great sense of humor and must have been amused by the proceedings.

#10

The cultural differences persist, though appearing in different ways. Santa Fe, for example, is now roughly half Hispanic and half Anglo. While English is the common language, roughly 40 percent of the students in the Santa Fe public schools are English language learners. There is generally little social interaction between the groups, particularly with Anglos who have arrived in the city in the last thirty years. The renowned museums and musical organizations, such as the Santa Fe Opera, were founded many years ago by Anglos and are still largely managed by them. The prevalent poverty is generally among the Hispanic population; 70 percent of the public school students come from backgrounds of poverty and are predominantly Hispanic. Despite these differences, the different cultures live in harmony.

#11

One of the children traveling to Wiesbaden was my grandmother, Susan Glasgow Carson. She was ten when the family left for Germany and in died in June 1928, six months before my birth. She was seventy-seven. My grandfather, Norman Bruce Carson, died in August 1931 at the age of eighty-six. Lane addressed Susan as "Suszy" in his letters.

#12

The three-year-old Sarah was my great-aunt, whom we called "Aunt Sarah." It was in her attic that the boxes of letters that had been retained by the Glasgow family were found at the time of her death in 1938 at the age of eighty. I don't know when she broke her hip, but with the state of medicine at that time, she was confined to a wheelchair the rest of her life. That is how I remember her. She had been a widow since 1914. Her husband, Newton Wilson, had been an enormously successful entrepreneur, first managing smelters in Mexico and then establishing the Industrial Lumber Company in central Louisiana. At one time it encompassed 200,000 acres, sawmills, a paper mill, and a company town, Elizabeth. Aunt Sarah was, as a result, extremely wealthy and contributed generously to Washington University and Mary Institute.

Acknowledgments

As always, the most important person to thank is my wife of fifty-eight years, Georgia, for listening and providing encouragement for many years as she watched me disappear into my office. Our daughters Chapin and Laura and son-in-law John have provided similar support from a distance. All have offered valuable suggestions.

None of this could have occurred without Kay Carlson, who somehow for years has managed to turn my scrawl into well-ordered typed pages while inserting witty and valuable comments. Marilyn Helmholtz has found important documents in both St. Louis and Chicago that have added important facts and color. Without Don Lamm's encouragement and important advice, I would probably have abandoned this project years ago. Rick Hendricks, the New Mexico State Historian, has made important observations and suggestions related to the New Mexico chapters. Bill Stewart has been particularly helpful in reading the final manuscript and making the suggestions of an experienced historian, writer, and good friend. Joyce Idema, another close friend, made valuable suggestions concerning the early chapters.

My father, William Glasgow Bruce Carson (1891–1976), made the book possible by salvaging Wm. Carr Lane's letters and in later years publishing many of them, accompanied by family trees and stories. It must be noted that the late Charles van Ravenswaay, director of the Missouri Historical Society and co-conspirator with my father in finally obtaining the letters, was particularly important. His comprehensive book, *Saint Louis, An Informal History of the City and Its People, 1764–1865*, has been invaluable. The Missouri History Museum is the repository of the personal material and other archives related to Lane, and its staff has been unfailing in responding to questions. Certainly, I retain responsibility for any errors in the text.

The personnel in the following organizations have been extremely helpful, even when working in an atmosphere of reduced staff and budget pressures.

- Archives & Special Collections, AC Long Health Sciences Library, Columbia University Medical Center, New York
- Coyle Fred Library, Chambersburg, Pennsylvania
- Filson Historical Society, Louisville, Kentucky
- Kenneth W. McClintock, Council Grove, Kansas
- Missouri History Museum, St. Louis, Missouri
- New Mexico History Museum and Palace of the Governors
- New Mexico State Library
- New Mexico State Records Center and Archives
- Prothonotary, Fayette County Courthouse, Uniontown, Pennsylvania.
- St. Louis Public Library
- Silver City Museum, Silver City, New Mexico
- U. Grant Miller Library, Washington & Jefferson College, Washington, Pennsylvania
- University of Pennsylvania Archives, Philadelphia, Pennsylvania
- Vincennes State Historic Sites, Richard Bay, Indiana
- Waidner-Spahr Library, Archives and Special Collections, Dickinson College, Carlisle, Pennsylvania

NOTES

PROLOGUE

1   Lane, William Carr. Diary, edited by Wm. G. B. Carson, *New Mexico Historical Review*, Vol. XXXIX, no. 4, October 1964.

2   Twitchell, Ralph E. *Historical Sketch of Governor William Carr Lane,* . Historical Society of New Mexico, November 1, 1917.

3   The spelling of the name of the fort can be found in historical accounts as both 'Fort Bellefontaine' and 'Fort Belle Fontaine.' The latter has been used throughout this book, because it is currently used in the history of the park at the site of the fort near St. Louis.

4   Darby, John F. *Personal Recollections.* New York: Arno Press, 1975, 350.

5   Wade, Richard C. *The Urban Frontier.* Chicago: The University of Chicago Press, 1959, 277.

6   Horn, Calvin. *New Mexico's Troubled Years.* Albuquerque, NM: Horn & Wallace, 1967, 49.

7   The frequent quotations from his letters and journals are taken directly from his writing and reflect his own often unique and peculiar spelling and grammar.

8   Wood, Gordon S. *Empire of Liberty.* New York: Oxford University Press, 2009, 315–31.

9   Wood, Gordon S. *The Idea of America.* New York: Penguin Press, 2011, 14.

10   Volcker, Paul. "What the New President Should Consider." *The New York Review of Books*, December 6, 2012.

Part I

11   Ellis, Franklin. *History of Fayette County Pennsylvania.* Philadelphia, PA: L. H. Everts & Co., 1882, 67.

12   Quackenbush, Nancy. *Some Northern Neck Lanes.* 1987. The details of the Lane family are contained in this comprehensive genealogy.

13   Ellis, Franklin. *History of Fayette County Pennsylvania,* Philadelphia, PA: L. H. Everts & Co., 1882, 486.

14   *Ibid.,* 488

15   Quackenbush, Nancy. "Appraisement of Pressley Carr Lane's estate recorded January 21, 1822, Shelby County, Kentucky." *Some Northern Neck Lanes,* Will Book 5, 251.

16   Lane, Wm. Carr. Letter to Mary Lane in Philadelphia. June 25, 1852.

17   Lane, Wm. Carr. Letter to Mary Lane in Washington City. July 3, 1852.

18   *Ibid.*

19   *Ibid.*

20   *Ibid.*

21   *Ibid.*

22   Lane, Wm. Carr. Letter to Mary Lane in St. Louis. July 17, 1853.

23   Lane, Wm. Carr. Letter to Anne Lane in St. Louis. June 12, 1853.

24   *Ibid.*

25   *Ibid.*

26   *Ibid.*

27   *Ibid.*

28   *Ibid.*

29   Lender, Mark Edward, and James Kirby Martin. *Drinking in America.* New York: The Free Press, 1982, 2.

30   *Ibid.,* 205–206.

31   Wooster, Robert. *The American Military Frontiers, The United States Army in the West, 1783, 1900.* Albuquerque, NM: University of New Mexico Press, 2009, 68.

32   *Ibid.,* 102

33   Lender, Mark Edward, and James Kirby Martin. *Drinking in America.* New York: The Free Press, 1982, 36.

34   Wood, Gordon S. *Empire of Liberty.* New York: Oxford University Press, 2009, 395.

35 Roosevelt, Theodore. *Life of Thomas Hart Benton.* Boston and New York: Houghton Mifflin, 1887, 57.

36 *Ibid.,* 395.

37 Earlier descriptions of Wm. Carr Lane's life have referred in error to Jefferson College in Chambersburg.

38 Smith, Joseph. *History of Jefferson College.* Pittsburgh, PA: J. T. Shryuck.

39 Rush, Benjamin. *A Plan of Education for Dickinson College.* 1785.

40 *Ibid.*

41 Steele, Volney. *Bleed, Blister, and Purge.* Missoula, MT: Mountain Press Publishing Company, 2005.

42 Mettler, Cecelia O. *History of Medicine.* Birmingham: AL: The Classics of Medicine Library, 1986.

43 *Ibid.*

44 *Ibid.*

45 Wood, Gordon S. *Empire of Liberty.* New York: Oxford University Press, 2009, 726.

46 Gillett, Mary C. *The Army Medical Department, 1775-1818.* Honolulu, HI: University Press of the Pacific, 2002, 6–7.

47 Wood, Gordon S. *Empire of Liberty.* New York: Oxford University Press, 2009, 129–130.

48 Wooster, Robert. *The American Military Frontiers: The United States Army in the West, 1783-1800.* Albuquerque, NM: University of New Mexico Press, 2009, 16.

49 Wilentz, Sean. *The Rise of American Democracy.* New York: W. W. Norton & Co., London, 2005, 149.

50 *Ibid.,* 150.

51 University of Pennsylvania. *Catalogue.* Philadelphia, 1825.

52 *Ibid.*

53 University of the State of New York College of Physicians and Surgeons. New York, 1811.

54 University of Pennsylvania. *Catalogue.* Philadelphia, 1825.

55 Appointment by President James Madison, January 20, 1816.

56 *Ibid.*

57 Gillett, Mary C. *The Army Medical Department 1775-1810,* Honolulu, HI: University Press of the Pacific, 2002, 214.

58 Carson, William G. B. *Glimpses of the Past.* St Louis, MO: Missouri Historical Society, 1940, pp. 66-67.

59 President and Members of the Board of Physicians for the First Medical District in the State of Indiana, May 4, 1818.

60 Carson, William G. B. *Glimpses of the Past.* St. Louis, MO: Missouri Historical Society, 1940, 56.

61 *Ibid.,* 57.

62 *Ibid.,* 57.

63 *Ibid.,* 58–61.

64 *Ibid.,* 58–61.

65 *Ibid.,* 63.

66 *Ibid.,* 63.

67 *Ibid.,* 63.

68 *Ibid.,* 65.

69 *Ibid.,* 68–71.

70 *The Early Histories of St. Louis.* St. Louis, MO: St. Louis Historical Document Foundation, 1952, 71.

71 *Ibid.,* 63.

72 Van Ravenswaay, Charles. *Saint Louis: An Informal History of the City and Its People, 1764–1865.* St. Louis, MO: Missouri Historical Society Press, 1991, 33.

73 *Ibid.,* 35.

74 *Ibid.,* 44.

75 *Ibid.,* 46.

76 *Ibid.,* 63.

77 Wood, Gordon S. *Empire of Liberty.* New York: Oxford University Press, 2009, 369.

78 Wilentz, Sean. *The Rise of American Democracy.* New York: W. W. Norton, 2005, 124–129.

79 Van Ravenswaay, Charles. *St. Louis: An Informal History of the City and Its People, 1764–1865.* St. Louis, MO: Missouri Historical Society Press, 1991, 149.

80 *Ibid.,* 149.

81 Wade, Richard C. *The Urban Frontier.* Chicago: University of Chicago Press, 1959, 89.

82 *Ibid.,* 188.

83 Primm, James Neal. *Lion of the Valley.* St. Louis, MO: Missouri Historical Society Press, 1989, 135.

84 Meacham, Jon. *American Lion.* New York: Random House, 2008, 29–30.

85   *Ibid.*, 338.

86   Van Ravenswaay, Charles. *Saint Louis: An Informal History of the City and Its People, 1764–1865.* St. Louis, MO: Missouri Historical Society Press, 1991, 196.

87   *Ibid.*, 197.

88   *Ibid.*, 193–194.

89   DeVoto, Bernard. *Across the Wide Missouri,* Boston: Houghton Mifflin, 1947, 24.

90   Darby, John F. *Personal Recollections.* New York: Arno Press, 1975, 350.

91   Horn, Calvin. *New Mexico's Troubled Years.* Albuquerque, NM: Horn and Wallace, 1963, 48.

92   Denton, Sally. *Passion and Principle.* New York: Bloomsburg, 2007. The author acknowledges that "Historiography has depicted John as a glory-seeking fraud and Jessie as a manipulative and overly ambitious shrew," 379, but takes a completely opposite and almost romantic view in believing that the Fremonts were an important and positive force in American history. In contrast, another highly respected Western writer called him more of a Path-publicizer than a Pathfinder (Wineapple, Brenda. *Ecstatic Nation: Confidence, Crisis, and Compromise, 1848-1877.* New York: Harper, 2013, 86).

93   Van Ravenswaay, Charles. *Saint Louis: An Informal History of the City and its People, 1764-1865.* St. Louis, MO: Missouri Historical Society Press, 1991, 205.

94   Berlin, Isaiah. *The Hedgehog and the Fox.* London: Orion Books, 2009, 1. Attributed to the great poet Archilochus.

Part II

95   Wade, Richard C. *The Urban Frontier.* Chicago: The University of Chicago Press, 1959, 175.

96   Primm, James Neal. *Lion of the Valley.* St. Louis, MO: Missouri Historical Society Press, 1981, 119.

97   Carson, William G. B. *Glimpses of the Past.* St. Louis, MO: Missouri Historical Society, July–September 1940, 75.

98   *Ibid.*, 75.

99   *Ibid.*, 84.

100   *Ibid.*, 81.

[101] *Ibid.*, 82.

[102] Howe, Daniel Walker. *What Hath God Wrought in the Transformation of America, 1815–1848*. New York: Oxford University Press, 2007, 148.

[103] Wilentz, Sean. *The Rise of American Democracy*. New York: W.W. Norton, 2005, 223.

[104] Carson, William G. B. *Glimpses of the Past*. St. Louis, MO: Missouri Historical Society, July–September 1940, 85.

[105] *Ibid.*, 86.

[106] Van Ravenswaay, Charles. *Saint Louis: An Informal History of Its People, 1769–1865*. St. Louis, MO: Missouri Historical Society, 1991, 205.

[107] *Ibid.*

[108] Wade, Richard C. *The Urban Frontier*. Chicago: The University of Chicago Press, 1959, 109.

[109] St. Louis, Missouri Board of Alderman Minutes, April 1823–April 1830, Works Projects Administration Municipal. Municipal Reference Library, City Hall, St. Louis, 1939.

[110] Lane, Wm. Carr. Letter to Sarah. April 1836.

[111] Primm, James Neal. *Lion of the Valley*. St. Louis, MO: Missouri Historical Press, 1981, 145.

[112] Van Ravenswaay, Charles. *Saint Louis: An Informal History of the City and Its People, 1764–1865*. St. Louis, MO: Missouri Historical Society Press, 1991, 190.

[113] *Ibid.*, 434.

[114] Carson, William G. B. "Anne Ewing Lane." *Missouri Historical Society Bulletin*, St. Louis, 1965, 88.

[115] Wade, Richard C. *The Urban Frontier*. Chicago: The University of Chicago Press, 1959, 189.

[116] Van Ravenswaay, Charles. *Saint Louis: An Informal History of the City and Its People, 1764–1865*. St. Louis, MO: Missouri Historical Society Press, 1991, 219.

[117] Carson, William G. B. *Glimpses of the Past*. St. Louis, MO: Missouri Historical Society, 1940, 87.

[118] *Ibid.*, 87.

[119] *Ibid.*, 87.

[120] *Ibid.*, 88.

[121] *Ibid.*, 89.

[122] *Ibid.*, 89–90.

[123] *Ibid.*, 90.

124   Lane, Mary Ewing. Letter to Wm. Carr Lane. September 19, 1824.

125   Van Ravenswaay, Charles. *Saint Louis: An Informal History of the City and Its People, 1764–1865.* St. Louis, MO: Missouri Historical Society Press, 1991, 233.

126   *Ibid.,* 233.

127   Message by William Carr Lane, Mayor of St. Louis, Mo., April 25, 1825, St. Louis, Missouri. Board of Aldermen minutes, April 1823–April 1830. Copied from St. Louis, Missouri, Board of Aldermen minutes by Works Progress Administration, St. Louis Public Library, 1939.

128   Ewing, Nathaniel. Letter to Wm. Carr Lane. November 20, 1825.

129   Darby, John F. *Personal Recollections.* St. Louis, MO: GI Jones, 1880, 344.

130   Wood, Gordon S. *The Idea of America.* New York: The Penguin Press, 2011, 142.

131   Carson, William G. B. *Glimpses of the Past.* St. Louis, MO: Missouri Historical Society, 1940, 90.

132   *Ibid.,* 91.

133   *Ibid.,* 92.

134   *Ibid.,* 92.

135   *Ibid.,* 95.

136   Lane, Wm. Carr. Letter to Aldermen in St. Louis. June 4, 1827.

137   Lane, Mary Ewing. Letter to Wm. Carr Lane. January 1, 1827.

138   Carson, William G. B. *Glimpses of the Past.* St. Louis, MO: Missouri Historical Society, 1940, 99.

139   Lane, Mary Ewing. Letter to Wm. Carr Lane. January 1, 1827.

140   *Ibid.*

141   Carson, William G. B. *Glimpses of the Past.* St. Louis, MO: Missouri Historical Society, 1940, 96.

142   *Ibid.,* 96.

143   *Ibid.,* 99.

144   *Ibid.,* 98.

145   Howe, Daniel Walker. *What Hath God Wrought in the Transformation of America, 1815–1848.* New York: Oxford University Press, 2007, 208.

146   Carson, William G. B. *Glimpses of the Past.* St. Louis, MO: Missouri Historical Society, 1940, 100.

147   *Ibid.,* 100.

148   *Ibid.,* 100.

149   *Ibid.,* 100.

150 Gamble, Archibal. Recorder of St. Louis County, Deed of Sale of Wm. Carr Lane to Russel Farnham. June 12, 1828.

151 Darby, John F. *Personal Recollections*. St. Louis, MO: GI Jones, 1880, 189.

152 Goodwin, Doris Kearns. *Team of Rivals*. New York: Simon and Schuster, 2005.

153 Meacham, Jon. *American Lion*. New York: Random House, 2008, 289.

154 Brands, H. W. *The Money Man*. New York: W.W. Norton, 2006, 72.

155 *Ibid.*, 64.

156 Howe, Daniel Walker. *What Hath God Wrought in the Transformation of America, 1815–1848*. New York: Oxford University Press, 2007, 379.

157 *Ibid.*, 380.

158 Lane, Wm. Carr. Letter to Mary in Vincennes, St. Louis. April 25, 1832.

159 Meacham, John. *American Lion*. New York: Random House, 2008, 3–4.

160 Howe, Daniel Walker. *What Hath God Wrought in the Transformation of America, 1815–1848*. New York: Oxford University Press, 2007, 420.

161 *Ibid.*, 344.

162 *Ibid.*, 420.

163 All of the following references are from this report delivered to the House of Representatives on Thursday morning, December 21, 1830.

164 Lane, Wm. Carr. Letter dated December 7, 1835.

165 Primm, James Neal. *Lion of the Valley: St. Louis, Missouri, 1764-1980*. St. Louis, MO: Missouri Historical Society Press, 1998, 132–133.

166 *Ibid.*, 135.

167 *Ibid.*, 135.

168 *Ibid.*, 143

169 All of the quotations come from the letters of that period. Carson, William G. B. *Glimpses of the Past*. St. Louis, MO: Missouri Historical Society, 1940, 104–114.

170 Van Ravenswaay, Charles. *Saint Louis: An Informal History of the City and Its People, 1764–1865*. St. Louis, MO: Missouri Historical Society Press, 1991.

171 All of the quotations and statistics concerning the 1832 and 1833 epidemic are from Van Ravenswaay, Charles. *Saint Louis: An Informal History of the City and Its People, 1764–1865*. St. Louis, MO: Missouri Historical Society Press, 1991, 269–273.

172 *Ibid.*, 388–391. Primm, James Neal. *Lion of the Valley: St. Louis, Missouri, 1764–1980*. St. Louis, MO: Missouri Historical Society Press,

1998, 154–157. All of the quotations and statistics concerning the 1849 epidemic are from Primm.

[173]   Carson, Wm. G. B. "Secesh." *Bulletin of the Missouri Historical Society.* St. Louis, January 1967, 129.

[174]   Wilentz, Sean. *The Rise of American Democracy.* New York: W.W. North, 2005, 712.

[175]   Van Ravenswaay, Charles. *Saint Louis: An Informal History of the City and Its People, 1764–1865.* St. Louis, MO: Missouri Historical Society Press, 1991, 276–295. This work details the violence and Lovejoy death.

[176]   Howe, Daniel Walker. *What Hath God Wrought in the Transformation of America, 1815–1848.* New York: Oxford University Press, 2007, 430–434.

[177]   Carson, William G. B. *Glimpses of the Past: Letters of William Carr Lane.* St. Louis, MO: Missouri Historical Society, 1940, 101.

[178]   *Ibid.,* 102.

[179]   *Ibid.,* 102.

[180]   Lane, Wm. Carr. Letter to Anne and Sarah. September 14, 1834.

[181]   *Ibid.* Lane, Wm. Carr. Letters dated August 4, 1835, to November 14, 1837 or 1838.

[182]   Lane, Wm. Carr. Letter to Anne and Sarah. April 12, 1836.

[183]   Lane, Wm. Carr. Letter to John F. Darby, Mayor of St. Louis. November 18, 1836.

[184]   The references to dollar amounts immediately raise questions about the equivalent amount today. Perhaps not surprisingly, there is no simple answer. The Measuring Worth tool provides six ways of calculating today's value of 1836 dollars, but they provide such varying results that there is not a clear answer. Using what appears to be the most appropriate measure would put Lane's $30,000 powder mill at $688,000 in 2013 and Fred's $480 annual salary at $109,000. The former is probably a little low and the latter a little high. But regardless, he was dealing with substantial amounts of money.

[185]   Cleland, B. *A Historical Account of All the Mayors, Since the Formation of the City Government of St. Louis to the Present Date - 1846, and Some Odes.*

[186]   Darby, John F. *Personal Recollections.* New York: Arno Press, 1975, 222.

[187]   *Ibid.,* 228.

[188]   Lane, Wm. Carr. Letter to Henry Kayser. November 29, 1839.

[189]   Darby, John F. *Personal Recollections.* New York: Arno Press, 1975.

190   *St. Louis City Council Board of Alderman Journal*, April 1839–April 1840, Vol. 5, 2.

191   Van Ravenswaay, Charles. *Saint Louis: An Informal History of the City and Its People, 1764–1865*. St. Louis, MO: Missouri Historical Society Press, 1991, 314.

192   Primm, James Neal. *Lion of the Valley: St. Louis, Missouri, 1764–1980*. St. Louis, MO: Missouri Historical Society Press, 1989, 140.

193   Lane, Wm. Carr. Letter to Mary Lane. April 16 and 18, 1840.

194   Carson, Wm. G. B. *Managers in Distress: The St. Louis Stage, 1840–1844*. St. Louis, MO: St. Louis Historical Documents Foundation, 1949, 53.

195   Gardner, Mark L. *Brothers on the Santa Fe and Chihuahua Trails*. Niwot, CO: University of Colorado Press, 1993. The descriptions of the early Glasgow enterprises come largely from pp. 2–14 and personal papers of William Bruce Carson Glasgow.

196   *Ibid.*, 28.

197   *Ibid.*, 40.

198   Van Ravenswaay, Charles. *Saint Louis: An Informal History of the City and Its People, 1764–1865*. St. Louis, MO: Missouri Historical Society Press, 1991, 303-305.

199   Lane, Wm. Carr. Letter to William Glasgow Jr. July 23, 1840.

200   Howe, Daniel Walker. *What Hath God Wrought in the Transformation of America, 1815–1848*. New York: Oxford University Press, 2007, 587.

201   *Ibid.*, 572.

202   *Ibid.*, 505.

203   Wilentz, Sean. *The Rise of American Democracy, Jefferson to Lincoln*. New York: W. W. Norton, 2005, 501.

204   *Ibid.*, 507.

205   Lane, Wm. Carr. Letter to Mary. August 18, 1842.

206   Lane, Wm. Carr. Letter to Sarah. July 26, 1840.

207   Van Ravenswaay, Charles. *Saint Louis: An Informal History of the City and Its People, 1764–1865*. St. Louis, MO: Missouri Historical Society Press, 1991, 334.

208   Primm, James Neal. *Lion of the Valley: St. Louis, Missouri, 1764-1980*. St. Louis, MO: Missouri Historical Society Press, 1981, 163.

209   *Ibid.*, 164.

210   Howe, Daniel Walker. *What Hath God Wrought: The Transformation of America, 1815–1848*. New York: Oxford University Press, 2007, 688.

Part III

[211] Lane, Wm. Carr. Letter to Wm. Glasgow Jr. August 19, 1846.

[212] Lane, Wm. Carr. Letter to Mary. March 1, 1847.

[213] Lane, Wm. Carr. Letter to Anne E. Lane in St. Louis. March 6, 1847 (personal collection of author).

[214] Lane, Wm. Carr. Letter to Sarah. March 27, 1847.

[215] Lane, Wm. Carr. Letter to Mary. March 29, 1847.

[216] Lane, Wm. Carr. Letter to Wm. Glasgow Jr. December 19, 1847.

[217] Lane, Wm. Carr. Letter to Mary. July 7, 1848.

[218] Lane, Wm. Carr. Letter to Mary. July 1, 1848.

[219] Lane, Wm. Carr. Letter to Anne. January 27, 1852.

[220] DeVoto, Bernard. *The Year of Decision—1846*. Boston: Little Brown and Co., 1943, 115–116.

[221] Van Ravenswaay, Charles. *Saint Louis: An Informal History of the City and Its People, 1764–1865*. St. Louis, MO: Missouri Historical Society Press, 1991, 394.

[222] *Ibid.*, 383–385.

[223] Howe, Daniel Walker. *What Hath God Wrought in the Transformation of America, 1815–1848*. New York: Oxford University Press, 2007, 688.

[224] *Ibid.*, 2.

[225] DeVoto, Bernard. *The Year of Decision—1846*. Boston: Little Brown and Co., 1943, 5–6.

[226] *Ibid.*, 265.

[227] Wilentz, Sean. *The Rise of American Democracy, Jefferson to Lincoln*. New York: W.W. Norton, 2005, 596.

[228] *Ibid.*, 594.

[229] Howe, Daniel Walker. *What Hath God Wrought in the Transformation of America, 1815–1848*. New York: Oxford University Press, 2007, 833.

Part IV

[230] Lummis, Charles F. *The Land of Poco Tiempo*. New York: Charles Scribner, 1933, 3.

[231] Ferguson, Erna. *New Mexico: A Pageant of Three Peoples*. New York: Alfred A. Knopf, 1951, 152.

232 Twitchell, Ralph Emerson. *The Leading Facts of New Mexico History*. Volume I. Santa Fe, New Mexico: Sunstone Press, 2007[1911], 363.

233 Brooks, James F. *Captives and Cousins*. Chapel Hill, NC: University of North Carolina Press, 2002, 104.

234 *Ibid.*, Appendix E.

235 Twitchell, Ralph Emerson. *The Leading Facts of New Mexico History*. Volume II. Santa Fe, NM: Sunstone Press, 2007[1912], 133.

236 *Ibid.*, 210–211.

237 Horn, Calvin. *New Mexico's Troubled Years*. Albuquerque, NM: Horn and Wallace, 1963, 21.

238 *Ibid.*, 26.

239 *Ibid.*, 32.

240 All of the quotations in this chapter, unless otherwise noted, are from Twitchell, Ralph Emerson. *Historical Sketch of Governor William Carr Lane, Together with Diary of His Journal, from St. Louis, Mo., to Santa Fe, NM, July 31st to September 9th, 1852*. Santa Fe, NM: Historical Society of New Mexico, 1917.

241 Lane, Wm. Carr. Letter to Anne. August 2, 1852.

242 Horn, Calvin. *New Mexico's Troubled Years*. Albuquerque, NM: Horn and Wallace, 1963.

243 Lane, Wm. Carr. Letter to Mary. September 19, 1852.

244 Chavez, Fray Angélico, and Thomas E. Chavez. *Wake for a Fat Vicar*. Albuquerque, NM: LPO Press, 2004. This and other specific information comes from pp. 7–16.

245 Horgan, Paul. *Lamy of Santa Fe*. New York: Ferrar, Straus, and Giroux, 1975, 108–109.

246 Twitchell, Ralph Emerson. *Historical Sketch of Governor William Carr Lane, Together with Diary of His Journal, from St. Louis, Mo., to Santa Fe, NM, July 31st to September 9th, 1852*. Santa Fe, NM: Historical Society of New Mexico, 1917, 10–11.

247 *Ibid.*, 58.

248 *Ibid*

249 Twitchell, Ralph E. *Historical Sketch of Governor William Carr Lane, Together with Diary of His Journey from St. Louis, Mo., to Santa Fe, NM, July 31st to September 9th, 1852*. Santa Fe, NM: Historical Society of New Mexico, 1917, 19.

250 Del Castillo, Richard Griswold. *The Treaty of Guadalupe Hidalgo: A Legacy of Conflict*. Norman, OK: University of Oklahoma Press, 1990, 56–57.

251 Twitchell, Ralph E. *Historical Sketch of Governor William Carr Lane, Together with Diary of His Journal, from St. Louis, Mo., to Santa Fe, NM, July 31st to September 9th, 1852*. Santa Fe, NM: Historical Society of New Mexico, 1917, 296.

252 Horn, Calvin. *New Mexico's Troubled Years*. Albuquerque, NM: Horn and Wallace, 1963, 47.

253 Worcester, Donald E. *The Apaches, Eagles of the Southwest*. Norman, OK: University of Oklahoma Press, 1979, 43.

254 Carson, Wm. G. B. *William Carr Lane Diary*. Missouri Historical Review, Vol. XXXIX, No. 4, October 1964. All quotations in the account of Wm. Carr Lane's trip from February 28 to April 28, 1853, are from this source.

255 Bieber, Ralph P. *Letters of William Carr Lane, 1852–54*. Santa Fe, NM: El Palacio Press, 1928, 193–194.

256 Much of the area Lane refers to as "the copper mines" is roughly ten miles southeast of Silver City, New Mexico, and has been engulfed by one of the world's largest open pit mines, which continues to operate in the southwest portion of the state.

257 Wilentz, Sean. *The Rise of American Democracy, Jefferson to Lincoln*. New York: W.W. Norton, 2005, 665.

258 Lane, Wm. Carr. Letter to John F. Darby. December 31, 1852.

259 Carson, Wm. G. B. *William Carr Lane Diary*. St. Louis, MO: New Mexico Historical Review, 1964. All quotations related to this period are from this source, unless otherwise noted.

260 Worcester, Donald E. *The Apaches, Eagles of the Southwest*. Norman, OK: University of Oklahoma Press, 1979, 58.

261 Bieber, Ralph P. *Letters of William Carr Lane, 1852-1854*. Santa Fe, NM: El Palacio Press, 1928, 194–196.

262 *Ibid.*, 196–197.

263 Twitchell, Ralph Emerson. *The Leading Facts of New Mexico History*. Volume II. Santa Fe, NM: Sunstone Press, 2007[1912], 295.

264 Horn, Calvin. *New Mexico's Troubled Years*. Albuquerque, NM: Horn and Wallace, 1963, 48.

265 *Ibid.*, 49.

266 Twitchell, Ralph Emerson. *The Leading Facts of New Mexico History*. Volume II. Santa Fe, NM: Sunstone Press, 2007[1912], 334.

267 Chavez, Fray Angélico. *Tres Macho—He Said: Padre Gallegos of Albuquerque, New Mexico's First Congressman*. Santa Fe, NM: William Gannan, 1885, 10.

268 *Ibid.*, 69.

269 Bieber, Ralph P. *Letters of William Carr Lane, 1852-1854*. Santa Fe, NM: El Palacio Press, 1928, 193.

270 *Ibid.*, 197.

271 Bieber, Ralph P. *Letters of William Carr Lane, 1852-1854*. Santa Fe, NM: El Palacio Press, 1928, 199.

272 All reported vote counts in New Mexico are taken from Lane's journal. He clearly had access to the official counts.

273 *The Missouri Historical Review*, Vol. II, April–July 1917, 267.

PART V

274 Carson, Wm. G. B. *William Carr Lane Diary*. Missouri Historical Review, Vol. XXXIX, October 1964, St. Louis, 326–327.

275 *Ibid.*, 328.

276 *Ibid.*, 328.

277 *Ibid.*, 330.

278 *Ibid.*, 330.

279 *Ibid.*, 332.

280 *Ibid.*, 332.

281 All references to the presentation, consideration, and decision related to the dispute are taken from the *Congressional Globe* (now the *Congressional Record*) and from the Committee of Elections' *Contested Election—New Mexico 33d Congress, ___ Session*, Rep N121, February 24, 1854.

282 Twitchell, Ralph Emerson. *The Leading Facts of New Mexico History*. Volume II. Santa Fe, NM: Sunstone Press, 2007[1912], 309.

283 Lane, Wm. Carr. Letter to Mary. January 22, 1854. Additional quotations concerning Annapolis are from same letter.

284 McPherson, James M. *Battle Cry of Freedom*. New York: Ballantine Books, 1980, 125.

285   Lane, Wm. Carr. Letter to Miss Mary Glasgow and Master Wm. Carr Lane Glasgow. March 16, 1854.

286   McPherson, James M. *Battle Cry of Freedom, The Civil War Era.* New York: Ballantine Books, 1888, 126.

287   *Ibid.,* 128–129. Quotations are from Lincoln's speech in Peoria on October 16, 1854.

288   *Ibid.,* 154. The other background and statistics related to the 1856 election come from the same source, pp. 154–162.

289   Van Ravenswaay, Charles. *Saint Louis: An Informal History of the City and Its People, 1764–1865.* St. Louis, MO: Missouri Historical Society Press, 1991, 412. The statistics related the growth of St. Louis in this period are from the same source, pp. 412–459.

290   *Ibid.,*

291   McPherson, James M. *Battle Cry of Freedom, The Civil War Era.* New York: Ballantine Books, 1888, 88.

292   *Ibid.,* 119.

293   *Ibid.,* 147–153, for all statistics related to the Kansas-Missouri violence and attack on Charles Summer.

294   *Ibid.,* 214, for all statistics related to nomination and election of Lincoln.

295   *Ibid.,* 290.

296   Van Ravenswaay, Charles. *Saint Louis: An Informal History of the City and Its People, 1764–1865.* St. Louis, MO: Missouri Historical Society Press, 472.

297   *Ibid,* 494–495.

298   Copy #1, 350–354, for all statistics and descriptions relating to Fremont's final weeks.

299   Van Ravenswaay, Charles. *Saint Louis: An Informal History of the City and Its People, 1764–1865.* St. Louis, MO: Missouri Historical Society Press, 1991, 521–522.

300   Carson, Wm. G. B. "Secesh." *Bulletin of the Missouri Historical Society,* St. Louis, January 1967, 133.

BIBLIOGRAPHY

Books

Abbink, Emily. *New Mexico's Palace of the Governors: History of an American Treasure*, Museum of New Mexico Press, Santa Fe, 2007.

Acemoglu, Daron and James A. Robinson. *Why Nations Fail*, Crown Business, New York, 2012.

Bancroft, Hubert Howe. *History of Arizona and New Mexico 1530-1888*. A facsimile of the 1889 edition. Horn & Wallace, Albuquerque, 1962.

Benton, Thomas Hart. *Thirty Years View: A History of the Working of the American Government 1820 to 1850*, D. Appleton and Company, New York, 1856.

Berlin, Isaiah. *The Hedgehog and the Fox*. Orion Books Ltd., London 2009.

Bieber, Ralph P. *Letters of William Carr Lane, 1852-54*, El Palacio Press, Santa Fe, New Mexico, USA, 1928.

Billings, Warren M., Editor. *The Old Dominion in the Seventeenth Century*, University of North Carolina Press, Chapel Hill, 2007.

Brands, H.W. *The Money Men*. W. W. Norton & Company, New York and London, 2006.

Brooks, James F. *Captives and Cousins*, University of North Carolina Press, Chapel Hill and London, 2002.

Bryan, William Smith. *A History of the Pioneer Families of Missouri*, John S. Swift & Co., St. Louis, 1876. Published by Forgotten Books, 2012.

Carson, Wm. G.B.
> *Managers In Distress, The St. Louis Stage, 1840-1844*, St. Louis Historical Documents Foundation, St. Louis, 1949.
> *The Theatre of the Frontier*. University of Chicago Press, Chicago, 1932.

Chavez, Fray Angélico. **Tres Macho--He Said:** *Padre Gallegos of Albuquerque, New Mexico's First Congressman*, William Gannon, Santa Fe, New Mexico, 1985.

Chavez, Fray Angélico and Thomas E. Chavez. *Wake for a Fat Vicar*, LPD Press, Albuquerque, 2004.

Chavez, Thomas E. *Spain and the Independence of the United States*, University of New Mexico Press, Albuquerque, 2002.

Cleland, B. Esq. *A Historical Account of All the Mayors, Since the Formation of the City Government of St. Louis to the Present Date - 1846, and Some Odes.*

Cobos, Rubén. *A Dictionary of New Mexico and Southern Colorado Spanish*, Museum of New Mexico Press, Santa Fe, 1983.

Darby, John F. *Personal Recollections.* G. I. Jones, St. Louis, 1880. Arno Press, New York, 1975.

Dary, David. *Frontier Medicine*, Vantage Books, a Division of Random House Inc., New York, 2008.

Davis, W.W.H. *El Gringo: New Mexico and Her People*, The Rydal Press, Santa Fe, 1938.

de Aragon, Ray John. *Padre Martinez and Bishop Lamy*,Pan American, Las Vegas, New Mexico, 1978.

D'Emilo, John and Estelle B. Freedman. *Intimate Matters, A History of Sexuality in America*, Harper & Rowe, New York, 1988.

Del Castillo, Richard Griswold. *The Treaty of Guadalupe Hidalgo*, University of Oklahoma Press, Norman, 1990.

Denton, Sally. *Passion and Principle*, Bloomsburg, New York, 2007.

DeVoto, Bernard.

Across the Wide Missouri, Houston Mifflin, Boston, The Riverside Press, 1947.

The Year of Decision, 1846, Little Brown and Company, Boston, 1943.

Drum, Stella M. *Down the Santa Fe Trail and into Mexico*, Diary of Susan Shelby Magoffin 1846-1847, Yale University Press, New Haven, 1926.

Elliott, J. H. *Empires of the Atlantic World, Britain and Spain In America 1492-1830*, Yale University Press, New Haven and London, 2006.

Ellis, Franklin. *History of Fayette County Pennsylvania with Biographical Sketches of Many of its Pioneers and Prominent Men*. Vols. I & II. L. H. Everest & Co., Philadelphia, 1882. Facsimile Reprint, 1986.

Emmett, Chris. *Fort Union and the Winning of the Southwest*, University of Oklahoma Press, Norman, 1965.

Etulain, Richard W. *New Mexico Lives: Profiles and Historical Stories*, University of New Mexico Press, Albuquerque, 2002.

Fergusson, Erna. *New Mexico: A Pageant of Three Peoples*, Alfred A. Knopf, 1951.

Gardner, Mark L.

Brothers on the Santa Fe and Chihuahua Trails, University Press of Colorado, Niwot, Colorado, 1993.

Wagons for the Santa Fe Trade, University of New Mexico Press, Albuquerque, 2000.

Gillett, Mary C. *The Army Medical Department 1775-1810*, University Press of the Pacific, Honolulu, 2002.

Goodwin, Doris Kearns. *Team of Rivals*, Simon & Schuster, New York, London, Toronto, Sydney, 2005.

Gregg, Josiah. *Commerce of the Prairies*, Bobbs-Merril and Company Inc., Indianapolis and New York, 1970.

Horgan, Paul. *Lamy of Santa Fe*, Farrar, Straus and Giroux, New York, 1975.

Horn, Calvin. *New Mexico's Troubled Years*, Horn and Wallace, Albuquerque, 1963.

Howe, Daniel Walker. *What Hath God Wrought in the Transformation of America, 1815-1848*, Oxford University Press, 2007.

Inman, Colonel Henry. *The Old Santa Fe Trail*, Macmillan Company, New York, 1897.

Jackson, Hal. *Following the Royal Road*, University of New Mexico Press, Albuquerque, 2006.

Keleher, William A. *Turmoil in New Mexico 1846-1868*, Rydal Press, Santa Fe, New Mexico, 1952.

Kennedy, John F. *Profiles in Courage*, Harper & Row Publishers, New York, Evanston and London, 1964.

Lamar, Howard R. *The Far Southwest 1846-1912, A Territorial History*, University of New Mexico Press, Albuquerque, 2000.

Lender, Mark Edward and James Kirby Martin. *Drinking in America*, The Free Press, New York, 1982.

Levy, Jonathan. *Freaks of Fortune: The Emerging World of Capitalism and Risk in America*, Harvard University Press, Cambridge and London, 2012.

Locke, Raymond Friday. *The Book of the Navajo*, Mankind Publishing Company, Los Angeles, 1976.

Mann, Charles C. *1493, Uncovering the New World Columbus Created*, Vintage Books, New York, 2011.

Matthiessen, Peter. *In the Spirit of Crazy Horse*, Penguin books, London, 1992.

McCandlass, Perry.
> *A History of Missouri*. Volume II, 182-1860. University of Missouri Press, Columbia and London, 1971.
> *Workers of the Writer's Program of the Work Progress Administration in the State of Missouri*, Duell, Sloanan & Pearce, New York, 1941.

McDermott, John Francis. *The Early Histories of St. Louis*, St. Louis Historical Document Foundation, St. Louis, 1952.

McPherson, James M. *Battle Cry of Freedom*, Ballantine Books, New York, 1980.

Meacham, John. *American Lion*, Random House, New York, 2008.

Merry, Robert W. *A Country of Vast Designs*, Simon & Schuster, New York, 2009.

Mettler, Cecilia. *History of Medicine*, The Classics of Medicine Library, Birmingham, Alabama, 1986.

Primm, James Neal. *Lion of the Valley, St. Louis, Missouri, 1764-1980*, Missouri Historical Society Press, St. Louis, 1989. Revised 1998.

Roosevelt, Theodore. *Life of Thomas Hart Benton*, Houghton, Mifflin and Company, Boston and New York, 1887.

Rozier, Firmin A. *Rozier's History of the Early Settlement of the Mississippi Valley*, G. A. Pierrot & Sons, St. Louis, 1890.

Rush, Benjamin. *A Plan of Education for Dickinson College*, 1785.

Saxon, Lyle. *Father Mississippi*, The Century Co., New York, London, 1927.

Scharf, J. Thomas. *History of St. Louis City and County*, Philadelphia, Louis H. Everts & Co., 1883.

Segale, Sister Blandina. *At the End of the Santa Fe Trail*, Columbian Press, Columbus, Ohio, 1932.

Smith, Joseph, DD. *History of Jefferson College*, J. T. Shryuck, Pittsburgh.

Steele, Volnay, MD. *Bleed, Blister and Purge,* Mountain Press Publishing Company, Missoula, Montana, 2005.

Stegner, Wallace. *The Gathering of Zion: The Story of the Mormon Trail,* University of Nebraska Press, Lincoln and London, 1964.

Thomas, Charles C. and Ralph H. Major. *A History of Medicine.* Vol. Two. Springfield, Illinois, 1954.

Thomas, David Hurst, et al. *The Native Americans: An Illustrated History,* Turner Publishing Inc., Atlanta, 1993.

Trask, Kerry A. *Black Hawk, the Battle for the Heart of America,* Henry Holt and Company, New York, 2006.

Twitchell, Ralph Emerson.

> *The Leading Facts of New Mexico History,* Volume I (1911)
> *The Leading Facts of New Mexico History,* Volume II (1912)
> *Old Santa Fe, The Story of New Mexico's Ancient Capital* (1925)
> *The Military Occupation of the Territory of New Mexico from 1846 to 1851* (1909)
> Facsimiles of original 1912 editions, Sunstone Press, Santa Fe, New Mexico, 2007.

Van Ravenswaay, Charles. *Saint Louis, An Informal History of the City and Its People, 1764-1865,* Missouri Historical Society Press, 1991, St. Louis.

Wade, Richard C. *The Urban Frontier,* University of Chicago Press, Chicago and London, 1959.

Weber, David J. *The Spanish Frontier in North America,* Yale University Press, New Haven and London, 1992.

Wilentz, Sean. *The Rise of American Democracy, Jefferson to Lincoln,* W.W. Norton & Company, New York, London, 2005.

Wineapple, Brenda. *Ecstatic Nation: Confidence, Crisis, and Compromise, 1848-1877,* Harper, 2013.

Wood, Gordon S.

> *The American Revolution, A History,* The Modern Library, New York, 2002.

Empire of Liberty, Oxford University Press, 2009.
The Idea of America, Reflections on the Birth of the United States, The Penguin Press, New York, 2011.

Wooster, Robert. *The American Military Frontiers, The United States Army in the West, 1783-1900*, University of New Mexico Press, Albuquerque, 2009.

Worcester, Donald E. *The Apaches: Eagles of the Southwest*, University of Oklahoma Press, Norman, 1979.

Journals and Unpublished Material

Carson, Wm. G. B.

Anne Ewing Lane. The Bulletin, Missouri Historical Society, St. Louis, January 1965.

Glimpses of the Past, Letters of William Carr Lane. Missouri Historical Society, St. Louis, 1940.

Secesh. The Bulletin, Missouri Historical Society, St. Louis, January 1967.

William Carr Lane Diary. New Mexico Historical Review, Santa Fe, 1964.

Quackenbush, Nancy. *Some Northern Neck Lanes (1987)*. First published in the *Magazine of Virginia Genealogy*. Vol. 24, #4, November 1986.

Twitchell, Ralph E. *Historical Sketch of Governor William Carr Lane, Together with Diary of His Journal, from St. Louis, Mo., to Santa Fe, NM, July 31st to September 9th, 1852*. Historical Society of New Mexico, Santa Fe, 1917.

Unpublished letters of Wm. Carr Lane (in possession of author).